Understanding Crime

AN EVALUATION OF THE NATIONAL INSTITUTE OF LAW ENFORCEMENT AND CRIMINAL JUSTICE

Understanding Crime

AN EVALUATION OF THE NATIONAL INSTITUTE OF LAW ENFORCEMENT AND CRIMINAL JUSTICE

COMMITTEE ON RESEARCH ON LAW ENFORCEMENT AND CRIMINAL JUSTICE
Assembly of Behavioral and Social Sciences
National Research Council

Susan O. White and Samuel Krislov, Editors

NATIONAL ACADEMY OF SCIENCES
WASHINGTON, D.C. 1977

NOTICE: The project that is the subject of this report was approved by the Governing Board of the National Research Council, whose members are drawn from the Councils of the National Academy of Sciences, the National Academy of Engineering, and the Institute of Medicine. The members of the Committee responsible for the report were chosen for their special competences and with regard for appropriate balance.

This report has been reviewed by a group other than the authors according to procedures approved by a Report Review Committee consisting of members of the National Academy of Sciences, the National Academy of Engineering, and the Institute of Medicine.

Prepared under Contract #J-LEAA-006-76 from the National Institute of Law Enforcement and Criminal Justice, Law Enforcement Assistance Administration, United States Department of Justice. Points of view or opinions stated in this document are those of the author and do not necessarily represent the official position or policies of the United States Department of Justice.

Library of Congress Catalog Card Number 77-088871
International Standard Book Number 0-309-02635-0

Available from:
Printing and Publishing Office
National Academy of Sciences
2101 Constitution Avenue, N.W.
Washington, D.C. 20418

Printed in the United States of America

COMMITTEE ON RESEARCH ON LAW ENFORCEMENT AND CRIMINAL JUSTICE

Members

SAMUEL KRISLOV (*Chairman*), Department of Political Science, University of Minnesota

ALFRED BLUMSTEIN, School of Urban and Public Affairs, Carnegie-Mellon University

DONALD T. CAMPBELL, Department of Psychology, Northwestern University

DONALD R. DESKINS, JR., Department of Geography, University of Michigan

EUGENE EIDENBERG, Vice-Chancellor, University of Illinois at Chicago Circle and Chairman, Illinois Law Enforcement Commission

MALCOLM M. FEELEY, Yale Law School, Yale University

JACK P. GIBBS, Department of Sociology, University of Arizona

CHARLES M. HERZFELD, Aerospace Electronics Components and Energy Group, International Telephone & Telegraph Corporation

ROBERT M. IGLEBURGER, Police Department (retired), Dayton

GARY G. KOCH, Department of Biostatistics, University of North Carolina

BERYL A. RADIN, The LBJ School of Public Affairs, The University of Texas at Austin

SIMON ROTTENBERG, Department of Economics, University of Massachusetts

RICHARD D. SCHWARTZ, School of Law, State University of New York at Buffalo

MARVIN E. WOLFGANG, Institute of Criminology, University of Pennsylvania

COLEMAN A. YOUNG, Mayor, City of Detroit

Staff

SUSAN O. WHITE, Study Director

FREDRICA D. KRAMER, Research Associate

MICHAEL A. ROSSETTI, Research Assistant

JUANITA L. RUBINSTEIN, Research Assistant

PAULETTE M. HOLMES, Administrative Secretary

DOROTHY E. JACKSON, Administrative Secretary

Contents

Preface

This report of the Committee on Research on Law Enforcement and Criminal Justice is the product of an intensive 18-month effort by a committee of individuals with a variety of scholarly, research, administrative, and technical skills and experience broadly associated with law enforcement research. The effort was undertaken at the request of the Law Enforcement Assistance Administration (LEAA) of the Department of Justice. Some members of the Committee previously had extensive acquaintance with the National Institute of Law Enforcement and Criminal Justice or with LEAA in various guises. Others among us had relatively little. All were aware that the Institute and LEAA, generally, were subjects of major criticism and national evaluation. Indeed, one of the reasons for undertaking the task was the assumption that such an assessment was a value to the Institute itself and to the country's effort to deal in effective fashion with the general problem of crime.

Because of the atmosphere in which much of the discussion of research on crime necessarily operates—an atmosphere that, to some extent, we document early in the report—we deliberately set out to minimize the filters of past judgments and past preoccupations. To that end we set out a very extensive program of Committee participation, not only in the general broad policy decisions and writing, but also in the very fiber of the evaluation of the Institute's work. As described in Appendix C, we set out a stratified sample of projects supported by the

Institute, and members of the Committee participated in the actual reading of the files of the projects. Virtually every member of the Committee read several files in addition to getting a broad overview of the program of the Institute. A large subcommittee of the Committee also heard presentations by the major contractors for technological projects developed by the Institute and included in our sample.

Our effort was to evaluate the work that has been done in as dispassionate a fashion as possible. In reaching judgments, we have tried to understand the nature of the arena in which the work was undertaken as well as to judge the product in an absolute sense. We have tried, too, to be as constructive as possible both in our evaluations and in our recommendations. Our aim is not to look back with recrimination but to look forward to improvement.

Throughout our discussions, we have tried to ask two fundamental questions: Should there be research on crime? Should there be a federal presence in that research? There are many points of view among Committee members, and our agreement on language sometimes represents a form of consensual bargaining. Most Committee members have been convinced through their own experience that the effort to develop research on crime is one that should be pursued and that an action-research orientation is the correct mode for such research. As will be evident in this report, we are not impressed with the results so far, and we do not preclude the possibility that further efforts will fail. But we do believe that the effort to find a style of research and a mode of work is one that should continue.

Our recommendations are that the Institute move toward political and administrative independence so that it can become both a more effective research structure and one that can serve users more effectively. Our belief is that this can be done through insulating the Institute from some of the pressures that result from a necessarily politicized situation and, even more importantly, by removing it from the day-to-day operations that, as students of all organizations know, continually drive attention away from longer-range efforts. In an organization where both research and day-to-day activity takes place, research takes a back seat, and that seat is pushed further and further back as time goes on.

In producing this report, the efforts of the Committee members were many and inestimable. The special skills of some of our members were most valuable, and the dedication of all impressed me throughout the period in which we worked. Because everyone did so much, I find it impossible to single out anyone without injustice. The text and recommendations of the report are the responsibility of the Committee.

Major portions of the text reflect background papers by both Committee members and staff.

The staff labored under tough deadlines and the loose reins of a Committee in which all were active leaders. They in many ways got to know more about the Institute than the Institute itself, and the report is shaped very much by their insights and their knowledge. Specific mention should be made of their individual contributions. Susan O. White, Study Director, had overall responsibility for the design and execution of the project as well as general editorial responsibility for the text. Fredrica D. Kramer, Research Associate, worked closely with the Chairman and the Study Director in planning various phases of the project and in formulating findings and conclusions, and she was primarily responsible for developing background materials on the history of the Institute, its planning process, and its technology development program. Michael A. Rossetti, Research Assistant, was responsible for developing data on the Institute's budget and funding patterns, for overseeing the complex logistics of the Committee's evaluation of a sample of Institute projects, and for preparing and analyzing the data from that evaluation. Juanita L. Rubinstein, Research Assistant, prepared a number of background papers covering the history of LEAA, the relationship of the Institute to LEAA programs and to other criminal justice research and professional organizations, and the Institute's evaluation and technology transfer efforts. Completion of the Committee's work and publication of this report would not have been possible without the hard work and dedication of Edith Wright, Paulette McNeal Holmes, and Dorothy E. Jackson, each of whom served as Administrative Secretary to the Committee during important phases of its life.

We are grateful to the staff of the Assembly of Behavioral and Social Sciences of the National Research Council. The Executive Director, David A. Goslin, and Associate Executive Director, Lester P. Silverman, were helpful mentors as well as administrators who eased the way for the work of the Committee. Eugenia Grohman, Executive Associate/Editor, provided exceptional assistance with problems of format and wording at the drafting stage as well as with a blue pencil at the editing stage.

The staff of the National Institute of Law Enforcement and Criminal Justice was most cooperative in providing virtually anything we asked for. Gerald Caplan, the director, Betty Chemers, John Pickett, Richard Linster, Geoffrey Alprin, and Paul Cascarano were especially helpful. A complete list of those interviewed for the project can be found in Appendix D.

Finally, I would like to thank several people whose comments and advice were particularly valuable to me: Robert Crew, James Q. Wilson, Frank Zimring, John Gardiner, Victor Navasky, Herbert Jacob, and Mitchell Joelson.

SAMUEL KRISLOV, *Chairman*
Committee on Research on Law Enforcement and Criminal Justice

REPORT OF THE COMMITTEE

Summary

OVERVIEW

The Committee on Research on Law Enforcement and Criminal Justice has completed an 18-month review of the research program of the National Institute of Law Enforcement and Criminal Justice of the Law Enforcement Assistance Administration (LEAA). This review has included a systematic examination of the Institute's projects, products, and processes.

We conclude that the Institute has not been the catalyst or sponsor of a first-rate and significant research program commensurate with either its task or resources. It has clearly had some successes with individual projects and has begun to develop some basic and vital data and a research community, both of which had previously been inadequate for society's needs, but structural and political constraints have all too often deflected the Institute from its true mission—to develop valid knowledge about crime problems. Furthermore, we conclude that, given those same restraints and extrapolating its marginal improvements over the years, the Institute in its present form is not likely to become a significant and quality-oriented research agency. We also conclude, however, that there is a need for a program of research on crime problems that is national in scope and therefore for a national institute of law enforcement and criminal justice supported by the federal government. Consequently, we recommend both structural and conceptual reordering of the Institute itself and of its research agenda.

The report has three sections: the first describes historical factors that have influenced the Institute's development and the LEAA structure within which it operates; the second reports the Committee's evaluation of the federal role in crime research and of the program developed and funded by the Institute; the third details the Committee's conclusions and recommendations. This summary presents the Committee's findings, conclusions, and recommendations in terms of the program, role, and goals of the Institute.

FINDINGS AND CONCLUSIONS

Program

The Committee undertook a detailed examination of a sample of Institute awards for the years 1969–1975. (For specifics of methodology and detailed findings, see Chapter 4 and Appendix C.) Our findings can be summarized in terms of four criteria: quality of the funded research, usefulness of the products, success in cumulating knowledge, and effectiveness of research administration.

Quality

The quality of Institute-funded research is not high, and much has been mediocre. Of the sample projects reviewed by Committee members, most could be labeled neither failures nor successes. Program weaknesses are, in our opinion, primarily the result of a lack of attention to research design and of related administrative failings. The phenomenon of the weak project occurred often enough to prompt grave concern over quality control in Institute procedures.

Usefulness

The usefulness of the Institute's work is more problematic to assess, in part because there have been few attempts to discover whether or not Institute products are in fact being used. The information that has come to the Committee from staff of State Planning Agencies (SPAS) and other potential consumers, although admittedly limited, clearly indicates that little of the material disseminated by the Institute is used in planning or program development by either SPA staff or practitioners. Furthermore, in assessing individual projects, Committee members found few that deserved high ratings for usefulness.

Cumulative Research

A major criterion of effectiveness of programmatic research is its contribution to building a coherent body of knowledge and to focusing that knowledge on solving problems. Despite rhetoric to the contrary, the Committee finds little evidence that the Institute has been committed to this kind of cumulative research. We conclude that the Institute's purpose would be better served by a research agenda based on program areas, such as deterrence and rehabilitation, within which funding could be focused toward developing a coherent body of knowledge.

Research Administration

The Committee finds serious shortcomings in research administration. These include a weak advisory system that limits access to program development, review procedures that range from nonexistent to ineffective, a research strategy that tends to exclude a large majority of the existing social science research community, and vulnerability to pressures that are detrimental to the development of a research program. Such weaknesses are not necessarily the fault of any individual, but rather the consequence of misjudging the means by which research can be made useful to an action program.

Role

The Committee finds that the Institute has been asked to carry too large a share of the burden of making LEAA effective and accountable. It has been required to undertake numerous tasks—such as technical assistance to SPAS, training programs, project evaluations, and other direct service obligations—that have turned its focus away from research.

The Institute has responded to pressures for instant solutions to what are complex problems instead of concentrating on a program for testing, developing, and cumulating knowledge. One result has been that problem solving has become the test of success—measured by crime or recidivism rates identified as "cure" rates. Predictably, the Institute has failed the operational tests (which are wholly inappropriate for any research program) while at the same time neglecting its primary mission of developing knowledge. The Institute has not had autonomy within LEAA, nor has it been able to establish independent stature as a research agency. Authority to approve grants and contracts is in the hands of the Administrator of LEAA, not the Director of the Institute. Therefore, the Committee concludes that the Institute has been unable to resist pressures that are inappropriate to a research role.

The Committee concludes that the Institute's role of direct service to LEAA programming has not been successful and probably cannot be adequately undertaken by a national research institute because such a role ties it to the pace and demands of a delivery system. The appropriate role of a national institute of law enforcement and criminal justice is to engage in research and development on a scale and a level and within a time frame that is impractical for the rest of LEAA.

Goal

The Committee finds that the Institute has often been expected to address directly the goal of reducing crime and to meet measures of effectiveness such as decreasing crime and recidivism rates. This is inappropriate for a research program. However, the Committee finds that in rejecting these direct goals, the Institute has denied the possibility that its program can contribute in any way to the reduction of crime and has concentrated instead on improving the operation of the criminal justice system.

We can know more about criminal behavior and about the effectiveness of various governmental responses to it, and this knowledge will ultimately be useful for crime prevention and control. For example, our public policies on punishment as a deterrent, on the use of criminal law to control deviant behavior, on techniques of law enforcement, on court processing, on techniques of dealing with criminal offenders, can be productively informed by carefully focused research. And, we can also learn what processes and behaviors cannot be affected by changes within the criminal justice system. It is important to understand that practical payoff from research is necessarily indirect and often long term. But there is clearly potential for developing better informed and therefore more realistic and effective public policies on controlling crime.

RECOMMENDATIONS

The Committee's 19 recommendations can be found in Chapter 5. This section presents a summary statement of those recommendations.

The role of the Institute should be to develop valid, generalizable knowledge about crime, criminal behaviors, and the effectiveness of crime control methods and policies. As a national research institute, it should develop the resources necessary to undertake research that is not feasible or appropriate at the state or local level.

To protect the integrity of the Institute's research program, the Committee recommends that the Institute be reconstituted as an independent research agency within the Department of Justice. Such independence would include final approval authority over all awards as well as control of the administrative budget, personnel, and detailed program review. The Director should be chosen from candidates with significant experience and recognition in both research and research administration. Furthermore, the Committee urges that a Criminal Justice Research Advisory Board be established, by statute, with members appointed by the President and including an appropriate mix of scientists and practitioners.

The Committee recommends that the Institute be organized around substantive program areas. These should be designed to provide a common focus on a theoretically interesting problem while at the same time exploiting the variety of perspectives that different disciplines can bring to bear. They should also be designed on the assumption that producing valid and useful knowledge is a cumulative process.

The Committee recommends that the Institute take steps to ensure quality in its research. One such step involves the process of project review. To ensure quality, that process requires more than a mail review of individual projects. It requires program area panels, meeting regularly, to ensure continuity in the use of criteria and in the cumulation of knowledge. The Committee recommends sub-panels for methodological review and, for panels, a mix of researchers and practitioners to provide proper guidance for the long-range development of program areas.

The Committee concludes that activities involving direct service to components of LEAA or practitioners—whether these be training, technical assistance, packaging and marketing of research results, or non-generalizable evaluations—cannot be undertaken effectively by a research institute. Therefore, they should be a part of LEAA's technical assistance program and not the responsibility of the Institute.

The primary goal for the Institute should be developing knowledge that is useful in reducing crime. At the same time, the Institute should maintain its concern with the fairness and effectiveness of the administration of criminal justice. The function of research is always to produce knowledge, whether for its own sake or for a socially useful purpose. Therefore, the Institute's program should be judged by the value of its contributions to our knowledge about crime and criminal justice rather than by operational measures such as crime and recidivism rates.

I

The Federal Government's "War on Crime": The Role of Research

Every examination of the Law Enforcement Assistance Administration, of which the National Institute of Law Enforcement and Criminal Justice (referred to interchangeably as the Institute or NILECJ) is a part, has begun with a review of the stormy period in which the Omnibus Crime Control and Safe Streets Act was debated and enacted by Congress. This Committee begins its report with a similar analysis—not because of an insular concern with history, but rather because of a conviction that certain aspects of the Institute's origin and history are critical to an understanding of both the potential and the limitations of its program of research.

A focus on immediate solutions permeated the Congressional debates of 1967 and 1968. The resulting public expectations placed excessive demands on the Safe Streets action program and created nearly impossible conditions for developing a productive research program. The consequent use of crime rates as measures of effectiveness by the Institute's critics—and at times by its leadership—was a significant factor in several major policy decisions. The use of the block-grant format for the action program and the creation of State Planning Agencies (SPAS) affected not only the operations of the Law Enforcement Assistance Administration (LEAA)—NILECJ's parent agency—but also the Institute's own user-constituencies.

Likewise, Congressional ambiguity about both the purpose of the LEAA action program and the role of the Institute has encouraged frequent shifts in direction. In this unstable environment, the research program was unable to set its own course or develop leadership appropriate to a research effort. Therefore, the Institute often became the creature of whatever trend happened to be current at a particular time. While there has always been some uncertainty about the Institute's mission within LEAA, however, its position in an agency designed to serve criminal justice practitioners has had a dramatic effect on the type of research and "solutions" that it has pursued.

Chapters 1 and 2 provide a brief delineation of the Institute's history and current situation, but they should not be interpreted as fixed limitations on the Institute's potential as a research institute. It is now 1977 and neither Congress and the public, nor the Institute itself, are caught up in the situation of 8 years ago. The Committee accordingly bases its recommendations on the need to understand and then transcend many of the problems discussed in this section.

1 LEAA and the Institute: Historical Development

INTENT OF THE FRAMERS

The Federal Role in Criminal Justice

Until the passage of the Omnibus Crime Control and Safe Streets Act of 1968, active participation of the federal government in the field of criminal justice had largely been confined to the direct enforcement of a limited number of major criminal statutes and the collection and distribution of the Uniform Crime Reports by the Federal Bureau of Investigation. As crime and civil violence sparked public concern and political debate during the 1960s, however, it became increasingly apparent that the federal role in this area would be expanded. The ensuing controversy about the federal role was in keeping with a decade noted for public acrimony.

In the United States, crime has historically been considered a local problem, and fear and distrust of a national police force have deep roots. Even advocates of increased federal involvement have affirmed that the foundation of the criminal justice system lies in the states and localities. However, with the emergence of the "law and order" issue in the 1964 Presidential campaign, the conviction grew that the national scope of the crime problem necessitated a federal response. The attempt to define this response continued for four years while adherents of various ideologies advanced differing notions of a desirable federal approach.

One approach involved attempts to abolish the grievances thought to motivate those involved in anti-social activities. Such efforts—characterized by their detractors as exercises in social engineering—were not noticeably effective in immediately reducing either crime or violence. Another approach was followed in early 1965, when a Presidential commission was established to investigate the causes of crime and recommend measures for its prevention and control.* A third approach was inaugurated later that year with the passage of the Law Enforcement Assistance Act of 1965 (Pub. L. No. 89–197). This measure accented the role of the federal government as a supporter of law enforcement innovation at the state and local levels, with a modest appropriation of funds for experimental, demonstration, and planning projects.

None of this resulted in a visible improvement in what many believed to be an intolerable situation, and Congressional demand rose for a "war on crime." The tenor of the times fostered the belief that crime—like poverty, like the attempt to reach the moon, like a host of domestic or social ills—could be dealt with by a major mobilization of resources and the development of a consistent national strategy. Since a national police force was unacceptable in American society, major direct involvement of the federal government was limited to financial support of local efforts. This did not mean, however, that federal participation in policy making for state and local jurisdictions was necessarily circumscribed. The urgency of the crime problem seemed to override the traditional concern that federal power follows federal funds.

Therefore, when the Crime Commission issued its final report in February 1967, it found a climate receptive to its proposals for action. The report advanced several theses: a belief that crime has social roots and that there was widespread ignorance about what to do about crime; a belief in the validity of a scientific and technological perspective on law enforcement; optimism over the potential for controlling crime if sufficient commitments were made to the task; and a view of the entire criminal justice apparatus—the melange of fiefdoms in the courts, the police, and corrections agencies—as a system. There was also a presumption that our knowledge about how to improve the process of law enforcement and the administration of justice was well ahead of practice and that the propagation of this information would be a major factor in improving the quality of practice. The Commission recom-

*The President's Commission on Law Enforcement and the Administration of Justice, herein referred to as the Crime Commission.

mended the institution of a major federal program of support. It justified such a program by noting that modern crime was a national phenomenon not respecting geographic or political boundaries; that important needs of individual jurisdictions could not always be met with limited local resources; and that federal funds could be used as a catalyst to encourage changes that would render the entire criminal justice system more effective and more fair.

Using the Crime Commission Report as its rationale, the Administration proposed a major federal effort in criminal justice through the use of categorical action grants. Adoption of this proposed effort would have entailed a major involvement of the federal government in crime control activities at the state and local levels. Despite Congressional desire to appear to be taking some effective action in the "war on crime," the proposal to expand the federal role in this fashion was by no means uncontroversial. During the ensuing debate, serious concerns were voiced about the maintenance of the appropriate Constitutional division of powers and responsibilities. The fear of federal control over local police departments became a major topic of discussion, although supporters of the bill continually maintained that the limits of federal legal power in criminal justice were so strict as to render infeasible any serious attempt at federal supervision of state and local criminal justice systems.

Meanwhile, local government officials lobbied intensively for direct federal funding via categorical grants. Mayors and city managers individually, the League of Cities/Council of Mayors, the International City Management Association, and the National Association of County Officials all participated in this effort (Rogovin 1973). Many localities at this time had retained their own grants people to "mine" the federal categorical grants programs of the 1960s. Local politicians saw anti-crime performance as an increasingly important factor in voter attraction and federal money (with local autonomy) as helpful in shaping political images.

The Omnibus Crime Control and Safe Streets Act (Pub. L. 90–351) as it finally emerged from the Congress in 1968 bore the marks of the divergence of concerns enunciated in the debate. The resulting structure of the Law Enforcement Assistance Administration, created by the Act, can be traced to a pluralistic resolution of severe ideological differences. The two administrative features of LEAA of interest to this report were an administrative troika, consisting of the director and deputy directors, and the block-grant method of funding; both were attempts to constrain the power attendant upon the granting of large sums of money.

Unanimous consent by the troika—at least one member of which, by law, had to be of the party in opposition to the President—was necessary for any important policy or administrative decision. This was intended to remove a great deal of funding discretion from the Attorney General's office and prevent the development of a single powerful "crime czar" within the federal government. The troika was singularly counterproductive, as it institutionalized the ideological conflict of the crime debate and thereby precluded the possibility of creative leadership. The troika continued to function (as a source of both paralysis and needless dissension) until 1973, when it was deleted by the Crime Control Act of 1973 (Pub. L. 93–83).

The second critical administrative feature of the Safe Streets Act, and the most radical alteration of the Administration's proposal, was the institution of the block-grant method of funding. Often described as a significant event in the history of federal/state relations, the block-grant system broke with the pattern of direct categorical grants to localities that had developed in the major social programs of the 1960s. Money for both planning and action purposes was to be transmitted directly to the states as block grants. (A smaller percentage of the LEAA budget was to be allocated as discretionary funds, to be granted at the discretion of the central LEAA administration; this included the research funds of the National Institute of Law Enforcement and Criminal Justice.) The block-grant system not only transformed a creation of the Great Society into a precursor of the New Federalism, but also gave rise to the development of a complex structure within LEAA to administer this funding mechanism. (The LEAA System with its component Regional Offices and State Planning Agencies is discussed in Chapter 2.) This structure and its corresponding impact on the Institute are integral themes of this report.

The Federal Role in Criminal Justice Research

The National Institute of Law Enforcement and Criminal Justice was created by the 1968 Safe Streets Act and placed within the LEAA structure. Initially the brainchild of a single Congressman, James H. Scheuer of New York, the idea of a national research institute devoted to topics of crime and criminal justice had long been advocated without arousing Congressional interest. In the midst of the crisis atmosphere and the confusion of the crime debate, the Institute was added as an amendment to the Safe Streets Act with relatively little Congressional discussion. In fact, Congressman Scheuer (in a June 17, 1976, interview with Committee staff) remarked that the major difficulty that he encountered was the massive indifference to the measure evinced by senior members of both parties.

Possibly because the Institute was something of an afterthought in the Safe Streets legislation, it never received the formal authority necessary to shape its own program. Until recently, the Institute's director was appointed by the administrator of LEAA; its budget still comes piecemeal from LEAA's budget, largely at the discretion of the administrator, who controls both personnel funds and the line item containing funds for "technology, analysis, development and dissemination"; and, indeed, final approval of all Institute awards (sign-off authority) is in the hands of the administrator of LEAA. These structural features made the research effort a creature of LEAA's action mission from the start, with no insulation from the pressures and demands that naturally surround such a program.

The enabling legislation authorized the Institute to award grants and contracts to public agencies, research centers, and institutions of higher learning for the support of research, demonstrations, and behavioral studies pursuant to the development of new or improved systems, techniques, approaches, and equipment for the purpose of the improvement and strengthening of law enforcement. It empowered the Institute to carry out continuing studies and behavioral research in pursuit of more accurate information on the causes of crime and the effectiveness of various methods of crime prevention and correctional procedures. Likewise, the Institute was instructed to disseminate new knowledge in the field through action recommendations and workshops; to carry out a program of collection and dissemination of all relevant information; and to establish a research center.* In the 1973 Crime Control Act, Congress enlarged the Institute's mandate to include the development and support of training programs, a three-year national survey of criminal justice personnel needs, and program evaluation. This last mandate, in particular, symbolizes the nature of Congressional expectations with respect to the Institute's role in the LEAA program.†

The intellectual heritage of the Institute, the recipient of this varied mandate, was sparse. In the first place, Congress never clearly articulated its understanding of criminal justice research. Neither the problems of federal research for local consumption, necessitated by the LEAA block-grant system, nor the implications of expecting research to meet measures of cure were given serious consideration. Furthermore,

*See Appendix A2 for discussions of the impact of these expectations.

†See Appendix A1 for text of Title I, Part D, Sec. 401 to 407, which authorized NILECJ.

NILECJ never had the benefit of extended intellectual debate. At its inception, the primary point of departure for criminal justice reform was the Crime Commission's report, *The Challenge of Crime in a Free Society* (U.S. President 1967). While this report discussed many facets of the crime problem, it focused major attention on shortcomings in the criminal justice system and its parts. That analysis prompted many interpreters to concentrate on "improving the system," especially the mechanistic kinds of reform so characteristic of LEAA programs. Unfortunately, the academic research community largely ignored the Crime Commission's Report as a basis for serious debate about the possibilities either for controlling crime or improving the system. From the beginning, they viewed NILECJ as simply an arm of LEAA and took a relatively dim view of its intellectual potential. Since academic social scientists tend to be ideologically liberal, they found it more comfortable to deal with problems like juvenile delinquency and rehabilitation than with law enforcement and control. The academic research community, in short, has not been eager to muddy itself in the crime debate, and consequently, a major source of research competence was isolated from the federal effort in criminal justice research.

In addition, NILECJ's political heritage was without a broadly pluralistic base. LEAA (and consequently the Institute) lacked a range of constituencies from the start and has continued to attract an asymmetrical set of interest and pressure groups, mostly practitioners and other government fund-seekers. Consequently, the influence and direction from the user community has been one-sided. For most of LEAA's history, the police—traditionally well organized and considered synonymous with law enforcement—have provided the most visible and effective source of influence. People in corrections and the courts have only recently developed significant access to LEAA resources. The views of victims, racial and ethnic minorities, women, and other citizens' groups—those whose diverse experiences with crime problems could contribute different perspectives on what is needed to control crime—have only recently entered LEAA's field of vision and have had almost no impact on program priorities. The Institute has made few attempts to seek the opinions of groups not originally perceived as its clientele or constituents. Accordingly, its outlook has been unnecessarily narrow and its research agenda has not benefited from a variety of perspectives on criminal justice problems. Finally, the federal/state relationship as reflected in the block-grant program has hindered the participation of an urban constituency, which traditionally has interests and needs different from those of state institutions. Since influences on LEAA often were, in effect, influences on

NILECJ, the implications of the block-grant system were relevant to the Institute even though it is not a direct participant in that system.

HISTORICAL DEVELOPMENT OF THE INSTITUTE

The administrative history of NILECJ can be divided into three phases, which reflect the development of LEAA and its impact on NILECJ and in part explain the character of the Institute's research (as described in Chapter 4). The first phase, which includes the directorship of several individuals, was clearly the period of gearing up. The second and third phases are each identified with a single director who had sufficient time to make an evaluable record.

Phase I: Gearing Up (1969–1971)

The first phase began in October 1968 with a limited attempt to plan a research structure that would fit the requirements of the 1968 Act.* Ralph Siu, then at the Department of Defense, was nominated to be the first director, but he was not confirmed and served only through the change in administrations after the 1968 election. Henry Ruth became the first confirmed director under the new administration and served for approximately one year. He was succeeded in 1970 by his deputy, Irving Slott, who served as acting director until early 1971.

Henry Ruth organized the Institute's work around five centers: the Center for Crime Prevention and Rehabilitation focused on research into the conditions underlying criminal behavior and on new methods of prevention and rehabilitation; the Center for Criminal Justice Operations and Management concentrated on the use of operations research for the improvement of law enforcement agencies; the Center for Law and Justice dealt with the appropriateness and fairness of criminal laws (the 1971 program plan added mention of community treatment, offender reintegration, and concern for the conditions from which an offender enters the criminal justice system); the Center for Special Projects administered the fellowship program; and the Center for Demonstration and Professional Services was responsible for translating knowledge into action through dissemination and technical assistance programs.

*This attempt was carried out by personnel in the Office of Law Enforcement Assistance, which had been created in the Department of Justice by the Law Enforcement Assistance Act of 1965 (Pub. L. 89–197).

Director Ruth felt strongly that the mood of Congress was anti-research.* Representative John Rooney of New York was especially critical of research efforts during this period and demanded that the Institute demonstrate its usefulness by producing immediate solutions. Much of Ruth's time was spent justifying the research role to such oversight groups, including his own administrative hierarchy. The LEAA troika reflected practitioner/political divisions that were never conducive to developing a research role in LEAA. Charles Rogovin, first LEAA Administrator, summarized Ruth's experiences (1973, p. 18):

> I had represented to him that he could design his own research program and enjoy real freedom and flexibility in implementing it. I have rarely been more in error. Time and again Ruth's initiatives were frustrated by the disagreements from Velde, Coster and myself [the troika]. Despite a wealth of experience in assessing the quality of research institutions and individuals during his service as Deputy Director of the Crime Commission and in academic life, he was second-guessed on every judgment.

Whether reporting to a hostile Congress or to a divided LEAA administration, the early directors had a political rather than a research task. This characterization of the role of Institute directors varies only in degree, never in kind, throughout the history of the Institute.

Phase II: The Danziger Period—Impact Programming (1971–1973)

Phase I ended with President Nixon's appointment of Jerris Leonard as administrator of LEAA and Leonard's appointment of Martin Danziger as director of NILECJ in the spring of 1971. The previous year had seen strong criticism of LEAA in Congress (see Appendix A2) because, among other things, the large sums already expended on various programs had not produced a decline in the crime rate. Since Congress had established LEAA with the expectation that crime would be reduced and LEAA had not taken issue with the assumption that crime could be reduced by programs to "strengthen law enforcement," there was no public basis for advocating a different measure of performance. Unfortunately, the new LEAA administration accepted—even welcomed—this "cure rate" standard. It thereby confounded, instead of clarifying, a problem that still troubles LEAA, especially its research program.

*Mr. Ruth made these comments during an interview in the fall of 1975. They were supported by several sources: other individuals who were on the staff of the Institute during that time have made similar comments in interviews, and Charles Rogovin, first administrator of LEAA, has made such comments in print (1973, p. 19).

The use of crime rates as a measure of performance is problematic for three reasons. First, crime rates are affected to a considerable degree by factors other than those under the control of the criminal justice system, and conversely, many who contribute to the crime rate do not pass through that system. Second, crime rates themselves are affected by higher citizen or victim reporting and police reporting procedures. It is quite possible for a program in citizen awareness, for example, to have the intended impact of higher reporting of crimes, therefore producing a higher crime rate. Third, and in this context most important, the use of crime rates as a measure of performance is based on wholly unrealistic expectations about the kind and extent of impact that is possible from research. There are many aspects of crime about which little is now known, and much of this knowledge can be useful in future efforts to prevent and control crime. For example, our public policies on punishment as a deterrent, on the use of the criminal law to control deviant behavior, on techniques of law enforcement, on court processing, on techniques of rehabilitating criminal offenders, all can be productively informed by carefully focused research. But it is important to recognize that practical payoff from research is necessarily indirect and often long term.

Nonetheless, increases and decreases in crime rates remained the focus of LEAA performance measures, and the criticism continued. One outcome of the criticism was LEAA's embarrassing discovery that it had almost no information about the impact of its programs. Therefore, a new effort was begun throughout LEAA to focus on crime reduction (rather than "system improvement") and on evaluating the impact of its programs. The interest in evaluation was encouraging, but it had unfortunate consequences for the development of the Institute: it hardened and intensified LEAA's commitment to the goal of directly controlling crime, even for the research program; it involved Institute staff in a lengthy and complex planning process using specific reductions in crime rates as performance measures; and it produced a sharp change in research and development (R&D) strategy.

The term "crime-specific planning" came into use throughout LEAA in 1971, in direct response to Congressional questions about the relationship between government anti-crime funding and the increasing crime rate (see discussion of the Monagan hearings in Appendix A2; also see Chelimsky 1976, pp. 3–16). The term meant that programming had to be tied to a specific crime and designed to bring about a specified level of reduction (or decreasing rate of increase) in the rate of occurrence for that particular crime. The total lack of realism in the expectations underlying crime-specific planning became clear very quickly, but the concept continued to have organizational impact even in the research program. Two years were devoted to making both the organization and programs of the Institute directly responsive to the goal of reducing crime. "Crime-specific" was relaxed to "crime-oriented" during this period, but the belief remained strong that research on crime could directly and immediately affect crime rates if only the right combination of planning and funding strategy was used.

Accepting the pressures of providing immediate, "crime-specific" results, Director Danziger reorganized the Institute. The new structure included a planning and evaluation staff and four divisions: Research Administration, Research Operations, Statistics, and Technology Transfer. The 1973 Program Plan, in which this system was most fully elaborated, admits that "this approach is basically the structure for an operational, action-oriented program," but asserts that "a research plan also can closely follow the design." This statement illustrates the extent to which the Institute during this period was engaged in an intensive drive to produce social change.

The funding program for 1973 was significantly different from previous years. NILECJ chose to limit its major funding to a few large-scale grants and contracts, on the grounds that this strategy would have the largest possible payoff. Large dollar amounts were committed to projects—for example, the Equipment Systems Improvement Program—several of which continue today.

The major example of the shift in research strategy was the Institute's involvement in LEAA's Impact Cities Program. The Institute's 1973 program plan describes the Impact Cities Program in the following way:

> This program channels a substantial portion of LEAA's discretionary and research funds to selected Impact Cities for the reduction of stranger-to-stranger crime and burglary. The objective is to halt the increase in the target crimes and to achieve a 5% reduction in two years and a 20% decrease in five years.

Apparently convinced that solutions could be found by concentrating large amounts of money at selected sites and believing that this would result in a more efficient use of R&D money than a fragmented grants program, Leonard and Danziger made the Impact Cities program a major recipient of LEAA and Institute funds. The expected payoff of gaining new knowledge about reducing crime did not materialize and that failure should have been anticipated. A more detailed discussion of Impact Cities appears in Chapter 4 and in the Case Study on Impact Cities, but one major point should be stressed here: the obviously political nature of the overall program dictated many aspects of its design and operation. For example, the cities themselves were chosen for political reasons, and the New Federalism requirements precluded mandating comparable programs or comparable data collection and evaluation designs. While the Institute was not responsible for these politically motivated requirements, the situation illustrates the highly political constraints within which the Institute operates, constraints that do not lend themselves to good research efforts. The Institute can be held responsible for committing its resources to programs that cannot be reconciled with research objectives.

In sum, the Danziger period produced an intensification of the Institute commitment to directly reducing crime. Goals, objectives, and planning were all tied to a belief that crime was a problem that could be solved: a war on crime on the model of the war on poverty. This effort has generally been considered not only a failure but wrong-headed as well; crime cannot be simply purged from society by committing massive government resources. While this judgment does not fault the good intentions of those who were part of LEAA's effort during that period, it does point to a major mistake in the agency's understanding of crime problems. In fact, given the political climate and bureaucratic complexities, it is clear that this period did not provide a good test of the validity of crime-reduction policies. And it is particularly clear that the research program was misused in the mistaken campaign for immediate solutions.

Phase III: The Caplan Period (1973–1977)

Gerald Caplan was appointed director of the Institute in fall 1973 by the new LEAA administrator, Donald Santorelli. The Caplan period received its earliest definition in the decision to deemphasize crime reduction as a goal. The experience with crime-specific and then crime-oriented planning was clear throughout LEAA; it simply was not possible to demonstrate that the various LEAA programs, let alone NILECJ research grants, had contributed to specific decreases in specific crime rates.

Since crime rates had not decreased significantly anywhere—indeed had increased more often than decreased—any claims for impact were probably unfounded from the start.* Caplan responded to this state of

*In fact, some experimental programs had the effect of increasing the crime rate—as measured by the FBI's Uniform Crime Reports—because they achieved their intended effect of increasing the number of crimes reported to the police.

affairs by explicitly disclaiming the reality of such expectations. Recognizing that it was wholly unreasonable to measure the effectiveness of a research program by specific "cure" rates, Caplan modified the Institute's approach. The Institute would no longer plan for direct and immediate impact on crime rates but instead would develop longer-range objectives that could be expected to contribute to a more realistic way to achieve an overall reduction in crime. Even the traditional focus on improving the system was recast so that efficiency and fairness became objectives in their own right rather than tools for reducing crime rates. The Institute and all of LEAA entered a new period of deflating expectations.

Later, Caplan also began efforts to develop and encourage a research community interested in more basic research questions. He moved away from the Danziger strategy of supporting a few large-scale efforts toward a policy of awarding a larger number of smaller grants, especially looking to the academic research community, and tried to develop close connections with a wider research community. He attempted to draw research ideas from among those who had never done work in criminal justice but who were interested in behaviors and social patterns that are clearly important for understanding crime phenomena. This approach, had it been carried forward with a major commitment of Institute resources, would have amounted to a whole new strategy: namely, directing the Institute efforts not to reducing crime rates but to understanding the social and behavioral phenomena that underlie crime. Unfortunately, there are only minimal signs that such a strategy was pursued on a major scale. The overall impression of the Institute's goals and objectives under Caplan's leadership is one of decentralization and eclecticism. No research agenda exists as a general guide to planning and funding. Instead, the organizational structure itself—traditional program areas plus major efforts in evaluation and technology transfer—seemed to generate the program. This report addresses the question of whether this reflects the maturing of an organization that, in its collective sense of itself, now realizes that a step-by-step, piece-by-piece approach is the best route to accomplishing its mission or whether this reflects the frustration of failure and the absence of any sense of mission.

CONCLUSION

The problems of locating a research program in an action agency have always been substantial. The pressures from the parent agency tend to favor immediate solutions and foster an unnecessary polarization of basic and applied research. NILECJ's position in an agency whose perceived mission is to service local criminal justice practitioners has narrowed its focus to the criminal justice system, and sometimes simply to crime rates, and has prevented the Institute from looking to larger research issues. Its outlook has been unnecessarily narrow and its research agenda has not benefited from a variety of perspectives on criminal justice problems.

These difficulties have been exacerbated by the political atmosphere and administrative conditions in which the Institute has had to function. This chapter's brief sketch of the Institute's historical development illustrates a confusion about NILECJ's basic mission that has plagued the agency since its inception. As each new director or administrator of LEAA brought to the office a different conception of the Institute's mandate, NILECJ's structure was reorganized and the research program overhauled. Given the confusion in the Department of Justice and the turnover within LEAA's leadership during the past eight years, the development and pursuit of a coherent research agenda has been a formidable task. The cumulation of knowledge through research has suffered as program priorities have changed before results could accumulate on any specific topics.

The Safe Streets Act and the agency that it created were attempts at a pluralistic resolution of severe ideological differences. The resulting structure of the new action agency (LEAA) was an intricate imitation of the federal system. The problems of federal research for local consumption were not systematically considered by the Institute's founders and remain a basic dilemma to the present day.

2 The Structure of LEAA

The National Institute of Law Enforcement and Criminal Justice has, since its inception, pursued its mission of research and development within the LEAA structure. The responsibility of servicing an action agency organized to distribute block-grant funds to the states has significantly affected the Institute and its programs. Consequently, some description of LEAA and the environment in which it operates is an essential preamble to an understanding of NILECJ. This chapter describes the structure and organization of LEAA.

LEAA includes both national programs and the block-grant program. The decentralized block grants are administered through a system that includes: Regional Offices (ROS), State Planning Agencies (SPAS), Regional Planning Units (RPUS), and Criminal Justice Coordinating Councils (CJCCS).* The national programs, under the direction of the administrator of LEAA, are administered through five offices: the National Institute of Law Enforcement and Criminal Justice, the Office of National Priority Programs, the National Criminal Justice Information and Statistics Service, the Office of Juvenile Justice and Delinquency Prevention, and the Office of Regional Operations. The organization chart for LEAA is shown in Figure 1.

*The 1971 Amendments to the Omnibus Crime Control and Safe Streets Act authorized the establishment of CJCCS in areas with a population of at least 250,000.

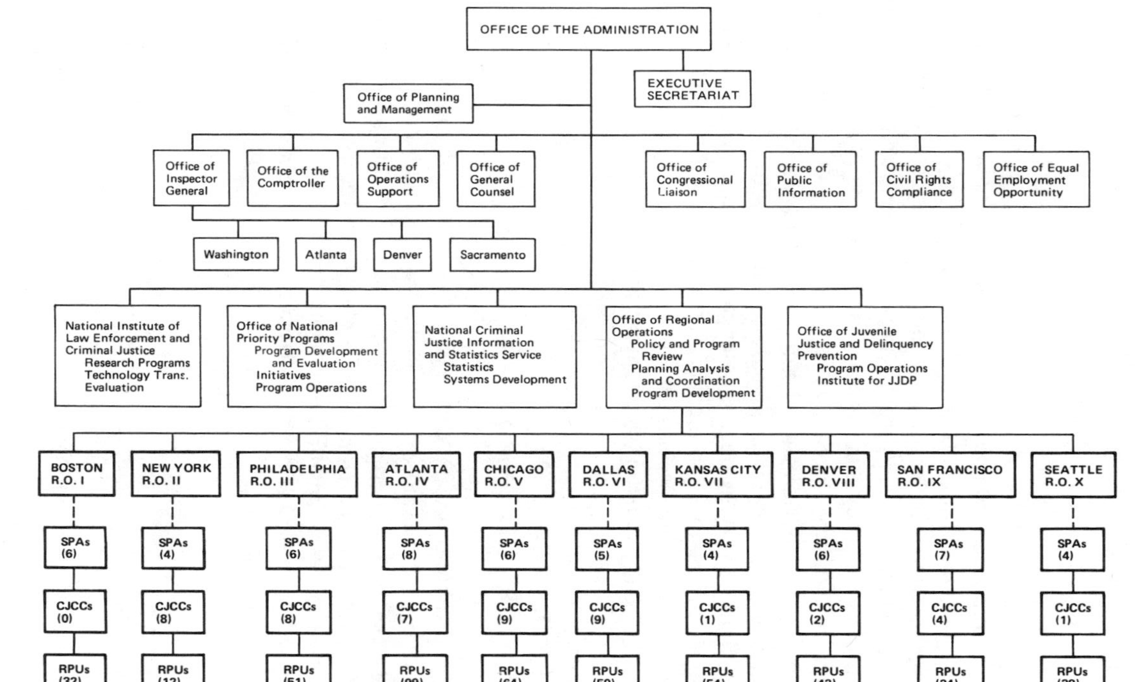

FIGURE 1 Law Enforcement Assistance Administration organization chart, 1976. SOURCE: *Two Hundred Years of American Criminal Justice: An LEAA Bicentennial Study*, Washington, D.C., 1976.

ADMINISTRATION OF THE BLOCK-GRANT PROGRAM

The primary mechanisms through which the block-grant program is administered are the State Planning Agencies. There are SPAs in each of the 50 states and in American Samoa, the District of Columbia, Guam, Puerto Rico, the Virgin Islands, and the Trust Territories of the Pacific Islands. These agencies, usually responsible to the governor, are charged with preparing and submitting to LEAA the annual comprehensive plans for the allocation of block-grant funds to the criminal justice programs in the states. In addition to their statutory responsibilities, SPAs perform a variety of tasks from grants monitoring and auditing to project evaluations. Many SPAs are also actively involved in special criminal justice studies, legislative programming, or system-wide budget review (LEAA Sixth Annual Report, 1974). Regional Planning Units, which are sub-state units, participate in both planning and funding decisions to varying degrees, depending on the state. They act as mechanisms to link LEAA to local criminal justice jurisdictions. The decentralized block-grant program is linked to the national headquarters through the Office of Regional Operations.

ADMINISTRATION OF THE NATIONAL PROGRAMS

The national programs are under the direction of the administrator of LEAA, aided by two deputies and eight management and support offices: the Inspector General, the Comptroller, Operations Support, General Counsel, Congressional Liaison, Public Information, Civil Rights Compliance, and Equal Employment Opportunity. The administrator is ultimately responsible for all management and policy decisions.

Office of Regional Operations

The Office of Regional Operations (ORO) is the major link between LEAA and the states, coordinating the implementation of the LEAA program through the 10 regional offices. ORO is intended to be a conduit of information, directives, guidelines, and policy decisions from the central LEAA office to the regional offices and then to the SPAs. The 10 regional offices have the responsibility for reviewing and approving the state comprehensive plans, as well as for technical assistance to the SPAS, RPUS, and operating agencies participating in LEAA programs.

ORO also funds and manages a number of discretionary and training programs,* some of which overlap with non-research responsibilities of NILECJ. Among the ORO programs that involve current NILECJ concerns are those in the Corrections Division, which develops and monitors nationally focused discretionary programs in corrections and assists the central and regional offices in dealing with corrections issues. This division also administers a technical assistance program for corrections agencies. The Organized Crime Section of ORO administers LEAA's programs directed at organized crime and corruption and the organized crime training program for prosecuting attorneys. The Narcotics and Drug Abuse Division coordinates LEAA's assistance to state and local drug enforcement activities and funds programs designed to reduce drug-associated crime. The Police Division provides technical assistance and funding to programs intended to improve the productivity of law enforcement agencies; furnishes technical assistance to the police specialists in LEAA regional offices; and represents LEAA in national police-oriented seminars and programs. The Adjudication Division performs similar functions for court programs. ORO also maintains an Education Division and its own program evaluation and monitoring staff.

Office of National Priority Programs

The Office of National Priority Programs develops crime reduction programs addressed to the nation's major crime problems. It includes four program divisions—Citizen's Initiative, Career Criminal Initiatives, Crime Prevention Initiative, and Standards and Goals Initiatives—and a division of Program Development and Evaluation, which undertakes planning, analysis, and evaluation functions for the other divisions.

National Criminal Justice Information and Statistics Service

The National Criminal Justice Information and Statistics Service (NCJISS) was established in 1970 and placed in NILECJ for a brief period after LEAA's 1971 reorganization. Its Statistics Division is responsible for generating criminal justice data on a national level. Prior to the

*The Crime Control Acts (Pub. L. 90–351, 91–644, 93–83) have always exempted a percentage of funds to be allocated at the discretion of the administrator.

division's creation, four separate agencies were responsible for providing statistics for criminal justice agencies: The Department of Health, Education, and Welfare provided data on juvenile delinquents; the Bureau of the Census provided relevant expenditure and employment data; the Bureau of Prisons published *National Prisoner Statistics;* and the FBI issued the *Uniform Crime Report.* The Statistics Division of NCJISS has assumed responsibility for all of these but the last.

The Statistics Division has also developed more than a dozen statistical series on various aspects of the criminal justice system and supports a research program. The National Crime Panel Survey is a major program designed to measure the extent and character of criminal victimization; it includes a continuous national survey and periodic surveys in selected cities. A second major program is composed of several system-wide surveys, including the annual survey of criminal justice expenditure and employment and the LEAA Directory of Criminal Justice Agencies. A series of surveys and censuses in the corrections field comprises the third major program of the Statistics Division; they include the National Prisoner Statistics, the Summary of Movement of Sentenced Persons, Characteristics of Admissions and Releases, and the Census of State Correctional Facilities. The Statistics Division supports research, primarily through grants to universities and non-profit organizations. Research has been funded on the self-reporting of crime, social indicators of personal harm, and the development of seriousness scales based on public perception of crime.

The Systems Development Division of NCJISS provides assistance to the states in the development of information systems of use to criminal justice agencies. This division monitors and coordinates the operations of Project SEARCH (System for Electronic Analysis and Retrieval of Criminal Histories), which is a multi-state consortium of representatives from the criminal justice community concerned with relevant information systems. It began in 1969 when six states were funded to develop cooperatively a uniform format for criminal history information and a prototype statistics system based on an accounting of individual offenders as they moved through the criminal justice system. By 1972, Project SEARCH had completed its original mission and was reorganized and expanded to include all 50 states, Puerto Rico, the Virgin Islands, and the District of Columbia. Charged now with the development and testing of prototype systems having multi-state use for the application of advanced technology to criminal justice, SEARCH has initiated programs in the upgrading of state identification bureaus, the development of information systems for courts and correction agencies, the standardization of police report forms, and the production of a nationalized central file for criminalistics laboratories (LEAA Sixth Annual Report, 1974).

Office of Juvenile Justice and Delinquency

In the Juvenile Justice and Delinquency Prevention Act of 1974 (P. L. 93–415), Congress enlarged LEAA's mandate by establishing an Office of Juvenile Justice and Delinquency Prevention and creating a second research institute to be housed within the new LEAA structure. The National Institute for Juvenile Justice and Delinquency Prevention (NIJJDP) was charged with conducting research, demonstration, evaluation, and training projects on topics of relevance to juvenile involvement with the criminal justice system. It is also responsible for the development of standards for the administration of juvenile justice at the federal, state, and local levels. With the creation of NIJJDP, which is parallel to and independent of NILECJ, NILECJ has largely withdrawn from sponsoring research on juvenile delinquency.

Since it began operating in 1975, NIJJDP has planned and undertaken the development of assessment centers through the country; a study of youth gang violence; a multi-year assessment of the national state of juvenile corrections; and an evaluation of community-based juvenile programs in the state of Massachusetts, which began after the 1972 abolition of state training schools. It has also undertaken some cooperative efforts with the National Evaluation Program (NEP)* of NILECJ's Office of Research Programs: grants were awarded in fiscal 1975 for studies of youth service bureaus, juvenile diversion, alternatives to incarceration, delinquency prevention projects, and alternatives to custodial detention and in fiscal 1976 for police juvenile units and juvenile court intake units. For these grants NEP follows normal contracting and monitoring procedures and juvenile justice maintains a monitoring role. The National Institute of Juvenile Justice and Delinquency Prevention received an appropriation of $6 million for fiscal 1976.

National Institute of Law Enforcement and Criminal Justice

Structure of NILECJ

The National Institute of Law Enforcement and Criminal Justice is the fifth national program. The Institute is divided into three Offices: the

*The National Evaluation Program is described in the Case Study on the Office of Evaluation.

Office of Research Programs, the Office of Technology Transfer, and the Office of Evaluation (See Figure 2). The Office of Research Programs (ORP) is divided into five program divisions: Police, Courts and Corrections, Advanced Technology, Community Crime Prevention, and Special Programs. The Office of Technology Transfer is divided into three divisions: Model Program Development, Training and Testing, and the Reference and Dissemination Division, which operates the National Criminal Justice Reference Service. The Office of Evaluation undertakes program evaluation and funds research in the development of evaluation tools and methodologies. (The Office of Evaluation, the Office of Technology Transfer, and the program in Advanced Technology in ORP are the subjects of three of the case studies in this report.) NILECJ's director is appointed by and responsible to the LEAA administrator who has final approval (sign-off authority) of all Institute awards. Table 1 shows the amount of LEAA funds budgeted to NILECJ vis-a-vis other program and management functions.

Consequences of NILECJ's *Setting*

Since the National Institute of Law Enforcement and Criminal Justice is the research organization of LEAA, NILECJ's immediate environment is its LEAA setting. Although it seems normal for the relationship of a research and development organization and its parent body to exhibit signs of strain, this phenomenon particularly characterizes NILECJ's relations with LEAA.

LEAA's policy-making and upper administrative levels are occupied largely by lawyers and practitioners from criminal justice agencies. These two groups have little sympathy for the complexities of social science research and an often inadequate grasp of the potential and limitations of research in the criminal justice field. Moreover, the history of LEAA itself has been characterized by intense political pressure, rapid growth, major policy changes, and turnovers in leadership.

The LEAA system is based on the 10 regional offices operated by the Office of Regional Operations (ORO) and on the 56 State Planning Agencies. On the whole, NILECJ has resisted close connections with this structure, despite Congressional mandates to provide technical assistance for project evaluation and other SPA activities. The Institute has traditionally viewed its audience as criminal justice practitioners rather than those in the LEAA structure. Local officials responsible for allocating resources to courts, correction and police agencies, and decision makers within criminal justice agencies were perceived by the

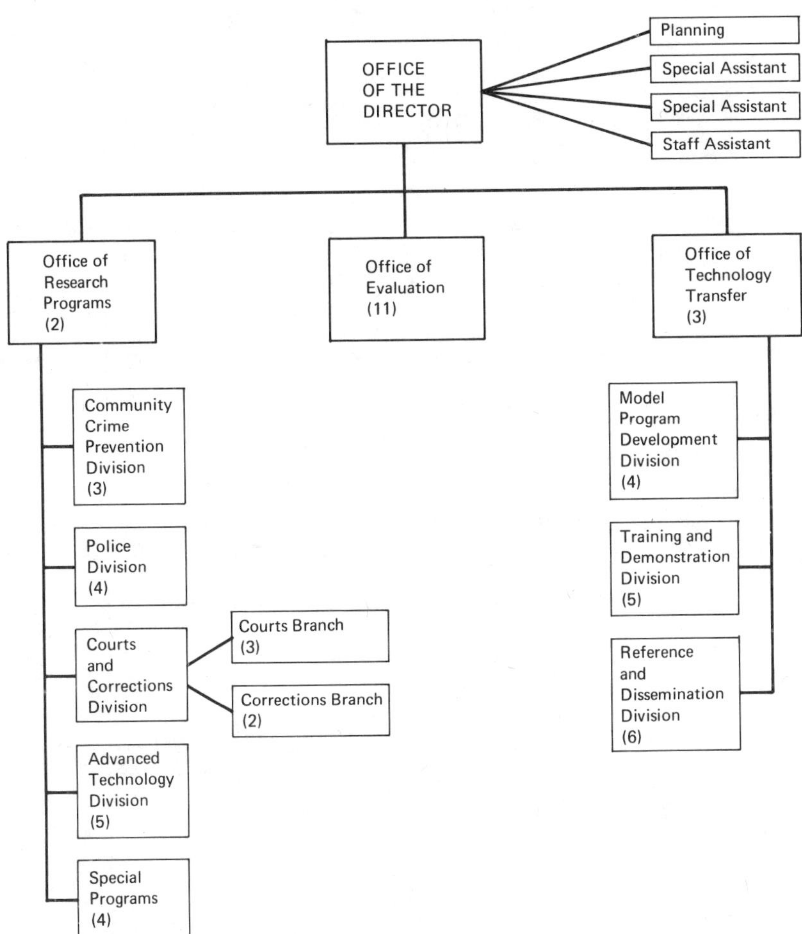

FIGURE 2 National Institute of Law Enforcement and Criminal Justice organization chart, 1976.

TABLE 1 LEAA Appropriations History (dollars in thousands)

	1969 Actual	1970 Actual	1971 Actual	1972 Actual	1973 Actual	1974 Actual	1975 Estimated
Grants for development and implementation of comprehensive plans (Part B)	$19,000	$ 21,000	$ 26,000	$ 35,000	$ 50,000	$ 50,000	$ 55,000
Matching grants to improve and strengthen law enforcement (Part C):							
(a) State block grants	24,650	182,750	340,000	413,695	480,250	480,250	480,250
(b) Discretionary grants	4,350	32,000	70,000	73,005	88,750	88,750	84,750
Aid for correctional institutions and programs (Part E)	—	—	47,500	97,500	113,000	113,000	113,000
Technical assistance	—	1,200	4,000	6,000	10,000	12,000	14,968
Technology, analysis, development, and dissemination (National Institute of Law Enforcement and Criminal Justice[a])	3,000	7,500	7,500	21,000	31,598	40,098	45,198
Manpower development (Part D: education)	6,500	18,000	22,500	31,000	45,000	45,000	45,000
Data systems and statistical assistance	—	1,000	4,000	9,700	21,200	24,000	26,500
Management and operations	2,500	4,487	7,454	11,823	15,568 –14,200[b]	17,428	21,734
TOTAL OBLIGATIONAL AUTHORITY	60,000	267,937	528,954	698,723	841,166	870,526	886,400
Transferred to other agencies	3,000	182	46	196	14,431	149	—
TOTAL APPROPRIATED	63,000	268,119	529,000	698,919	855,597	870,673	886,400

SOURCE: Law Enforcement Assistance Administration.

[a]Budget of the National Institute.

[b]Transferred to other agencies in the U.S. Department of Justice pursuant to P.L. 93–50.

Institute staff as a more appropriate clientele than the SPAS. The somewhat unwieldy system of the ORO, regional offices, and state planning agencies, each defensive of territorial claims, appeared to Institute staff as, at best, an indirect approach to the practitioner, and at worst, an obstruction. Despite NILECJ's resistance, however, there has been an effort on the part of the Administrator's Office to increase interaction between the Institute and LEAA. NILECJ has been encouraged to emphasize the LEAA system as its avenue of approach to practitioners and as the object of increased technical assistance. This has been most effectively observed in the operations of the Office of Technology Transfer (see the Case Study on the Office of Technology Transfer).

In summary, the Institute's location within the structure of an action agency and the accompanying requirement that it be responsive to the needs of action programs necessarily affects the nature of its research programs. While NILECJ is, by conception and purpose, a mission-oriented research institute, a question can be raised about the appropriate conditions under which its mission should be pursued. Certainly its location in LEAA has made the Institute vulnerable to the kinds of leadership tensions and intra-agency pressures described in Chapter 1. Whether this vulnerability has resulted in poor quality or less than useful research is an issue considered in the evaluation presented in the following chapters.

II Evaluating the Federal Role in Crime Research

The task of evaluating the research program of NILECJ is necessarily wider in scope than the record of Institute-funded research. It requires reaching judgments about a number of related factors that establish a frame of reference for research into serious social problems. These factors include the nature of criminal justice in our society, the proper federal role for research in criminal justice, and the various possible techniques for developing useful knowledge. Therefore, the first chapter in Part II, entitled "Basic Issues," lays the general groundwork for the more specific judgments made in the following chapter, "The Institute's Research Program," which evaluates the Institute's work.

3 Basic Issues

One of the central purposes of government is keeping the public peace and order and enforcing a system of assigned rights and corresponding duties. The criminal justice system is the primary instrument for achieving that purpose. It is a system that gives the authorities strong powers of coercion to control the behavior of the public. It is important that this coercive authority be exercised as fairly and benignly as is consistent with the efficient achievement of the public purpose that the system seeks to serve. The United States is large and enormously diverse in those properties that affect the equitable and efficient performance of the criminal justice system. The power to define criminal behavior and to take decisions within the limits of wide discretion in the administration of criminal justice is, therefore, quite rightly, decentralized and diffused, lodging mostly in state and local jurisdictions.

RATIONALE FOR A FEDERAL RESEARCH ROLE IN CRIME PROGRAMS

What is the mission of a national institute of law enforcement and criminal justice, in the context of a largely locally administered law enforcement and criminal justice system? Much of what follows in this report is intended to provide a detailed answer to this question. But a short, introductory answer is that extensive knowledge about crime and criminal behaviors and about the operation of the criminal justice system is necessary in order to develop governmental responses that are both fair and effective. The employment of the socially appropriate quantity of resources in the search for information and the discovery, acquisition, and assimilation of the necessary amount of information requires that criminal justice research be a national mission in the public sector.

Such a mission makes sense on the assumptions that there is, in fact, a stock of information to be discovered; that that information is capable of being discovered if research is undertaken; that the cost of discovery is smaller than the value of the information, once discovered; and that the relevant information is not yet known or, if known to some, has not been disseminated to those who could use it in developing criminal justice policies and in the administration of the criminal justice system. These seem to us reasonable assumptions.

The performance of policing, prosecutorial, and judicial functions is the responsibility of so many different institutions and personalities and are administered in so large a variety of phenomenological contexts in this country that it seems fair to conclude that an enormous body of experience of very great complexity has been built up over time. The extraction of nuggets from that stock of experience should provide usable information of value to law enforcement and criminal justice authorities.

In addition, basic research in many disciplines has created a large stock of knowledge about the physical properties of the world, some of which can be expected to have applied uses in law enforcement and in the administration of criminal justice. Some applied uses of that knowledge have been discovered for other fields; this can also be expected for criminal justice.

A more problematic question is the potential for gaining useful information about criminal behaviors and the conditions under which such behaviors flourish. Exclusive attention to the system of laws and their enforcement is of limited value since the incidence of crime is only minimally affected by that system. In fact, there are important indications that much crime is not even touched by the criminal justice system: surveys of victimization, which attempt to measure crime rates directly rather than through police records, tend to show a considerably higher incidence of crime than is ever reported to the criminal justice system;* and the rate at which police "clear" crimes by arrest is

*For example, surveys of victimization in the nation's five largest cities during 1972 discovered that only 44–51 percent of violent crimes and 28–33 percent of property crimes had been reported to the police; see Table 6, p. 61, of *Criminal Victimization Surveys in the Nation's Five Largest Cities* (U.S. Department of Justice 1975).

very low—for example, only 21 percent of all Index Crimes in 1975 (Federal Bureau of Investigation 1976, p. 166, Table 18). While we presently have little systematic knowledge about this submerged mass of the crime problem, it is clearly an important target for a large-scale research effort. But it is a very difficult target, requiring methodological ingenuity and considerable patience. There is no existing stock of knowledge that can simply be mined or translated from one field into another. A national research institute that can command the necessary resources of funding and skills is essential in order to adequately confront such a task.

Some caveats are warranted. Since law enforcement is mainly a local function in the United States, there can be no complete assurances that research discoveries will be assimilated by the local authorities, nor that they will recognize the usefulness of those discoveries in guiding their own practice, nor, even if they know them to be useful, that they will put those discoveries to use.

Criminal justice research promoted through a national institute is, therefore, inevitably a risky business. To achieve a payoff from that research requires wise judgment in the selection of research to be promoted and in differentiating research results that do and do not have useful applications, and it requires the intensive dissemination of useful research discoveries and the promotion of their use among the local law enforcement and the appropriate officials in the criminal justice system. Even so, it can be expected that some of those officials are more given to introducing innovation than others and that some who are committed to current practice will be unwilling to introduce change. Criminal justice research, even when successful in the sense of producing clear guides to the improvement of the system, may have only spotted effects upon practice.

Nonetheless, the magnitude of the crime problem necessitates a major effort to develop and disseminate reliable knowledge. For this purpose it is appropriate for the federal government to mount a long-range research program.

THE NATURE OF A FEDERAL RESEARCH ROLE IN CRIME PROGRAMS

Because the federal role in criminal justice research came about as part of a much larger action program, it is important to be clear about the nature of the relationship between the two. As detailed in Chapter 1, Congress was ambivalent about assigning any federal role in state and local criminal justice activities. Its solution to the problem of federal interference was to set up a framework of block-grant funding under which state and local decision makers are supposed to retain programmatic authority, although their actions are reviewed by federal officials. The federal role was essentially to provide the funds. But Congress also established a centralized structure for the purpose of performing some functions that were not considered feasible at the state level, principally a national crime statistics center and a research and development (R&D) effort. Since it was assumed from the beginning that the national interest in crime was to serve local needs, a federal R&D effort was not for the purpose of solving crime problems at the national level but rather to help state and local jurisdictions deal with their crime. A basic premise of the Safe Streets Act, therefore, was that the federal R&D effort was to service state and local planning.

Alternative Strategies

What kind of strategy will best serve that purpose? There are several possible answers to that question. One is to assume that serving state and local planning means providing information to the administrators of block-grant funds (the state planning agencies) about which programs being considered for funding are likely to be effective. The "what works and what doesn't work?" question has been posed insistently to NILECJ by SPAS from the early days, indicating that they at least perceive NILECJ's service role in terms of providing immediate solutions and that they wished to use the information in their planning. It will not surprise researchers that NILECJ was unable to respond to such requests. While the question itself is important and should be addressed—and it was even encouraging that SPAS asked it—it is naive to pose it in terms of immediate solutions. There is no more complex area of social phenomena than crime. Since researchers do not yet understand the basic causes of crime, it is naturally difficult for them to come up with quick prescriptions for stopping it. In short, the "immediate solution" strategy places the Institute in an impossible position.

Another strategy would place the Institute in the role of providing programmatic solutions for local crime problems but without the pressure of immediacy. Such a strategy would keep NILECJ in its direct service relationship with the block-grant structure and thereby force it to focus on the programmatic concerns of state and local criminal justice planners. Because of the nature of block-grant funding, this strategy would probably mean that the Institute's effort would be predominantly oriented to traditional practitioner needs. Thus, a major focus would be operational: improving the efficiency of the criminal justice system. Throughout much of its history, the Institute has pursued a very similar strategy. But, as will be illustrated in later chapters, the strategy has not successfully served SPA programming needs and has produced mostly mediocre research.

A third strategy would put the Institute in the primary business of planning and implementing large demonstration projects. Such a strategy would have the mixed purpose of synthesizing research results (from any source), testing appropriate implementations, and disseminating model programs to practitioners. It would probably tie the Institute's efforts to SPA programming less than would the first two strategies and make it more directly responsive to the practitioner community. It would also decrease substantially NILECJ's role in planning and sponsoring primary research. The Institute has engaged in some of this activity, but it is not at all clear that a demonstration strategy requires the guidance of a research institute. LEAA has its own office and funds for this purpose and could probably pursue such a strategy as effectively on its own or with minimal methodological advice from NILECJ.

A fourth possibility, and one that is far more appropriate for a national research institute, would be for NILECJ to emphasize that aspect of the "safe streets" legislation that encourages innovative anti-crime programming and, therefore, to focus its efforts on developing and testing alternative approaches to crime problems. Such a program would tend to de-emphasize operational questions except insofar as they were directly related to crime control (e.g., patrol strategies); it would work with non-traditional approaches to crime and criminal behavior in an effort to develop a new understanding of crime; it would attempt to bring to bear thinking and research from a variety of disciplines not now focusing on crime and encourage multidisciplinary research efforts; and it would concentrate on testing hypotheses under experimental and quasi-experimental conditions to obtain results that are reliable for use in developing programs. This strategy would tie the Institute more to the research community and permit resources to be allocated on grounds that are largely independent of political demands or system pressures. It would also require a risk-taking posture toward ideas and research possibilities. This kind of activity is necessary, we believe, in order to justify the existence of a national research institute. If encouraged to develop properly, this strategy will eventually serve state and local crime control needs far better than the more agency- or practitioner-dominated alternatives.

The nature of these alternative strategies reveals some important features of the relationship between research and action programming in LEAA. The role of SPAs is to administer the block-grant funds, which amount to approximately 5 percent of the total criminal justice expenditures in any state. Consequently, if the LEAA program is to have any impact, the SPAs must use action funds in strategic and innovative ways. To do so requires careful analysis of local crime problems, law enforcement patterns, and system needs. While few SPAs have yet developed this kind of analytical capacity, those that have find it both necessary and natural to conduct their own "immediate solution" research. The critical connection is between programming and research. Research, in this context, becomes totally a tool for planners with specific problems to solve. The case is similar for evaluation. The SPAs need to be able to evaluate particular programs with an eye both to refunding decisions and introducing changes to make existing programs more effective.

While this kind of research and evaluation has not yet developed extensively in the SPAs, it is clearly an appropriate and productive function. The Committee believes, however, that it is not a function that a national research institute can perform effectively. The relationship between a particular program's need for information and the deployment of resources to obtain the required knowledge is a matter of intra-organizational response. To place the responsibility for responding in the hands of a research institute that is remote from the particular needs defined by 56 SPAs is to ignore the natural dynamic in favor of an unnatural and inevitably unworkable relationship. A further complication is the fact that the canons for valid scientific research often conflict with the needs and style of program administrators. Since the basis of the relationship is service and that relationship runs in one direction only (with research serving program), the likelihood is that research canons will be compromised more often than administrators inconvenienced. Even when the research staff succeeds in protecting the integrity of its work, the constant struggle is likely to be debilitating.

The current relationship between SPAs and the Institute ranges from indifference to hostility. The SPAs resist programming that is not developed to meet a specific and, they argue, unique need; they also resent the intrusion of the federal presence whenever the Institute funds a demonstration or evaluation program in their state. By the same token, the Institute resents SPA expectations that the Institute should be providing readily applicable knowledge for local programming and their general lack of understanding of the nature of research. We believe that this mutual hostility is inevitable.

We suggest that there is another way to view the Institute's role in serving state and local needs. Rather than intruding upon the relationship between research and programming, which occurs most fruitfully at the SPA level where it is both organizationally sound and part of the dynamics of planning, the federal research effort should concentrate on developing and testing innovative approaches to crime problems. This strategy, which has already been outlined above, is particularly appropriate for a national institute. First, a major research commitment will often be required in order to thoroughly develop and adequately test new approaches to crime problems. The scale of such a commitment—both in resources and time frame—is beyond the capacities of SPAS. Second, the range and degree of scientific competence necessary to mount a highly sophisticated research effort are not normally available at the SPA level. Third, an undertaking that has a long-range time frame but no clearly specifiable product, and is risky as well, is simply inappropriate for an action agency such as an SPA. Therefore, the proper mission of a national institute of law enforcement and criminal justice is to engage in research and development on a scale and a level and within a time frame that is impractical for the rest of the system. Such a mission must not be all-inclusive because there is much valuable "immediate solution" evaluation and research that should be done (and would be better done) at the SPA level. In short, the nature of a federal research role in crime problems depends not only on the needs to be served but also on the capacities that exist or can be developed at the various levels of the system.

The Concept of Applied Research

To opt for a research strategy based on developing and testing innovative approaches to crime problems is not to exclude what is usually called applied research. The range of contributions that is appropriate necessarily spans a wide variety of research, development, and evaluation activities. But it is important to be clear about two matters: first, what is excluded and why; and second, the essentially eclectic (sometimes serendipitous) nature of what is included.

The preceding argument outlined what is excluded, namely, "immediate solution" research: this is research that is (or ought to be) tied directly to the planning process of an operating or funding agency and therefore to action programming. Another equally inappropriate undertaking for a national institute is simply gathering information on aspects of crime problems—building an inventory, if you will. This is what practitioners often think of as applied research and then feel frustrated when the piles of "data" do not tell them anything.

On the other hand, the example of data collection is a good point of departure for understanding the complex concept of applied research. Data collection and archiving must be carefully planned to be productive. One must, in effect, design a number of potential research projects in order to determine what data are necessary to answer important questions. In this speculative and informal design process, the significance of the questions, and therefore of the information that will become data, arises from the nature of the problems one is interested in. Research, whether its purpose is to understand a problem better or to try to solve it, is always a matter of stating and testing hypotheses. In short, applied research is not a singular activity that is unrelated to the more general process called research or to the normal canons of scientific methodology. It is part of a continuum that ranges from the abstract to the concrete; whatever differences that exist are matters of degree.

Differences do exist, of course, and they are important and instructive. Defining a problem for applied research means, minimally, starting with a practical problem rather than one that derives from theory; it also means that the researcher is concerned with finding a way of solving the problem rather than simply of understanding it better. Consequently, while so-called basic research is not constrained to produce a certain kind of answer, applied research always has a peculiar stake in its own results. For this reason, applied research is often more difficult to design than is basic research. It requires the perspective of practitioners, of program planners, and of researchers—an inherently conflicting mix—as well as the kind of creativity that permits one to understand and conceptualize social problems in terms of their possible solutions. A role for the Institute that emphasizes applied research is in many ways a more difficult assignment than conducting or sponsoring basic research.

There is a tendency to insist upon dichotomizing basic and applied research in such a way that many fruitful approaches are excluded. So-called basic research is considered inappropriate or so unrelated to problems as to be irrelevant. Research problems are defined as problems of practice, requiring only the application of proper technology for solution. Researchers are hired to survey the state of the art and then apply it: this is the model of "immediate solution" research, but without the specific problem and the programming function to make it useful. Furthermore, the approach tends to exclude the normal process of research: namely, generating alternative hypotheses from relevant theory and then testing one or more hypotheses to determine which variables and relationships are explanatory in a particular case. To say that applied research is problem-oriented does not mean that it cannot be informed by theory. Studying the problem of recidivism surely requires knowing something about attitude formation; studying problems of caseload and administrative discretion requires the application of organization theory as much as management technique; testing preventive patrol strategies requires an understanding of various possible behavioral responses in order to ensure that the proper measures are built into the experiment. The point is that the kinds of research that the Institute should be doing necessarily include aspects of both basic and applied research.

THE GOAL FOR A RESEARCH PROGRAM ON CRIME PROBLEMS

The goals for the Institute research program were set by Congress, in the Safe Streets Act and its amendments, and by LEAA throughout its history. The historical account in Chapter 1 reveals important shifts in these goals, as the urgency of the "law and order" mandate first intensified and then faded and the difficulty of pursuing immediate solutions became clear. The Committee has carefully considered both these lessons of history and the compelling nature of the social problem being addressed. Accordingly, we offer our own view of the proper goals for a national program in criminal justice research.

As noted in Chapter 1, crime reduction was a major goal of the Safe Streets Act and of LEAA programming from the beginning. It was responsible for the early emphasis on law enforcement and later for crime-specific and crime-oriented planning and, eventually, for the Institute's involvement in a disastrous "research" effort as part of the Impact Cities program.* These were all simplistic approaches to the problem and never got beyond the frustrating stage of trying to manipulate crime rates for the short term.

Only recently have LEAA and Institute officials been willing to quarrel publicly with the feasibility and appropriateness of crime reduction as a program goal. For example, former Institute Director Gerald M. Caplan, in speaking of the kinds of research discoveries that are and are not possible in the criminal justice field, said (1975):

> . . . the wiser view is that it will be through improved understanding of human behavior, rather than application of the laws of physics or chemistry, that gains will be made. Here, knowledge about controlling our worst impulses has grown but little over the last few thousand years. The suggestion is that crime control

*See the Case Study on Impact Cities for extended comments.

is not one of those fields of study where the word "breakthrough" is applicable. Progress in the acquisition of knowledge, such as it has been and such as it is likely to be, will come slowly, haltingly, unevenly, on occasion steadily, but rarely with rushing speed. It is best to think in time spans of 10 or 20 years, rather than of crash programs of six months, a year, or even several years.

Later, Caplan wrote (1975a, p. 13):

Finally, what can be said about our crime reduction capacity? Not much that is encouraging. We have learned little about reducing the incidence of crime, and have no reason to believe that significant reductions will be secured in the near future.

Unfortunately, the Institute's most recent response has been to deny its capacity to produce useful knowledge about crime problems at all and to substitute as its focus of concern the operation of the criminal justice system. We do not wish to belittle efforts to improve the operations of the criminal justice system or to exclude them entirely from the purview of the Institute, but many of these efforts are not properly a matter of research interest. Furthermore, while some are very important to the effective control of crime—such as studies of the formative conditions for police performance—others are remote from that concern. The danger we see is an Institute that avoids the hard questions of knowledge about crime and criminal behaviors in favor of easier but relatively trivial studies of system operations. It is understandable that an agency would respond negatively to a painful and unproductive history, but the Committee believes that the Institute's response is correct only with respect to expectations of immediate payoff. The goal of controlling crime for which LEAA and the Institute were originally established remains a valid objective, although a complex and difficult one.

Clearly, there were serious problems with LEAA's approach to crime reduction. If Congress expected that it could mount a program that would defeat crime, these expectations were plainly overblown. And certainly LEAA's frantic attempts to meet those expectations were ill-advised. But the Committee believes it would be a mistake to abandon the goal of reducing crime as if it were beyond the capacity of this society to cope with crime. The difficulty with crime reduction as a goal lies in a lack of understanding about how to approach the problem of crime and how to measure the impact of our efforts, not in the inherent intractability of the problem. No one is going to eradicate crime, just as no one is going to "cure" poverty or end wars. But we as scientists and citizens would be irresponsible if we abandoned our efforts because immediate solutions are not in sight. The fact is that we can know more about criminal behaviors and about the effectiveness of various governmental responses to them. And furthermore, this knowledge will ultimately be useful for crime prevention and control.* Therefore, we strongly urge that LEAA restore the control of crime as its primary goal and that NILECJ define its primary role as building knowledge toward that end.

If the goal of crime reduction is re-introduced, it should be clearly understood that gimmicks like 5-year deadlines for 20-percent reductions in burglary rates are seriously misleading, even for action programs, and certainly a mistaken measure of research productivity. In the first place, we do not yet have accurate or informative measures of crime rates, so the use of crime-rate measures as indicators or "tests" of anything is highly suspect. But even if we did have useful measures, it would be foolish to apply them to research programs. The National Institutes of Health have a cancer research program but no reasonable observer measures its effectiveness or usefulness by cancer cure rates (or death rates). It is obvious that the knowledge-building process in cancer research is long-term and unpredictable; the same is true for the process of building knowledge about crime and criminal behaviors. It is simply wrong to judge a research program by operational measures. It should be judged by the intelligence and coherence of its approach to crime and problems related to crime and by its capacity to cumulate and focus knowledge toward solving those problems. The Committee believes that such a program is feasible—and that it is the only legitimate basis for the existence of a national institute of law enforcement and criminal justice.

OBTAINING QUALITY RESEARCH

The requirements for successful research in any area of complex social phenomena are both stringent and problematic. They are stringent in part because of the difficulty of the problem being addressed, but more importantly because the cumulation of knowledge toward a solution is itself a particularly difficult task. They are problematic because no one strategy is clearly more effective than others.

From a process point of view, a research strategy has three critical features: planning and review procedures, proposal generation, and procurement practices. The following discussion is intended to clarify

*See Chapter 5 for specific recommendations about research on crime problems.

the alternatives of each feature and indicate the Committee's judgment of what is at stake in each case for a research program on crime problems. A research institute can develop elaborate program plans, using outside advice or not, and then require potential grantees to fit into one of the planned categories, or it can rely on the potential grantees to generate the ideas, on a sort of laissez-faire theory of research payoff. It can use a variety of kinds of outside review processes or rely on in-house review. It can procure research by grant or by contract, piecemeal with the pieces building on each other or in comprehensive packages. All of these alternatives have been followed at one time or another by both private and public funding agencies in the social sciences. None are clearly unacceptable, but there are advantages and disadvantages of each.

The programming approach is appealing in crime research, where there is a specified but highly complex purpose. Developing a productive program is a long-term process requiring broad knowledge and continuous involvement with developments in various disciplines. The programming approach is susceptible to severe parochialism unless outside advice is seriously sought and used. But if heavy reliance on internal programming is to be avoided, a research institute must be able to call upon an existing research community to develop its own creative response to the problems needing solution, or it must make a concerted effort to mobilize researchers across relevant disciplines to become interested in particular questions.

In criminal justice research, the nature of the research community has been a major problem. Few academic researchers outside the field of criminology have been interested in studying criminal behaviors, and even fewer have concentrated on the effects of law enforcement practices or on compliance problems. While a specialized research community in crime is increasingly available in research organizations, the university-based research community (which continues to be of major importance in the social sciences) has not been deeply involved in criminal justice. Until recently, Institute strategy was not designed to broaden the criminal justice research community: programs were either highly specialized or so grandly conceived that researchers based in traditional disciplines could find no point of departure for a response. This narrow strategy makes it all the more important that the Institute develop formal links to the most competent people in the research community.

A related issue is the Institute's approach to proposal review procedures. Proposal review procedures are important in ensuring that a range of expert views are brought to bear on the substantive importance of the proposed research. They are also the appropriate means for ensuring that research design and methodology meet accepted standards of rigor. In research operations within mission agencies, there is a real danger that staff, who are naturally and properly in advocacy positions, will dominate the substantive review process to the exclusion of a variety of perspectives and a range of expertise. It is especially important to broaden the base of substantive review when the traditional frameworks of discipline and theory-centered criteria are not applicable. Furthermore, staff in such mission agencies—even those whose interests and training naturally put them in research management—are normally not methodologists. The Institute needs a system of outside peer review because most staff are not trained methodologists and because they are in advocacy positions with respect to program objectives. This is not to say that traditional peer review systems always perform adequately, but the Committee believes that such systems, even with their shortcomings, are preferable to a system that relies on internal substantive and methodological review.

Another important issue is procurement practices. A research institute must decide whether it will fund solely (or largely) by grants or solely (or largely) by contracts. The conventional wisdom about the difference between the two emphasizes that grants are difficult to control while contracts ensure performance. This is an over-simplified view, to say the least. Grants have traditionally been used in the university-based research community because they permit the kind of flexibility that is required for creative research. Few (if any) of the interesting questions in social and behavioral science research can be dealt with as if they were cut-and-dried purchase orders. While this fact may be frustrating to those seeking immediate solutions, it is indeed a fact. This does not mean, however, that grantee research is inherently non-accountable or uncontrollable; it does mean that grantee research is not, and cannot be, performance-coded as if it were serial responses to a set of commands.

The contract procedure, usually through a request for proposals (RFP), is appropriate in some cases, notably where the purchase-order analogy is telling: that is, highly specific research such as data collection and data analysis projects in which the required expertise is located in a research organization. For more generalized research needs, however, there are several consequences of the procurement model that can work against creating a quality research program. The RFP process (whether by contract or by grant) usually excludes university-based researchers, who comprise a major portion of the social science research community, partly because of time constraints. The time period for responding with a detailed proposal is usually so short (often about six weeks) that academic personnel, with on-going responsibilities for teaching and for research already underway, are unable to commit the resources necessary to quickly develop an adequate proposal. Furthermore, the work statement in a contract RFP is often so specific that it does not permit any flexibility for reconceptualizing the problem or considering a different set of questions. By trying to control for performance and product, the contract precludes creative responses. Another consequence of using a contract procedure stems from the legal requirements surrounding competitive bidding: that is, bidders are not permitted to discuss their proposal or the contract work statement with anyone but contract officers. As a result, the potential for fruitful exchange between researchers and program staff before a proposal is accepted is prevented.

A common procurement strategy in federally sponsored applied research has been the use of large contracts that address a whole problem. We think such a strategy deserves some comment because of its particular relevance in criminal justice research. Normally, such contracts include several phases, from state-of-the-art reviews through a final report. We believe that this kind of contract, which delegates exclusive control over a problem, tends to transfer too much responsibility for thinking from the program staff to the contractor. Further, it inhibits creative thinking about the research questions of a problem. The contractor is bound to deliver certain already specified pieces and therefore has no incentive to deal with unexpected results or to follow up on emerging ideas as the research proceeds. In short, this strategy tends to constrain the normal research process in unproductive and even destructive ways.

Another consequence is perhaps even more destructive. The large, "whole problem" contract is a tempting vehicle for the immediate-solution response to social problems because it tends to force the commitment of large amounts of resources to a single mode and prevent a more tentative, incremental approach. This tends to lead to massive programs, but the state of our knowledge about a particular social problem at any time has never been adequate to support massive programming. The mentality of believing in immediate solutions, furthermore, is susceptible to a certain closed-mindedness about alternatives.

In sum, we believe that the Institute should rely primarily on grants, and on a combination of flexible RFP procedures and unsolicited proposals, in order to develop a research program that is suited to the requirements of social science research. This approach excludes no qualified scientist and provides the optimal conditions for a creative and productive research effort. We do not argue that grants are always better than contracts, that RFPS based on a rigid procurement model are never appropriate, or that university-based researchers are preferable to research organizations. We do argue that the largest segment of the social science research community—university-based researchers—should not be excluded from the Institute's program. While this has not yet occurred (see Figures 2, 3, and 4 in Chapter 4), we have observed a pronounced trend toward more contracts and more rigid RFPS addressed to large-scale problems. To the extent that this trend continues, the Institute will become more and more isolated not only from university-based researchers but also from the normal processes of social science research. Many well-qualified researchers work in research organizations, but the procurement model under which they usually operate is so constraining that their efforts are often pedestrian and of limited value in generating a body of knowledge.

All of these factors must be taken into account in evaluating the Institute's research program, for they are the choices and constraints under which the Institute has lived through the seven years of its existence. We believe that the Institute has sometimes been forced to accept constraints that are inappropriate and destructive to its mission and that it has made some choices that are equally inappropriate and destructive. The description and evaluation that follows provides evidence for this conclusion.

4 The Institute's Research Program

This chapter discusses the Committee's evaluation of the program funded by the Institute during the years 1969–1975. The first part of the chapter describes the program as it developed over time; the second part sets forth the Committee's approach to evaluating the program; and the third part presents the findings of that evaluation.

DESCRIPTION OF THE PROGRAM

Scope

As suggested by the historical and structural descriptions in the previous chapters, NILECJ is a product of diverse and transient expectations. It is not surprising to find, therefore, that it has chosen to support a variety of kinds of projects or that it has shifted research strategies over time. The evidence indicates that the Institute's programming has responded to many different demands—indeed, that the Institute has attempted to be all things to all people.

In terms of its overall program, NILECJ is not and has never been strictly a research and development operation. The present organization of the Institute (see Figure 2) reflects the variety of work it performs. Following the Institute's three major functional categories, research received the bulk of the funds in fiscal 1975:

Research Programs	$23,623,194	(68%)
Evaluation	6,572,028	(19%)
Technology Transfer	4,502,849	(13%)
TOTAL	$34,698,071	(100%)

Included in the major categories, however, are model programs, demonstrations, training programs, impact evaluations, data archives, and a series of publications designed to disseminate ideas for action programming. The variety of work was mandated by Congress in a clear attempt to connect the Institute's program to the overall action mission of LEAA and especially to the efforts of SPAs to mount effective programs in the states.

The Committee found it necessary to delineate 13 categories of funding in order to provide a comprehensive description of the Institute's program. These categories are: research, evaluation, data collection, hardware development, software, dissemination, innovation, training, demonstrations, technical assistance, standards, feasibility studies, and fellowships. In many instances, these categories are not exclusive since any particular award can include, for example, research, data collection, evaluation, and dissemination components. It is important to realize that, as a consequence of this diversity, no single set of evaluation criteria could be employed to assess all Institute awards. This was true even for those that were nominally research awards as opposed to technology transfer or evaluation.

Distribution of Awards

From 1969 through 1975, the Institute has spent over $150 million; its program has grown from an annual funding level of $2,900,000 in fiscal 1969 to $42,500,000 in fiscal 1975. (See Table B-2 in Appendix B for a detailed breakdown.)

Table 2 indicates the distribution of awards by type of project. It should be noted that in order to construct this table, it was necessary to create a substantive typology that was both informative and an accurate representation of the allocation of Institute resources and then to categorize each award according to the typology in order to present a distribution. This required sometimes arbitrary choices when particular projects conceivably belonged in more than one category. The resulting table may be somewhat different than other representations of Institute awards by category.

TABLE 2 Characteristics of NILECJ Program, by Percentages of Annual Dollar Amounts, and Percentages of Annual Number of Projects (dollars in thousands)[a]

Program Area	Fiscal Year 1969		1970		1971		1972		1973		1974		1975		Total, 1969–1975	
	%	N	%	N	%	N	%	N	%	N	%	N	%	N	%	N
Advanced technology																
Dollar amount	14	$ 407	22	$1,704	25	$1,926	33	$6,537	35	$7,940	32	$6,613	23	$9,267	29	$34,394
Number of projects	15	14	19	20	25	34	22	9	24	11	15	10	5	7	17	105
Courts																
Dollar amount	9	255	20	1,479	11	816	3	559	7	1,497	11	2,346	8	3,185	8	10,137
Number of projects	12	11	16	17	12	16	12	5	15	7	13	9	13	19	13	84
Police																
Dollar amount	22	624	13	998	8	602	0.5	88	9	1,954	5	975	7	2,592	7	7,833
Number of projects	23	22	13	14	9	12	7	3	20	9	13	9	11	16	13	85
Corrections																
Dollar amount	14	411	7	522	10	787	4	699	6	1,369	8	1,536	10	4,134	8	9,458
Number of projects	15	14	13	13	10	13	15	6	11	5	15	10	14	20	13	81
Juveniles																
Dollar amount	15	420	2	160	10	797	5	998	1	305	2	439	7	2,708	5	5,827
Number of projects	13	12	[illegible]	[illegible]	[illegible]	[illegible]	[illegible]	[illegible]	[illegible]	[illegible]	[illegible]	[illegible]	[illegible]	[illegible]	[illegible]	[illegible]

Community crime prevention																
Dollar amount	2	$ 45	6	$ 443	10	$ 738	1	$ 104	2	$ 543	10	$ 2,104	3	$ 1,381	4	$ 5,358
Number of projects	2	2	8	8	4	5	2	1	4	2	3	2	6	9	5	29
Drug rehabilitation																
Dollar amount	4	114	—	—	2	172	2	320	2	428	—	—	1	503	1	1,537
Number of projects	2	2	—	—	1	2	5	2	2	1	—	—	1	2	1	9
Criminal justice topics[b]																
Dollar amount	15	424	12	933	14	1,113	6	1,206	3	773	11	2,327	35	14,024	17	20,800
Number of projects	13	12	11	11	7	10	17	7	11	5	16	11	28	42	15	98
Specific crimes																
Dollar amount	7	194	11	858	6	480	1	121	—	—	1	258	2	801	2	2,712
Number of projects	5	5	14	15	9	12	5	2	—	—	3	2	4	6	7	42
Fellowships																
Dollar amount	—	—	5	382	4	323	—	—	—	—	1	209	1	339	1	1,253
Number of projects	—	—	2	2	19	25	—	—	—	—	12	8	10	15	8	50
Impact Cities/Pilot Cities[c]																
Dollar amount	—	—	—	—	—	—	46	8,900	34	7,600	18	3,657	2	939	18	21,096
Number of projects	—	—	—	—	—	—	5	2	4	2	3	2	1	2	1	8
TOTALS																
Dollar amount	100	$2,894	100	$7,479	100	$7,754	100	$19,532	100	$22,409	100	$20,464	100	$39,873	100	$120,405
Number of projects	100	94	100	104	100	135	100	41	100	46	100	67	100	148	100	635

SOURCES: Directory of Grants, Contracts, and Interagency Agreements; 1974 Annual Report of NILECJ; 1975 Annual Report of NILECJ; Status of Funds Report (various fiscal years).

[a]Expenditures do not include pass-through awards to DEA and other programs.

[b]Includes studies of the entire criminal justice system. For 1975, includes expenditures on the Institute's NEP, RAP, and MEP programs.

[c]Expenditures were derived by assuming the ORO to be the grantee for these programs. The actual number of projects is therefore greater.

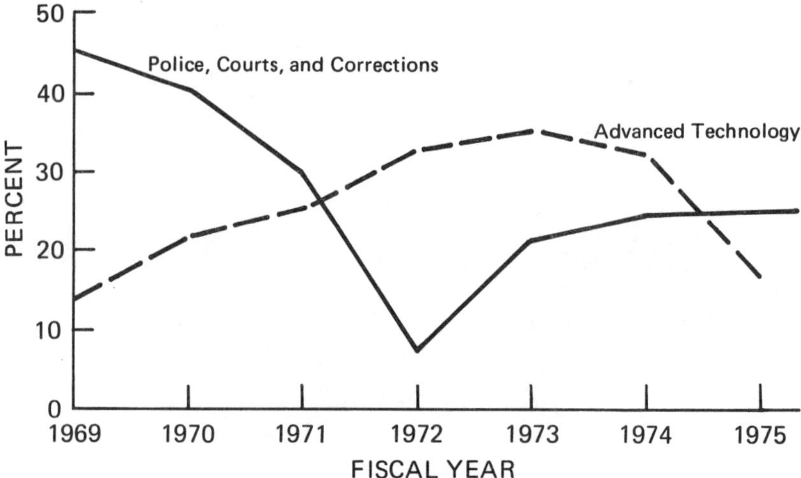

FIGURE 3 Comparison of percentage of NILECJ funds spent on the program areas of police, courts, and corrections and of advanced technology, 1969–1975. SOURCES: See Table 2.

Accepting the typology, some substantive conclusions are apparent. Two categories—advanced technology and the Pilot/Impact Cities program—have dominated the Institute's budget. Pilot/Impact Cities expenditures began in 1972 and were largely ended by 1975, so its domination was brief. Technology projects have maintained a large claim through the Institute's history, although the current trend is down.* The traditional criminal justice program categories—police, courts, corrections—have together maintained a fairly constant claim, biggest in the early years and smallest during the period of Impact Cities domination (see Figure 3). It should be noted, however, that the Impact Cities program included planning and evaluation funds for the criminal justice system in each city.

In our typology, "criminal justice system topics" is to some extent a residual category. But the fact that these projects could not easily be assigned to specific categories indicates that the Institute has supported some projects that cut across traditional boundaries. The dramatic increase in that category in fiscal 1975 directly reflects Director Caplan's efforts, notably the long-term Research Agreements Program (RAP) with Yale University, Northwestern University, the

*Because such a large share of Institute resources has been allocated to these two categories, a case study of each was prepared; see Case Studies in this volume.

RAND Corporation, and Stanford University's Hoover Institute, and the broad-scale National Evaluation Program (see below).

Table 3 shows the distribution of Institute awards in another way: the allocation of Institute funds by type of performer over time, showing both dollar amounts and numbers of projects. This typology distinguishes among the various kinds of expertise that the Institute has selected: research organizations and universities and national and professional associations (e.g., International Association of Chiefs of Police, National Center for State Courts) in criminal justice; national government agencies with special development expertise and testing facilities (e.g., the Department of Army and the National Bureau of Standards); performers among state and local government agencies, including police departments and prosecutors' offices; performers from private industry, including Westinghouse, which has handled environmental design, and General Electric, which holds the contract for the National Criminal Justice Reference Service.

As illustrated in Tables 3 and 4, research organizations, particularly Federal Contract Research Centers (e.g., the Mitre Corporation, the Rand Corporation, the Aerospace Corporation), have captured the lion's share of Institute resources through its entire history. Figure 4 shows that this same performer group received the largest percentage increase in funds as the Institute's budget grew over the years. When examined in terms of number of projects rather than dollar amounts (see Figure 4), the largest number of performers are universities. The difference between Figures 5 and 6 illustrates the expected difference in the nature of the tasks performed by the two major performer groups, with research organizations receiving far larger dollar amounts for large-scale efforts while university researchers absorb smaller dollar amounts for a larger number and wider variety of projects. The research strategy implicit in each case is obviously important to the success of a research program, discussed in the evaluation below.

APPROACH TO THE EVALUATION

Major Questions

The first part of this chapter described the Institute's research program in terms of the allocation of Institute funds. While informative, this description says little about the quality or usefulness of the program. What do we want to know about the program in order to speak to these

TABLE 3 Characteristics of NILECJ Performers, by Type, Percentages of Annual Dollar Amounts, and Percentages of Annual Number of Projects (dollars in thousands)

Type of Grantee	Fiscal Year														Total, 1969–1975	
	1969		1970		1971		1972		1973		1974		1975			
	%	N	%	N	%	N	%	N	%	N	%	N	%	N	%	N
Research organizations																
Dollar amount	25	$ 732	21	$1,588	22	$1,711	29	$ 5,583	35	$ 7,871	32	$ 6,566	42	$16,831	34	$ 40,882
Number of projects	16	15	18	19	19	25	24	10	28	13	25	17	32	47	23	146
Universities																
Dollar amount	31	911	26	1,923	31	2,380	13	2,454	13	3,012	8	1,693	24	9,419	18	21,792
Number of projects	47	44	40	42	32	43	29	12	33	15	21	14	33	49	34	219
National and professional associations																
Dollar amount	15	445	18	1,333	12	910	4	768	2	491	11	2,313	7	2,619	7	8,879
Number of projects	10	9	10	10	7	9	20	8	7	3	15	10	11	16	10	65
National government agencies																
Dollar amount	14	400	14	1,070	18	1,391	8	1,565	11	2,555	15	3,033	7	2,889	11	12,903
Number of projects	6	6	8	8	13	18	10	4	13	6	[illegible]	[illegible]	[illegible]	[illegible]	[illegible]	[illegible]

Dollar amount	14	$ 397	18	$1,322	11	$ 847	1	$ 267	4	$ 876	4	$ 895	5	$ 2,080	6	$ [illegible]
Number of projects	20	19	18	19	13	17	12	5	13	6	12	8	9	13	14	87
Corporations—private industry																
Dollar amount	—	—	2	134	5	414	—	—	—	—	10	2,000	12	4,709	6	7,257
Number of projects	—	—	2	2	2	3	—	—	—	—	1	1	1	2	1	8
Individuals and fellowships																
Dollar amount	—	—	1	109	1	101	—	—	0.02	4	1	244	1	387	1	845
Number of projects	—	—	4	4	15	20	—	—	2	1	13	9	9	13	7	47
Other																
Dollar amount	0.3	9	—	—	—	—	—	—	—	—	0.3	65	—	—	0.1	74
Number of projects	1	1	—	—	—	—	—	—	—	—	1	1	—	—	0.3	2
Impact Cities/Pilot Cities[b]																
Dollar amount	—	—	—	—	—	—	46	8,900	34	7,600	18	3,657	2	939	18	21,096
Number of projects	—	—	—	—	—	—	5	2	4	2	3	2	1	2	0.1	8
TOTALS																
Dollar amount	100	$2,894	100	$7,479	100	$7,754	100	$19,532	100	$22,409	100	$20,464	100	$39,873	100	$120,405
Number of projects	100	94	100	104	100	135	100	41	100	46	100	67	100	148	100	635

SOURCES: Directory of Grants, Contracts, and Interagency Agreements; 1974 and 1975 Annual Reports of NILECJ; Status of Funds Reports (various fiscal years).

[a]Not including pass-through awards to DEA or other programs.

[b]Impact and Pilot Cities awards were determined by using ORO as the grantee.

TABLE 4 Dollar Amounts Awarded by NILECJ to Federal Contract Research Centers, 1969–1975 (in thousands of dollars, number of projects in parentheses)

Federal Contract Research Center	Fiscal Year 1969	1970	1971	1972	1973	1974	1975	Total, 1969–1975
RAND Corporation	—	$171 (1)	$110 (1)	—	$ 506 (1)	$ 19 (1)	$1,229 (4)	$ 2,035 (8)
MITRE Corporation	—	—	—	$3,000 (1)	—	396 (1)	776 (3)	4,172 (5)
Aerospace Corporation	—	—	—	1,850 (1)	5,185 (1)	3,100 (1)	6,400 (1)	16,535 (4)
Institute for Defense Analyses	—	146 (1)	—	—	116 (1)	—	—	262 (2)
Center for Naval Analysis	—	—	1 (1)	—	—	—	—	1 (1)
TOTAL	—	317 (2)	111 (2)	4,850 (2)	5,807 (3)	3,615 (3)	8,405 (8)	2,305 (20)
Percent of R&D expenditures[a]	—	4%	1%	25%	26%	17%	21%	19%

SOURCES: See Table 2.

[a]Does not include expenditures on DEA or other pass-through programs.

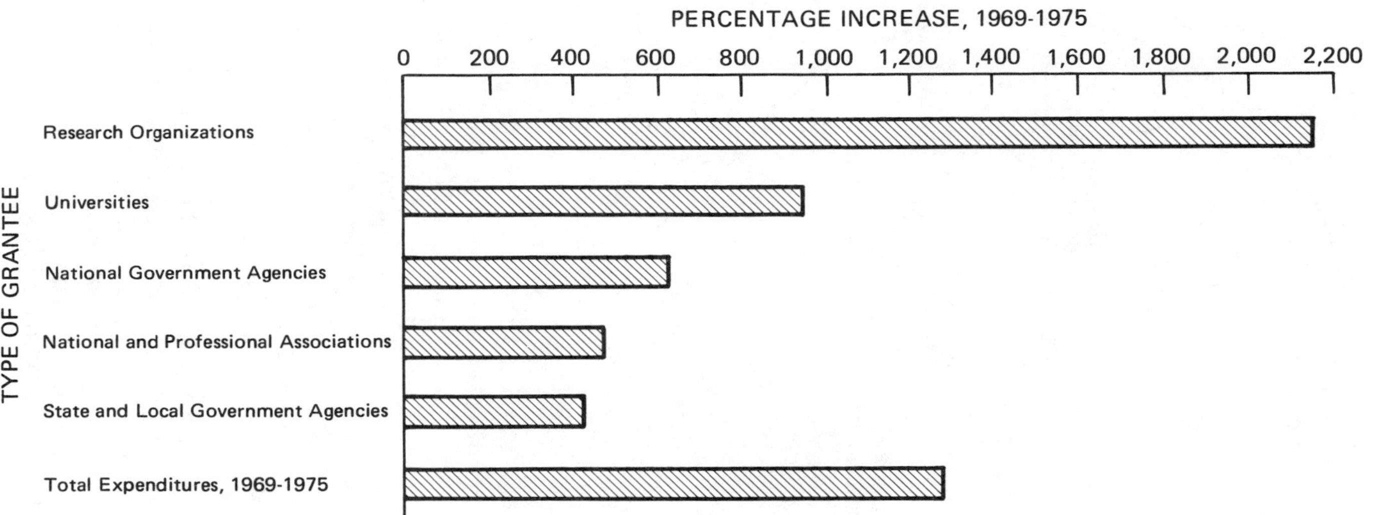

NOTE: Four types of grantees, which are not represented in every year, are not shown above: Impact/Pilot Cities, Corporations, Individuals, and "others."

FIGURE 4 Percentage changes in dollar amounts awarded to various types of NILECJ grantees, between fiscal years 1969–1975. SOURCE: See Table 2.

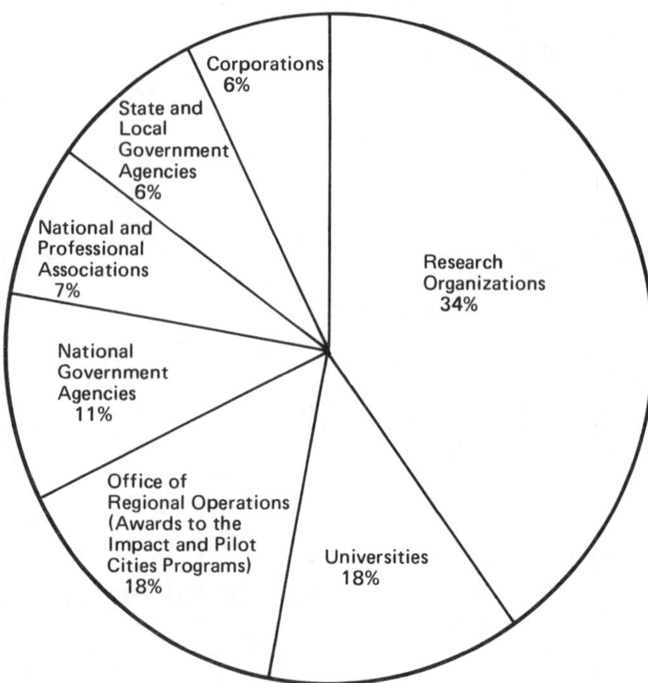

FIGURE 5 Percentage distribution of NILECJ dollars by type of grantee, 1969–1975. SOURCES: See Table 2.

issues? What questions must be asked in order to evaluate this massive research and development program in criminal justice?

In the Committee's view, there are four broad criteria that should be applied to such a program. First, a judgment must be made about the quality of the research that the Institute has funded; this requires looking at both the products of the research and the design of individual projects. Second, the usefulness of the program must be assessed: What kind of impact has the program made? What are its successes and (inevitable) failures? Where does the program stand in terms of meeting social priorities?

In addition to these two obvious criteria are two others that have more to do with managerial competence. One is the issue of cumulating knowledge: Has the Institute succeeded in developing a program in which research products build on one another, or is the program repetitive and haphazard, with no continuity of planning toward objectives? The other is the issue of the competence of the administra-

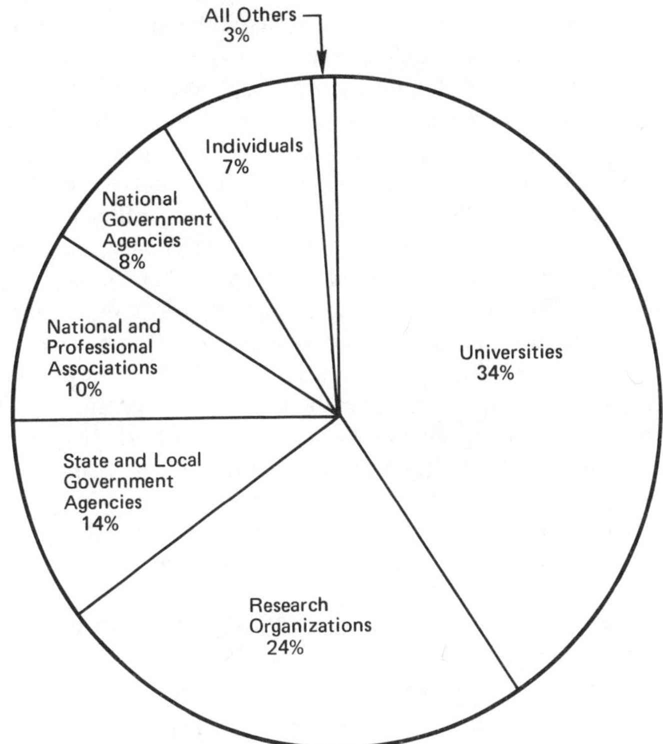

FIGURE 6 Percentage distribution of NILECJ project awards by type of grantee, 1969–1975. SOURCES: See Table 2.

tion of the program: Has the Institute developed effective strategies for obtaining quality research? Is it playing a significant leadership role in efforts to cope with crime? (Each of these criteria is elaborated in the third part of this chapter, which presents the Committee's evaluation of the research program.)

Data

In its effort to evaluate the Institute's programs, the Committee has relied on the wide range of perspectives and diverse areas of academic and professional expertise represented by its members. Recognizing that the questions posed above are both important and difficult to answer, the Committee also made use of three different means of developing the information needed to provide the answers (see Appendixes C and D for more detailed descriptions).

The first kind of information came from staff interviews with a number of individuals who have been involved in developing the Institute's program over the years or have been in key positions to observe that development. These included most current professional personnel, some individuals who formerly held critical positions in the Institute or LEAA, some major LEAA administrative and Department of Justice personnel, and individuals who carry out similar research administration tasks in other agencies and organizations. Comments were also obtained from respondents to a mail questionnaire sent to all individuals listed by the Institute as having served it in an advisory capacity. In addition, Committee members received informal comments from their colleagues about experiences with the Institute. This information provided firsthand knowledge of current Institute operations, from general planning down to funding procedures, and of various historical events and practices. It also provided diverse perspectives on the Institute, on LEAA, and on their relationship over the years.

The second kind of information came from direct exchanges between Committee members and current Institute staff and contractors. Conferences were held on evaluation, on technology transfer, and on the advanced technology program, which are special Institute functions that absorb significant portions of the Institute's resources. Subcommittees met with all Institute staff of the Office of Evaluation, of the Office of Technology Transfer, and of the Advanced Technology Division. In addition, a subcommittee held three days of conferences with representatives of major technology contractors: the MITRE Corporation, the Aerospace Corporation, the Law Enforcement Standards Laboratory of the National Bureau of Standards, and the Department of the Army's project on lightweight body armor. These sessions produced both firsthand accounts of the kinds of work being done in these categories and valuable exchanges of views between Committee members and Institute staff.

The third kind of information came from reading a sample of the Institute grants and contracts files. The Committee decided that it needed to develop its own independent knowledge of the Institute's program by examining as many Institute awards as possible. It was decided that the files would provide the widest range of information about each award—from proposal to final report—and about Institute procedures. Since there was neither time nor resources to examine every file, a sample of awards was drawn (see Appendixes C2 and C3 for a detailed description of the sample design). The sample was stratified by year and dollar amount so that the large awards were over-represented; this was done on the assumption that the categories of large resource commitments required, and deserved, the closest examination. With few exceptions each file was read by at least two evaluators including, in most cases, at least one (and usually two) Committee members.

In order to make the review of files as systematic as possible, a set of instruments was developed covering the 13 categories of Institute funding. The instruments (some of which are reproduced in Appendix C3) included questions common to each category as well as questions designed to assess the particular characteristics of each category. The instruments provided for detailed coverage of the issues that the Committee felt should have been considered by Institute staff and accorded appropriate attention in making funding decisions and in monitoring projects. These criteria included, for example, conceptualization and design, usefulness, adequacy of funding, significance, and contribution to cumulating knowledge. Each file reviewed was assigned to one principal category, but instruments representing other relevant categories were also applied as appropriate.

The reading of grants and contracts files provided the Committee with a rich supply of information about the Institute's program—information that could not have been gotten in any other way. The process of comparing notes on the basis of this common experience proved invaluable for Committee deliberations, and much of the assessment that follows is drawn from Committee discussions of the grants and contracts files. A note of methodological caution is in order, however: the Committee does not make any statistical inference from the sample that can or should be construed as applying to the entire population of Institute awards. While our sample was drawn in an unbiased manner, its (intended) stratification prevents it from being strictly representative in a statistical sense. The sample is a large cut from the population, however—138 of 601—and provides a solid base for a close and detailed study and evaluation of the program that has been funded by the Institute.

EVALUATION

Quality

The Committee's judgments about the quality of Institute research rest on evidence gained by Committee members' own examination of grants and contracts files, from the other sources described above, and reports from colleagues in criminal justice on their experiences with the Institute. That is, in addition to its own first-hand assessment of a sample of Institute work, the Committee's judgment relies on the reputation earned by the Institute among researchers and practitioners in the field.

The Committee finds that the projects funded by the Institute have been predominately mediocre. There are successes and failures, but the latter are more visible and certainly more renowned. The successes appear to be related more to the quality of the performers involved than to the Institute's own capacities for creative planning and research design. While there are exceptions, most Institute successes cannot be attributed to any particular competence of the Institute. The failures, on the other hand, can often be traced to some facet of Institute or LEAA operations.

Sources of weaknesses are clear and fundamental. The most obvious is lack of attention to, competence in, and even awareness of research design. A common Institute practice is to fund a project on the basis of a slightly elaborated concept paper in which rigorous design of the proposed research is (apparently) neither expected nor offered. Several of the projects reviewed by Committee members were well into their funding cycles before the most basic preliminary design functions had been fulfilled. One of the most striking consequences of our evaluation process by Committee members was the experience of reading files on projects that had been funded without requiring the most basic showing of methodological rigor or technical competence. The number of projects whose weakness could be attributed to this kind of defect was considerable.

One version of the problem deserves particular mention: the kind of project that might appear to escape the requirements for methodological rigor because it is not really research—such as technical assistance or training or demonstrations. The lack of rigor in these projects is usually no more excusable than in research projects. The most obvious (but not the only) example of this kind of failure is Impact Cities (see Case Study), where Institute funds were committed without regard for ensuring the scientific validity and usefulness of the projects.

Although the Institute appears to have produced more than its share of weak projects, most of the projects in our sample could be labeled neither failures nor successes. We make this judgment on the basis of several different measures of quality. We developed an index of generalized quality based on 7 questions that were common to most of our 13 instruments. The questions dealt with methodology, overall adequacy of the research component, scientific contribution, contribution toward cumulating knowledge, utility, adequacy of level of expertise, and adequacy of level of support. (See Appendix C3 for complete questions.) Index scores were developed based on scaled (from 0 to 100) responses to the questions. Table 5 presents scores on the two major funding categories—research and evaluation—by the three time periods of the administrative phases of the Institute (discussed in Chapter 1). Table 6 presents the index scores for the five key questions across all the funding categories.

The questions regarding levels of support and expertise (Tables 7 and 8) must be interpreted separately because they were scaled differently on the instruments: the highest rating for these two questions was "adequate," and there was no midpoint comparable to the "average" or "acceptable" midpoints on the other scaled responses. Less than half of the ratings of these two questions were at the "adequate" level. Scores for the five key measures of methodology, utility, scientific contribution, contributions to cumulating knowledge, and overall adequacy of the research component all cluster at the midpoint of the 0-100 scale. These scores are products of evaluator choices and not an artifact of measurement procedures. Furthermore, the ratings by categories show considerable variation—scores from 13 to 76—indicating evaluators had made sharply discriminating judgments. Those questions specifically comparing Institute projects with general work in the field show the same middling or fair ratings. We do not wish to place too much stress on these findings, partly for statistical reasons and partly because baseline data are in any event strangely

TABLE 5 Index Scores for Selected Questions for the Combined Categories of "Evaluation" and "Research" in the Grants and Contracts Sample, by Administrative Phases of NILECJ

	Administrative Phase			
Question	I 1969–1971	II 1972–1973	III 1974–1975	Average Index Score, Phases I–III
Methodology	52	41	53	52
Knowledge-building	48	51	52	51
Research component	51	48	53	51
Scientific contribution	44	51	51	48
Utility	56	57	58	58
Summary index score	50	50	53	52

Scale: 0–20, far below average; 21–40, somewhat below average; 41–60, average; 61–80, somewhat above average; 81–100, far above average.

TABLE 6 Index Scores for Selected Questions Across Categories

Question	Category (number of projects in parentheses)														
	Data Collection (10)	Evaluation (25)	Research (32)	Hardware (0)	Software (10)	Training (2)	Innovation (1)	Dissemination (17)	Demonstration (4)	Technical Assistance (5)	Standards (8)	Feasibility Study (1)	Fellowships (2)	Miscellaneous (4)	Weighted Average Across Categories
Methodology	—	50	53	—	—	—	—	—	46	—	53	13	13	33	50
Knowledge-building	55	48	53	—	52	—	—	—	54	37	56	0	0	36	49
Research component	—	52	51	—	49	76	75	64	52	—	53	25	25	53	53
Scientific contribution	—	49	47	—	—	—	—	—	44	45	—	—	—	50	48
Utility	—	61	55	—	58	25	50	—	60	38	—	50	50	75	56

Scale: 0–20, far below average; 21–40, somewhat below average; 41–60, average; 61–80, somewhat above average; 81–100, far above average.

TABLE 7 Levels of Support: Percentage Distribution of Scaled Responses in the Grants and Contracts Sample

Question	Scaled Response	Percent
Level of support	Not applicable	2
	Clearly inadequate	7
	Adequate, but strained	10
	Adequate, good fit	42
	Adequate, some slack	13
	Clearly unnecessary slack	9
	Can't tell	17

NOTE: Figures may not add to 100% due to rounding.

lacking in the evaluation literature. It does not, however, seem harsh to expect better performance from projects funded at an average of more than $100,000 than from standard research, normally undertaken with little or no support.

Another measure of quality from our evaluation of grants and contracts files is based on responses to the single question that appeared on every instrument and was thus answered for every project in our sample:* "If it were your decision to fund this project, would you have funded it?" Table 9 presents responses to this question. Since each project had more than one evaluator, the disagreement rate (17%) is noted in the table. For 48 percent of the projects reviewed, the evaluators agreed that they would have funded the projects. For 7 percent of the projects, the evaluators indicated they would have funded the projects "only with changes." For 29 percent of the

TABLE 8 Level of Expertise: Percentage Distribution of Scaled Responses for Question in the Grants and Contracts Sample

Question	Scaled Response	Percent
Level of expertise	Not applicable	2
	Clearly inadequate	11
	Adequate, but strained	11
	Adequate, good fit	49
	Adequate, some slack	6
	Clearly unnecessary slack	3
	Can't tell	18

NOTE: Figures may not add to 100% due to rounding.

*This does not include large technology awards that were evaluated in a different manner.

projects, the evaluators agreed that they would not have funded the projects at all.

Since it is clear from the historical discussion in Chapter 1 that different research strategies have been employed over time, a relevant question is whether the quality of the program has varied over time. Our only basis for answering that question is to examine our ratings of projects in the sample arrayed chronologically. To do so meaningfully, we divided the history of the Institute into three administrative phases representing the major directorships as discussed in Chapter 1. While recognizing that some overlap occurs between phases because of longer-range funding, we consider the representation to be reasonably accurate. (We caution again, of course, that we are not making statistical estimations to the entire population of funded projects.) Table 5 above shows our ratings of research and evaluation projects combined and Table 10 shows our ratings of all projects in the sample to which the questions applied. Again, the index scores on our five common questions tend to cluster around the midpoint in each period, although the tendency overall is upward. We conclude that there has been some trend toward better quality over time, but the magnitude of change is relatively small—certainly less than might have been expected after seven years and the Institute's cumulated experience.

Thus far we have considered only the projects actually funded by the Institute. In addition, the Committee evaluated a sample, stratified by year, of rejected concept papers and proposals. (The design and detailed results are shown in Appendix C4.) In general, we find that the

TABLE 9 Responses to the Evaluation Question, "If It Were Your Decision to Fund This Project, Would You Have Funded It?"

Decision	Percent	N
Y	48	58
O	7	8
N	29	35
YN	17	20

Y, yes, would have funded; O, only with changes; N, no, would not have funded; YN, yes/no (disagreement between evaluators).

TABLE 10 Index Scores for Selected Questions across All Categories, by Administrative Phases of NILECJ (0–100 scale)

	Administrative Phase		
Question	I 1969–1971	II 1972–1973	III 1974–1975
Methodology	47	48	51
Knowledge-building	46	48	52
Research component	54	50	54
Scientific contribution	44	45	50
Utility	53	53	59

overall quality of the rejected proposals was low. Virtually all rejected applications reviewed were unsolicited.

The Committee, however, does not consider that to be justification for the Institute's apparent reluctance to fund unsolicited proposals. Since that reluctance has been well known among established researchers for several years, the more experienced and knowledgeable investigators in the research community are probably aware that the unsolicited proposal route is not promising at NILECJ. In the initial years of the Institute when substantial funding occurred through a normally unsolicited and unplanned framework, a good percentage of projects were competent enough to receive favorable ratings from Committee evaluators. Given the assumption that top-quality researchers now have less reluctance to pursue Institute funding, the circumstances suggest that the Institute would benefit from reviving its interest in unsolicited proposals. This would leave, one hopes, increasing room for the unexpected and potentially creative proposal to surface. Under present conditions, this is unlikely to occur except when an individual has established entry into the Institute in some other manner—at least by name recognition, and at worst, by simple cronyism.

Commitment to a more open research program would at least be an investment in better relations with the research community at large. Currently, it is clear from reading the files and from discussions with Institute contractors and grantees that relationships between NILECJ and its researchers are often characterized by nitpicking, haggling, and not a small degree of unfriendliness. More than in most agencies, those who come closest to it are the most annoyed by it.

Usefulness

The usefulness of the Institute's work can be examined from a number of perspectives, all of which are illustrated by specific programs designed for practical application. These include the Impact Cities program, a variety of evaluation projects, dissemination efforts (or technology transfer), technology development, and projects aimed at improving criminal justice system operations. We have already stated that the Institute's research mission should be to build knowledge and focus it toward solving problems of crime. Therefore, a major criterion of usefulness is a program's contribution to that end. Other criteria are specific to the particular category of program being assessed.

Before discussing the usefulness of particular programs, however, it is important to address the more general question of whether the Institute has met its responsibilities under the Safe Streets Act. According to the Act and its amendments, the Institute is supposed to serve the programming needs of State Planning Agencies and, perhaps less directly, the operational needs of practitioners. As a first measure of usefulness, therefore, it is reasonable to consider the Institute's impact on these service constituencies. Unfortunately, the Institute has not itself developed data to provide such a measure. It has only recently begun to include evaluation forms in conference and training materials and in the various publications of the Office of Technology Transfer (OTT). It has not surveyed in a systematic way the extent to which either practitioners or SPA planners have made use of the program ideas disseminated through OTT's publications. This seeming lack of interest in the kinds of effects it is producing is curious, given the Institute's service mandates.

The Committee's own contacts with SPA staff in a number of states yields the strong impression that the Institute and its products have little visibility within the LEAA block-grant program and even less impact on LEAA's dealings with practitioners. Although the Institute may have been helpful to some practitioners directly, we have found no evidence of a productive relationship. The exceptions to this finding are few—primarily the National Criminal Justice Reference Service (which receives many good comments from SPA staff) and conferences in which a mix of practitioners, researchers, and planners can exchange views.

As a general matter, therefore, the Committee finds that the Institute has not met its service responsibilities under the Safe Streets Act. We have already commented on the unrealistic expectations that characterize that legislation, especially the expectation that the Institute can and should undertake to provide immediate solutions to problems of crime. The fact that the Institute has not achieved visibility within the larger LEAA and practitioner community may be due, at least in part, to these unrealistic expectations.

*Impact Cities**

The Impact Cities program was started by LEAA in 1972 as a means of concentrating large amounts of resources on controlling urban crime. In terms of evaluating the Institute's research effort, the central fact about the Impact Cities program is that it had no research value at all.

The Institute's role in the Impact Cities program was to measure the impact on crime of this large-scale action program—on its face, an appropriate task of evaluation research. However, the design for the program as a whole precluded the application of even minimal standards of methodological rigor. For example, there was no standard technique for data collection and no specification of the kinds of data required in order to compare measures across projects or across cities; in fact, the guiding political premise of the program—the "New Federalism"—required that the participating cities individually choose what kinds of projects that they would fund, as well as the means of implementing them. In short, Impact Cities was not designed to produce reliable knowledge. For the Institute's purposes, therefore, it was a wholly inappropriate use of resources.

We emphasize, however, that evaluation research is an appropriate use of Institute resources when it is carefully designed and focused on producing reliable knowledge. Unfortunately, the Institute has often been asked to design, support, and promote a limited form of evaluation, usually called "impact evaluation," in order to satisfy Congressional concern for results and agency demands for "intelligence" about particular projects. The need to force accountability in social programming is important, but a national research institute should play a carefully circumscribed role in such activities, if any at all. This is not to say that highly specific policy interventions (or natural experiments)—such as stringent gun control laws or determinant sentencing—should be ignored by evaluators; it is possible to design good evaluation research to test the effects of such policies in a manner that will yield generalizable results. However, the more narrow and

*See the Case Study on Impact Cities for a discussion of Institute involvement in this program, including details on problems of planning and implementation.

immediate purpose of providing decision makers with feedback is not a role for a national research institute.

*Office of Evaluation**

The present Office of Evaluation in the Institute has funded a variety of programs, ranging from impact evaluations to projects on the development of evaluation methodology. The Committee believes methodological development to be an area of potential importance and usefulness to the advancement of the state of the art of evaluation and an appropriate concern of a national research institute. Therefore, further commitment to methodological development should be encouraged.

Two major evaluation programs now being conducted by the Institute were mandated by the LEAA Evaluation Policy Task Force† in its 1974 report—The Model Evaluation Program (MEP) and the National Evaluation Program (NEP). MEP was intended to serve as a capacity-building program, encouraging the development of program evaluation at the SPA and regional planning unit (RPU) level. It has proven a costly failure, providing only minimal and largely idiosyncratic evaluation capacity within the block-grant structure of LEAA. While the Committee believes that increasing the capacity of SPAS and RPUS to evaluate their action programs is a useful and necessary function, it is more appropriately performed through the Office of Regional Operations and the LEAA regional structure. The placement of the program in the Institute was ill-advised not only because it diverted resources from good evaluation research, but also because the relative isolation of NILECJ from the SPAS renders it an ineffective agent for capacity building.

The National Evaluation Program, on the other hand, is an example of an evaluation program appropriate to the mission of a criminal justice research institute. Designed as a knowledge-building program, NEP has involved the purchase of phased evaluations of projects and approaches for selected topics (e.g. alternatives to incarcerating juveniles, court information systems, specialized police patrol operations). The first phase consists of a brief analysis of the selected topic to determine what is currently known, what further information could be provided by evaluation, and the estimated value and cost of obtaining that information. The second phase, not yet underway, will implement the evaluation design contained in the Phase I analysis. The

*The programs of the Office of Evaluation are discussed in more detail in the Case Study on the Office of Evaluation.

†The LEAA Evaluation Policy Task Force was established in 1973 in response to the mandate for evaluation.

program should provide a useful synthesis of current knowledge in criminal justice practice and research.

*Office of Technology Transfer**

Dissemination The dissemination activities of the Institute have been carried out by the Office of Technology Transfer (OTT). These activities are aimed at practitioners and at planners within the SPAS and RPUS. OTT makes use of the traditional dissemination tools—printed materials, demonstrations, and conferences—with a heavy emphasis on printed materials. The Committee has found that these materials range markedly in quality and notes that the usefulness of printed materials in communicating research results to practitioners remains debatable (Yin *et al.* 1976). NILECJ has only begun to make an impact analysis to determine who is using their disseminated materials. From its acquaintance with reactions of SPA staff and practitioners, the Committee infers that the Institute's materials are largely ignored. The Committee strongly urges the completion of a rigorous impact analysis on the dissemination efforts of OTT and its National Criminal Justice Reference Service (NCJRS).

Further, the Committee notes that much of OTT's activities involve capacity building and technical assistance rather than the dissemination of research results. OTT has begun using Prescriptive Packages and Exemplary Project manuals and validation reports as technical assistance in its dealings with state and regional planners. It has also established an Evaluation Clearinghouse within NCJRS for the use of SPA staff. These functions are important and useful to both the LEAA and criminal justice system—but would more appropriately and more adequately be performed within an action agency. While the publication of research results and of new knowledge in a format useful to researchers and practitioners is clearly an appropriate and integral function of an institute of criminal justice research, marketing and capacity building are inappropriate and, in some cases, compromising activities for a disinterested research institute.

Advanced Technology† The Committee's major concern with the Institute's advanced technology program is its usefulness. Our first conclusion is that the technology program is not integrated with the rest of the Institute's research program. The consequences of this iso-

*The programs of the Office of Technology Transfer are discussed in more detail in the Case Study on the Office of Technology Transfer.

†The advanced technology programs are treated in greater detail in the Case Study on Advanced Technology.

lation for the technology development program have been striking. The hardware projects that the Institute has undertaken are not part of a repertoire of approaches to a particular criminal justice problem, but rather are isolated and discrete efforts. The limitations of a narrow technological approach were often apparent in the hardware projects.

The Committee finds that the Institute's project on police body armor is an example of technically good development, but limited by the absence of any analysis of its ultimate usefulness to society or even of a thoughtful consideration of such immediate concerns as motivating intended users to actually use the technology. The Committee finds the citizen alarm—which requires a receiver within 500 feet of a transmitter in order to be effective and which is incapable of locating an alarm-wearer with any more specificity than a 500-feet radius—is an example of a project poorly designed and totally lacking an analysis of its practical applicability. Contrasting examples of projects that the Committee finds are well conceived and well developed are the work on an anti-burglar door striker plate and on the police helmet.

Even in successful hardware projects, however, one consequence of the separated technology program is the potential for over-allocation of resources to specific projects in relation to the rest of the research program. The Committee believes there must exist some mechanism for assessing technological against other solutions and for generally integrating technological thinking with substantive program areas.

System Operations Institute projects in improving criminal justice system operations share some of the same problems. Such projects have been beneficial to a point, but the Committee notes the danger of overestimating the usefulness of these programs and the consequent over-commitment of resources to them. Just as technological solutions are an extremely narrow approach to solving crime problems, so are criminal justice systems operations a narrow focus. While the Committee does not deny the existence of a role for technological and operation-oriented solutions, it notes that the present structure isolates these projects and inhibits consideration of questions about social priorities in criminal justice research and the issue of crime reduction. Systems improvement, per se, is a worthwhile goal for the criminal justice system—but a goal better pursued by an action agency.

Knowledge-Building in the Research Program

Any organization charged with program-oriented research must be judged in part by the usefulness of its research program for the systematic accumulation of knowledge and the long-term contribution of that knowledge to solving relevant problems. However, the demand that every piece of research have immediate usefulness can lead to a narrowly conceived program of applied development or a program heavily weighted toward immediate-solution research. Criminal justice and its relevant disciplines contain too many unanswered questions to be totally amenable to such a program. Similarly, many functions that are clearly useful in a criminal justice or law enforcement agency are counter-productive when mandated for a research institute.

While a large proportion of the Institute's awards continue beyond one year, the Committee found little evidence that the Institute has been committed to cumulative research. Too many research projects appeared isolated, developed without any historical context. This is particularly disturbing because the Institute has repeatedly professed to have committed itself to a coherent research agenda. Recent developments, such as the Institute's National Evaluation Program, are attempting a cumulative interaction between projects, although final results are not yet available. There is also very little evidence to suggest that the work funded by the Institute has been influential in the work of other researchers including, of course, other Institute research projects. The Institute's favoring of atheoretical projects, and the lack of any patterns between and among these, is noteworthy considering its avowed programmatic aims. Since managed, sponsored, or initiated research is more common within the Institute than in agencies like the National Science Foundation, one might have expected that the interaction between projects would be greater. To some extent the annual nature of appropriations may be a handicap, but other federal agencies have annual budgeting and cumulative research programs.

A subcommittee of the Committee examined cumulativeness in the program by looking at all funded grants and contracts. It was unable to locate any evidence of a multiple approach to particular problems. This does not mean that some topics have not been funded year after year, but the subcommittee was not able to determine what orchestration, if any, was taking place for the purpose of filling out an area of knowledge. This is not to say that the Institute never systematically addresses the issue of cumulativeness: the Institute's annual program plans over the years have frequently discussed with concern the orderly filling of areas of knowledge. The 1973 Program Plan states (p. 23):

> [NILECJ] is sponsoring a number of projects to facilitate case flow. Data from these efforts will be assessed before additional projects are undertaken. Projects aimed at improving the quality of justice will analyze and develop

sentencing procedures and guidelines, and analyze and develop criminal code and criminal law reform.

There is no evidence, however, that the Institute followed this agenda. The 1974 Program Plan (p. 4) makes cumulation an important criterion in selecting projects to be funded, noting:

> Continuity is a fundamental research need—both to enable good researchers to pursue their work to fruition and to *permit structural accumulation of a body of knowledge* in a given area. Individual researchers and the research community cannot ignore the need to proceed through the various research phases—problem identification, basic research, program development and program evaluation. Each year's Plan must, therefore, emphasize continuing, promising research projects.

However, Program Plans have been published after most funding commitments have been made for that year; only in fiscal 1976 was this not the case. But an examination of the fiscal 1976 Program Plan reveals that many of the program areas are represented by single-grant commitments, with knowledge-building reduced to a purchasing program in which all facets of a problem become the funded product of a single grantee. Thus a premium is placed on packaged solutions.

While we have found exceptions to our basic findings on cumulativeness—environmental design, the Phase I National Evaluation Program (NEP), and the Research Agreements Program (RAP)—most of the projects have an essentially isolated focus. Issues involved in community crime prevention are perhaps given the most lip service for common focusing of related ideas. The quality that we call cumulativeness must have, as necessary conditions, the goals of a common focus and of integration—or bringing evidence to bear on centralized concepts. Without such centralization, researchers' efforts are fortuitous, spinning off in all directions with explorations that are unrelated to each other.

There are legitimate reasons for pursuing a diverse research program, but research on a wide range of subjects can be conducted within the framework of a predetermined research agenda. The Institute's failure to pursue an integrated program of research is one reason for the lack of cumulative knowledge emanating from its program.

Each change in Institute directors has caused shifts in strategy and goals. Frequent shifts of research goals have a deleterious effect on the production of top-quality, useful research. A strong degree of cumulativeness in program planning and project design would reduce opportunities for these shifts to occur. Quite probably, a cumulative tradition would even act as a buffer against frequent changes in leadership at the working levels of the Institute.

The Committee believes that another crucial reason for the lack of cumulativeness is the poor state of the project files. (A recent report by the U.S. General Accounting Office [1976] was also critical of the Institute's files.) Evaluators who read the project files were invariably left with the impression that the kind of material available did not lend itself to the development of programmatic and cumulative research. Indeed, if any cumulation of knowledge and carry-over of information exists, it is in the private files of individual monitors or in their own memories. Given the extent of staff turnover and the methods of operation of the agency, one can understand why the files do not contain more indication of what is going on and why they are not more comprehensive. Perhaps most distressing is the large number of files that are not available at the Institute or that are missing altogether, with no auxiliary records available. This haphazard arrangement of important research records, in the Committee's opinion, can only work to the detriment of the Institute's ability to cumulate existing knowledge.

Administration of the Research Program

We wish to emphasize that, throughout the Institute's history, the director has never had the capacity to shape the research program. The major tool for controlling a research program—final approval of awards, or sign-off authority—has never resided within the Institute: that is, all grants and contracts and purchase orders exceeding $10,000 must be approved by the LEAA administrator. Consequently, all individual proposals considered for funding must be sent outside NILECJ for approval. This requirement and the consequent weakness in the authority of the NILECJ director for shaping the program has had a deleterious effect on the administration of the program.

Research Strategy

The Institute has employed a variety of strategies in planning its research program. The variation is reflected in the sample projects (see Appendix C2). However, we have found little evidence that the Institute has pursued a coherent research agenda or effective means for structuring advice from users, researchers, or others during the planning process.

Currently, the planning process is diffused throughout the Institute—technically controlled by the management by objectives (MBO) system used by LEAA. In fact, there is little in the way of substantive control over Institute objectives through MBO. The general goals are so broad that they provide little guidance for selecting priorities, and budget constraints, continuation funding, political demands, and general LEAA priorities combine to determine Institute priorities.

The overall planning function appears to be managerial rather than substantive. Within the Office of Research Programs, for example, the program desks represent the traditional parts of the criminal justice system and each submits requests for funding on the basis of a canvass of its own program needs. This procedure has led to a lack of coordination and exchange of ideas across units within the agency. The result of the reliance on managerial planning has been a research program characterized by few imaginative projects, by an emphasis on traditional modes and topics for research, and by concentration on system improvement rather than innovation.

The Committee finds that the absence of substantively integrated research objectives in the Institute's planning process is also reflected in its use of solicitation. The potential effectiveness of formal solicitations has been severely limited by the Institute's general strategy. Invitations to submit concept papers are sent out primarily to a number of researchers and research institutes with whom NILECJ has had prior dealings; or, in the case of contracts, the request for proposals (RFP) is printed in *The Commerce Business Daily*. The Committee believes that the Institute would find it advantageous to place more stress on advertising its intentions to a broader research community through major program announcements rather than relying almost solely on soliciting its past constituency for specific projects. Furthermore, the limited time period allowed for response to these solicitations (often 30 days) makes it extremely difficult to achieve thoughtful and carefully structured designs.

The Institute has over the years employed various strategies—contracting, granting, formal and informal solicitation—all with a "development" model of procuring research. The Committee feels that this emphasis rests, in part, in a mistaken judgment about the Institute's own mission and purpose and a resulting disinterest in a kind of research and community of researchers. The Institute has sought to fund applied, immediate-solution research. Although the intent, it claims, is changing, the Institute appears to have avoided those kinds of research questions that it feels are part of basic rather than applied research. In part, it contrasts itself with other research operations whose missions are less service-oriented. As we have discussed in Chapter 3, many important social questions suggest elements for both basic and applied research; adhering to a rigid distinction often obscures the best available research designs and the most appropriate researchers.

The Institute has tended to cultivate a specialized and narrow research community. It does so in the mistaken belief that applied or program-oriented research naturally suggests single undertakings that will bind together research and application. It therefore attempts to order these pieces of research by relying heavily on solicitation, often with precise prescriptions for the projects. There are three important consequences to this strategy.

First, the strategy assumes that a development approach to social science research is valid. A development approach treats the research process as if it were a series of purchases with the products already or easily specified. We disagree with the assumption that social science research is amenable to such an approach. But more importantly for the current discussion, we find that the Institute's apparent acceptance of this assumption has led to mistaken administrative practices. The Institute relies extensively on solicitations that outline a problem for which knowledge is required and specify the pieces of research that will fulfill the requirement. A single "bidder" is then selected from among those who compete to perform the specified research. Such a procedure places the major responsibility for conceptualizing research on the staff, who are somehow expected to create single-handedly what generations of social scientists have never achieved—namely, a well-defined set of research tasks leading to clearly applicable knowledge about solving crime problems. This approach requires the staff to accomplish the impossible; it is not surprising, therefore, that their solicitation efforts are sometimes reduced to simplistic requests.

A more realistic—and ultimately more productive—approach would be to organize the staff around important research topics, such as deterrence and rehabilitation; for each such topic, a wide range of researchers working in related fields could be encouraged, by means of broad program solicitations, to submit proposals out of which the most promising ones would be funded. This kind of approach involves the staff directly in structuring the sets of issues to be researched, but opens the process to contributions from active researchers and promotes a creative exchange between program planners and performers. The sort of solicitation that the Institute presently uses puts an inordinate strain on staff competence, particularly a staff that is isolated, and in turn reduces their credibility with that community that might well serve their purpose. While the patterns of solicitation vary among different divisions in the Institute, and there are examples of well-designed solicitations, the dangers of depending on solicitation and the development approach are worth stressing.

Second, the Institute in recent years has characteristically funded large projects, averaging about $265,000 (see Figure B-4, in Appendix B). It feels these large projects are inappropriate or unattractive to individual researchers and conversely assumes that large institutions like Federal Contract Research Centers and nonprofit research organizations are best suited to supply the desired product. Whether intended or not, the Institute's argument for large project procurement is self-fulfilling. Though the number of university-based Institute grantees has increased in recent years, the Institute's interest in large grantees rather than individual researchers is openly stated. This is a widespread trend in federal research funding, but the consequences should be well understood. The business of research organizations is to provide answers to questions posed by the funding agency, not to conceptualize or restructure questions nor to select their own questions for research. Thus, the Institute is correct in its assumption that it will get "solution-oriented" answers to the questions it poses and less equivocal prescriptions than might be anticipated from academically based researchers. This strategy precludes a research style that is capable of developing questions that arise from the subject matter. The question that the Institute staff poses initially becomes all-important, and that staff's ability to pose central questions—as opposed to defining areas of concern—is therefore paramount. When this strategy is used to solicit large, multiphased projects, the staff is even removed from the long-term process of working through the issues.

The strategy also has a tendency to exclude academically based researchers. When solicitations—formal or informal—require a short response time, the process attracts only those who are either already working on the topic or those in the business of answering proposals. Academic researchers who are already involved in the topic and are, therefore, able to respond quickly are not likely to want to restructure their research to specific NILECJ requirements, while other academic researchers who might be interested in getting into the topic could not possibly respond within the short time frame. On the other hand, research organizations that have a sizable commitment to proposal writing have a staff whose express role is to fulfill that need and are therefore content with such constraints. Staff in such organizations are often generalists whose major skill is to make the standard (acceptable) responses to procurement requests; they may not be the best researchers.

Finally, the strategy precludes a creative interaction between staff and researchers in designing projects. The strategy of other research funding agencies—for example, the National Institute of Mental Health—results in a markedly different style. In such agencies, once a decision has been made to encourage a grantee through proposal stage, the program staff become intimately involved with assisting, supporting, and cultivating the research design; the final decision then is made by an outside review panel. As a result, there is an opportunity for creative exchanges between the applicant and the program officer, and ample opportunity as well to make judgments in a nonadversarial environment about the competence of the applicant and the ultimate productivity of the design.

It is also the Committee's impression that the Institute has, in addition to de facto exclusion of many academically based researchers, alienated a large segment of the potential grantee community. First, by funding without any apparent patterns, and throughout the year, the Institute appears to follow capricious funding cycles. Second, through solicitations that tend to dictate research questions and stifle creativity rather than simply control for quality, the Institute turns off researchers who might wish to pose and structure their own innovative research questions. The Institute has also made the mistake of asking well-known social scientists to submit ideas, informally, for possible funding, and then neglecting to follow up on the response. Whatever the Institute's intent in such cases, the impression left is that its solicitation approach is either parochial or less than candid. Third, the commitment to a solicitation strategy leaves little room for unsolicited work, thereby reinforcing the disinterest of a large segment of the research community.

Proposal Review and Project Monitoring

The Committee is concerned about the number of weak projects approved by the Institute staff. We believe this is a direct result of the lack of any proper peer review or commitment to serious consideration of the opinions of outside evaluators. If properly used, peer review provides a careful check on methodological questions and some breadth and exchange of views on the theoretical and social significance of proposals.

Currently, the Institute makes use of a peer review process in three ways. First, it requests from its technical assistance contractor a mail review of a selected number of proposals, at a cost of $300,000 a year. We note that mail review is the least potent form of peer review, especially in a multidisciplinary field, and even this weak form is not always used by the Institute. Further, there is ample evidence both from interviews with Institute staff and from the files that staff have ignored advice they disagreed with and promoted advice that supported their views; such behavior is understandable, but hardly consistent with the purpose of review. Review by a panel of outside experts, meeting together periodically, would counteract the tendency of staff to use the process as a political cover rather than a means of getting expert opinion.

Second, NILECJ engages in a self-proclaimed form of peer review by creating ad hoc panels of Institute staff. Such panels are useful devices for integrating diverse expertise within the Institute and thereby providing a common substantive focus for a variety of perspectives, but they cannot substitute for individual proposal review by outside review panels.

Third, the Institute has made increasing use of outside panels that exist not to review a proposal but rather to advise the grantee through the course of the project. The Committee considers such panels a salutary device for some monitoring purposes, and especially as a means of gaining the continuing advice of eminent social scientists on major projects. But these panels should not be relied upon, as they sometimes have been, to salvage projects that were badly designed to begin with and should never have been funded at all.

On a somewhat different level, the Committee's review of grants and contracts files suggests that the Institute has failed to integrate the contributions of practitioners and researchers in the most productive way. Balanced advice from both practitioner and research communities is essential to a well-planned and methodologically sound program. The Institute cannot achieve a productive substantive base for a research program without joining the two perspectives. Mail review is no substitute for face-to-face exchange among experts, both practitioners and researchers, who have the responsibility for advising those making funding decisions. The current review procedures are largely a pretense, although there have been some recent indications of more rigorous project review.

The lack of adequate review also places a strain on the monitoring process, since problems are almost always discovered when it is too late for any significant alteration. This is inherent in the process and renders questionable the Institute's insistence on the importance of monitoring as a means of control. Indeed, for a good deal of the

Institute's social science research, monitoring is necessarily inappropriate because monitoring can discover problems only after the data have been collected; by that time, a flaw in the project design can be cured only by returning to the field at enormous costs. Through its review of NILECJ files, the Committee found that monitors are overly occupied with administrative detail in the early stages of projects. Monitor concentration on budgetary detail and staffing at the early stages tends to postpone interest in substantive results until the final few months of a one- or two-year grant.

In addition to the possibility of improving existing projects, intensive monitoring is justified by a desire to get increased feedback about future funding, but the NILECJ files do not show evidence of such flow of information. On the contrary, there are indications of both individual researchers and organizations being re-funded to repeat the same work without any awareness on the part of the monitors that this is a twice-told tale. The Institute's experiences with monitoring reinforce the argument for strengthening the initial review: many of the remedies suggested toward the end of the project could be intelligently implemented through contract and design arrangements in the initial stages—but are useless when the project's life is half spent.

Overall the Committee finds that the Institute has neglected the obvious avenues for gaining highly sophisticated and broad-based advice. As a consequence, it has continued to fund weak projects and then to engage in futile salvage efforts. A properly designed review system would at least screen out the weak projects, if not produce good ones.

Staff Capabilities and Institute Role

The Committee's assessment of the relations between Institute staff and grantees and applicants indicates a considerable lack of rapport. To bring about any meaningful change in this regard and to effect strong direction of research design and implementation, the Institute must first recognize that it has alienated a large part of the potential grantee community. This has been due to a combination of factors: its politicized image, its arbitrary funding procedures, and a generally held low opinion of its intellectual stature. Some of this is reputation, a legacy of past attitudes. The presumption that federal efforts against crime were ideologically motivated and the perception on the part of the intellectual community that these efforts lacked genuine research value are part of that legacy. However, the Committee has heard numerous complaints that speak to the tone of the Institute's relationships with the research community and the lack of understanding of the research process that remains a characteristic of these relationships. There is something fundamentally wrong about the image of social research in an uncharted area planned and executed by a staff that lays only limited claims to research capacity or experience—indeed, that claims, if anything, skill in management rather than research.

Any long-run success for NILECJ's programs requires the development of a professional Institute staff that can capably deal with experienced researchers, make intelligent judgments about research design, and effectively monitor projects. The staff should have the capability to work with a proposal's principal investigator in the development of project design and methodology. Accordingly, staff members should be current in the field, both in substance and methodology, able to function as active professionals in their own right. Building substantive involvement must include active contact with the user and research communities. This in turn would create a level of confidence in the staff, increasing their capacity to deal effectively with the range of problems that confront research on crime. The Institute itself must become a visible entity in the research world. Staff publications should be strongly encouraged along with other activities to enhance professional development. Upgrading of the Institute's stature in these ways should ultimately result in a more collegial and productive relationship with the research community.

The Institute's leadership role in the criminal justice research community is of major importance. As an organization, NILECJ has had a dual responsibility for developing both a research agenda and a research community. The Committee finds that NILECJ has been reasonably successful in creating a community of research organizations, but has often misused them through its procurement strategy. On the other hand, the Institute has underused the academic research community. Because academic researchers maintain a tradition of publication of findings, increased use of and relations with that community of researchers would serve the Institute in seeding ideas and developing the disciplines relevant to criminal justice research.

SUMMARY

In evaluating the Institute's research program, the Committee has applied four criteria: the quality of the funded research, the usefulness of its products, success in cumulating knowledge, and the effectiveness of research administration.

The quality of NILECJ funded research has been largely mediocre. Of the sample projects reviewed by the Committee members, most could be labeled neither failures nor successes. Program weaknesses are, in our opinion, largely the result of a lack of attention to research design and of related administrative failings.

The usefulness of the Institute's work is more problematic to assess. A major criterion of usefulness for programmatic research is its contribution to building a coherent body of knowledge and to focusing that knowledge on solving relevant problems. Despite rhetoric to the contrary, the Committee finds little evidence that the Institute has been committed to cumulative research. Further, the Committee finds the usefulness of specific programs limited by the structural isolation of various programs within the Institute and by pressures on the agency to perform functions inappropriate for a research institute.

We believe that the Institute's methods of procuring research and its preference for large, multiphased projects from a narrow research community have alienated a large portion of the research community and overburdened staff resources. The result has been a research program characterized largely by naive funding decisions and unimaginative research. Finally, the Committee finds that the administration of the research program within the Institute has been seriously hindered by the fact that the director does not have final approval for Institute awards and, consequently, that it lacks the independence necessary to shape a legitimate research program.

III Knowing About Crime

5 Conclusions and Recommendations

We begin our conclusions with two observations about the character of the Institute. First, NILECJ has never established the stature necessary to command the respect or involvement of the larger research community in its activities and therefore has never been able to exert significant influence in criminal justice research. Second, NILECJ has an appropriate role to play in serving state and local criminal justice needs, but that role has been distorted by its relationship to LEAA.

To play a leadership role in criminal justice research, the Institute's relationship with the research community and with LEAA will need major restructuring. We offer recommendations about the nature of the research that is needed, about the manner in which it ought to be administered, including the kinds of questions that ought to guide priorities, about the overall mission of the Institute, and about the conditions under which it ought to operate. The first part of this chapter contains findings, conclusions, and recommendations on the Institute's program, administration, and operating condition; the second part is a discussion of research priorities.

RESEARCH AND DEVELOPMENT PROGRAM

The Institute has had low visibility in much of the research community from which it might have drawn imaginative and productive research; it has maintained some mechanisms for procuring research that exacerbate that situation, and the quality of its research has been largely parochial and, overall, mediocre. If the Institute is to play a major role in criminal justice research, its grantee community must be widened, through direct contacts and through changes in solicitation policy. At this point in the development of knowledge about crime, the ideas from a broadened research community, and different approaches within chosen priority areas, ought to control funding decisions more often than the delivery of specific and immediately applicable products.

Program Quality

Findings

The Institute has, through its different phases, undertaken worthwhile ventures and strategies. But the importance of such efforts has frequently been dwarfed by major failures or highly criticized programs. In short, the projects funded over the 7-year history of NILECJ have been of notably uneven quality. The major source of weakness was poor research or project design, but it is important to note three other major weaknesses as well.

First, the program has been disproportionately concerned with testing conventional administrative devices and narrow technological innovations. Few of the Institute's research projects have shown much imaginativeness or daring. For example, despite obvious and continuing deficiences in police-community relations, the Institute has not taken the lead in developing alternative models of police organization and behavior. The Committee also notes the conspicuous absence of research on emerging social phenomena to elucidate crime causation: for instance, on the increasing number of women offenders to expand our understanding of socialization to crime or on the effects of prolonged economic insecurity on individual propensities to commit crimes. Furthermore, the Institute has not been adequately interested in research on important problems, like official corruption, not now on the conventional roster of major crimes.

Second, there has been little longitudinal continuity in Institute programming and even less coherence across different NILECJ organizational components. Consequently, any gains in knowledge have not been developed to full advantage. Similarly, whether the intent was there originally, there is no evidence that a common focus within broad subject areas has been used for funding decisions or that different pieces of research have been adequately integrated to cumulate knowledge. Consequently, knowledge-building from project to project has been severely handicapped.

Many projects the Committee evaluated were fuzzily defined attempts to answer a broad set of questions. Individual grants have been of poor quality often enough—badly designed or lacking a specifiable product—that it might have been difficult in any case to integrate findings from different projects. Projects were frequently defined from a narrow substantive perspective so that opportunities for creative thinking or alternative approaches to a particular set of problems were largely eliminated. And often the strategy was to attempt a solution to a major problem with a single project, rather than adopting more realistic, differently paced, or more modest designs that would use different grantees suited to different aspects of the task. In addition, staff have scrapped program areas and program strategies prematurely because they became enervated by bureaucratic minutia and are impatient for immediate payoff. Administrative convenience has too often dominated research needs. Overall, there do not appear to be any significant changes in the trend over time.

Finally, though the Institute has attempted a mix of strategies—contracting, granting, formal and informal solicitation, cultivation of different research communities—it has still drawn from a narrow set of grantees and perspectives and placed major emphasis on procurement. Complex problems have often been researched by a single grantee or contractor. Research tasks have at times extended all the way from state-of-the-art research, through testing of specific hypotheses derived from that research, to delivery of prescribed program implementation at the practitioner level. Many design weaknesses are due to structuring grants that are so broad and ill-defined that only superficial answers to complex problems can result. Specific mechanisms like large umbrella contracts, consortiums, and large multiphased grants have been used at different times. Though recent indications suggest the Institute is trying to change that process, its chosen procedures are uneven in their potential for accomplishing the goal of enlisting a broader research community.

Conclusions

Although research agendas may have been set at different times in the Institute's history, none have served adequately as a framework in which judgments could be made about what is known, what needs to be known, what alternative strategies may be undertaken, and what ultimate usefulness or applicability the research might have. While the

Institute has used mechanisms—like those in the MBO format for project review—that require some systematic, pro forma planning for each project, our grant evaluations suggest that adequate retrospective and prospective analysis is not being done. The Committee concludes that because priorities have been short-lived and rarely explored through a variety of research efforts, the strengths that they might have provided to program planning and project design have been often wasted.

A stable, guiding research agenda could have served as a constant reminder of basic goals. Moreover, within the boundaries of a respected set of basic goals and substantive interests, the Institute might have felt freer to take more risk in the analysis of those interests and the funding of specific research. A research agenda allows for a systematic and coordinated assessment of appropriate tasks, overall program planning, and project-by-project planning. It also allows a program planner to consider in retrospect what his or her projects have accomplished and plan accordingly for the appropriate next steps within the framework of a particular problem area. These sorts of features have been clearly lacking in the Institute's research program.

A well thought-out set of research priorities, along with the systematic involvement of prestigious research advisors and respected practitioners, could have acted as a protective buffer from the Institute's highly politicized environment. Without such a buffer, it was difficult for the Institute to pursue intellectually daring and imaginative projects in a professional and disinterested way. Instead, the Institute has taken a reactive stance that has made it overly sensitive to outside pressures and geared it toward a search for immediate gains and, in their own words, "short-term winners." It is hard to reconstruct in retrospect the chicken-and-egg dilemma: did changes in leadership in both LEAA and NILECJ destroy priorities, or did the Institute's anticipation of such changes force it to set priorities in a climate of crisis? The fact that the Institute has not controlled its own budget certainly contributed to its inability to cope with these pressures. It is clear that the lack of a stable direction has had a negative effect on the quality of research.

As noted, the Institute has not taken full advantage of a varied community of researchers that might have enhanced the quality of the research, in part because it emphasizes a process of solicitation and a kind of research that is skewed toward one community of researchers. The Institute often assumes that by the process of solicitation it can order defined pieces of research, as if a development model could be used for applied social science research or as if solutions to a whole category of problems can be procured through the purchase of comprehensive packages of research. It holds to the belief that applied research naturally suggests single undertakings including research and application and attempts to order these pieces of research by relying heavily on solicitation, often with precise prescriptions for the projects.

The Institute assumes that its own mission and purpose dictate a primary emphasis on immediate-solution applied research. Although the intent, it claims, is changing, the Institute appears to have worked hard at avoiding those kinds of research questions that it feels are part of basic rather than applied research. Even if the narrow emphasis on applied research were correctly chosen, an emphasis with which the Committee disagrees, the development approach to social science research is inappropriate. The development approach assumes that social science research is analogous to technology development: that the necessary knowledge exists and what is needed is to translate that knowledge into a form that is applicable to crime problems. It also assumes that staff will be in a position to initiate and administer the development process. The Committee concludes that both assumptions are incorrect and that Institute procedures that are based on these assumptions should be changed. It also notes that contracting, even more precisely aimed at getting specific deliverables and more encumbered by bureaucratic complexities than granting, may exacerbate the tendency to enlarge the scope of projects.

While the patterns of solicitation vary among different divisions in the Institute—and there are examples of well-designed solicitations—the dangers of depending on solicitation and the development approach are significant enough to stress. RFPS requiring quick responses attract only those who are either already working on the topic or those in the business of answering proposals. Organizations having a sizable commitment to proposal writing employ a staff whose express role is to fulfill that need and are therefore content with such time constraints. Furthermore, the formal, even legalistic, environment in which proposal competitions often operate eliminates the opportunity for creative exchanges between the applicant and the program officer, and the opportunity as well to make judgments in a nonadversarial manner about the competence of the applicant and the ultimate productivity of the research design. It is also the Committee's impression that seemingly capricious funding cycles, and solicitations that tend to dictate research questions and stifle creativity rather than simply control for quality, alienate a particular community of researchers who might wish to pose and structure their own innovative research questions. The Committee believes that a strategy that inhibits researchers from developing questions that arise from the subject matter is largely inappropriate for advancing the state of knowledge as it currently exists in criminal justice.

Recommendations

The Committee recommends that the Institute program be structured to foster the development of a coherent set of program areas that will suggest research questions with manageable limits for good research design and be a productive base for cumulating knowledge.

1. The Institute should develop more programs that are cumulative in nature. Programs like the Research Agreement Program (RAP), the National Evaluation Program, and some large-scale efforts at data archiving are good examples of this. The key to quality, open-ended projects like the RAP, however, is the Institute's ability to select competence in the investigators and to recognize competence in the execution of the work. Since success is necessarily uncertain, caution should be exercised in giving exclusive control over research in any particular subject area to a single grantee or institution.

2. The Institute should use a long-range set of priorities (like those discussed below) to guide individual project choices and should not require promises of immediate payoff. Overall, the Institute should aim for a mixed strategy with a balance between basic and applied research, and grants or contracts, as the individual research project and specificity of outcome dictate.

Within the research priorities, some important fraction of the Institute's program should be committed to testing approaches and funding researchers who are non-traditional, recognizing that if the result of any of these ventures is failure, discovering the cause of the failure provides new knowledge.

The dichotomy between basic and applied research should be invoked only as it helps to structure discrete research questions at different levels of a problem and to suggest appropriate outcomes and applications of each research project. Serious consideration of all aspects of a problem could require elements of both basic and applied research, and the dichotomy should not be used to determine appropriateness of Institute funding.

3. The Institute should use devices for making funding choices that would force it to take deliberate and systematic stock of what related research has already been undertaken, to tighten research designs, and to determine appropriate grantees and contractors. Devices to tighten design include exploratory funding, separation of state-of-the-art reviews from design and implementation, and pre-grant awards for design. Pre-grant awards of, say, $5,000–10,000 for exploring a topic could be given without the necessary expectation of funding the same grantee for the ultimate project. Small, perhaps $5,000, pre-grant awards could also be given to the chosen grantee specifically for design, prior to full funding.

Closer relationships should be maintained with other federal agencies and other research institutions in similar pursuits. Projects should draw on knowledge available from others in related fields.

A consideration of the appropriate audience should be one of the primary criteria for project selection and design. All research designs should include recognition of both the use and the limits of applicability of products that flow from it. The assumption should be that the practitioner is the consumer of some research products and that other research activities are appropriately directed toward other researchers.

4. *Upon completion of their projects, all* NILECJ *grantees and contractors should make their data available for secondary analysis, replication, and verification.* The Institute should consider each project as part of a potential continuum of knowledge. All grantees and contractors should ensure that in collecting data appropriate protections of confidentiality and other legal constraints are respected and maintained consistently in all research.

5. *The Institute should use announcements of areas of interest as the primary means of generating concept papers and proposals, rather than relying heavily on solicitations with precise specifications of research design.* By relaxing its solicitation strategy, the Institute can work toward broadening its potential source of grantees so that a wide range of disciplines and perspectives may be brought to bear on research problems.

Ample room should be left within program areas for innovative and individualized research approaches. Broadly advertised and carefully articulated program announcements can help develop a broad criminal justice research community, such that a more natural balance could develop between formal solicitations and ideas that are generated from an expanding research community.

When advertised solicitations or announcements are used, program descriptions by staff should be researched carefully enough so that they articulate important issues in the area, but allow researchers sufficient freedom and flexibility for serendipity to function.

6. *The presumption should be in favor of granting rather than contracting as the Institute's method for obtaining research. Within*

the chosen set of priorities and specific research interests, contracting should be limited to those projects with precise and known deliverable products, which would ideally be performed by contract and research organizations. The Institute has too frequently made premature decisions to contract before fundamental issues have been researched and understood. The presumption ought to be in this kind of social science research that the grant is the appropriate funding mechanism unless the research issue is already thoroughly investigated and products can be easily specified.

7. *The Institute should use a variety of mechanisms to establish more positive relationships with a broadly defined research community and to enrich the dialogue between staff and quality researchers.*

a. *The Institute should raise its visibility in various potential grantee communities.* Mechanisms to accomplish this include: encouraging staff publications in the refereed journals; organizing panels at professional meetings of the social science disciplines on criminal justice research issues; encouraging periodic visits by staff to research centers and universities to scout for interesting research; facilitating periodic staff seminars and leaves to attend university workshops; facilitating frequent and positive contact with SPAS and operating agencies to make known Institute work and to learn about operating problems that may be candidates for research or evaluation.

b. *The Institute should make use of extended leave and exchange programs, to give researchers experience in grant development and administration and to give administrators who have been trained in research the opportunity to engage in research in academic settings.* Such exposure would increase the Institute's visibility to a wide range of research disciplines and enhance staff capabilities.

c. *The Institute should clearly articulate its priority-setting and funding procedures to the research community.* The need to eliminate any real or perceived capriciousness in selecting grantees is clear. Wide advertising of program area interests, as suggested, is one mechanism for accomplishing this. Compliance with advertised funding cycles is another. The annual program plan should include a clearer overall description of program areas and procedures and be widely distributed across disciplines and research institutions.

8. *The Institute's budget should not be increased in the near future. The Institute should change its emphasis to smaller proposals within the program areas suggested below or of a pilot nature and to the major data efforts suggested below; it should reassess its position with respect to the knowledge it will have developed in 3 to 5 years hence.*

The evidence suggests that the roughly $35 million the Institute has had available in recent budgets has not been well spent; further, if the funds were allocated in the same ways, it is clear that comparable spending levels would not be productive in the future. More modest funding for the program would considerably assist the process of transition from its current program to that which we recommend.

During this period, efforts should be directed toward developing and piloting a comprehensive and practicable program of research. When and if such a program is developed, its implementation may well require an increase in resources well beyond the present level of funding.

Program Administration

Expert opinion and emphasis on substantive program areas should govern program planning and project administration. The Institute has not created accountable advisory mechanisms that would afford staff the best possible advice on overall priority setting, project planning, and review. Review capability should include assessment of both scientific validity and user applicability. Strict peer review procedures and a statutorily authorized advisory board should govern funding decisions. Administration—problem analysis, program development, and project funding—should be organized around substantive research areas, not artificial organizational divisions.

Findings

With little exception, the internal structure of the Institute has neither developed out of nor facilitated analysis of substantive research problems. Despite many superficial changes in its organization, the Institute's program has been administered within separate organizational divisions based more on the traditional functions of the criminal justice system and on several statutory mandates than on substantive research considerations. Hence, the expertise of staff in different parts of the agency has often been unavailable when important program planning questions were raised. Problems have been analyzed and projects funded within unnecessarily narrow perspectives. Tensions created simply by organizational lines have interfered with the staff's ability to make more informed judgments about planning and funding. Research problems are viewed as, for example, technological or nontechnological, as relating to courts or police. The formulation of research problems should not be dictated by narrow, functional concerns.

In addition, the Institute has not exploited the capacity of the research community to assist staff and advise on funding decisions; rather it has relied on tight, in-house control. The Institute has not made systematic use of experts in the field to suggest broad program areas or assist in individual funding decisions, and the recommendations they have received have not always been seriously considered. In fact, the staff is not accountable to the judgments of consultants, and the consultants are not held to account for their advice by any continuity of information or review. Typically, these advisors do not know what advice is followed or what resulted from their advice. Finally, since there is no effective mechanism for long-range, overall planning in the agency, the capabilities of outside experts are applied piecemeal rather than systematically.

In the absence of an adequate intellectual framework and a stable and continuing advisory group, staff is left to zigzag from one idea in vogue to another, never pursuing one long enough to carefully assess what has been learned and what should be pursued next. Enthusiasms are catching; the requirement to justify changes is absent.

Review procedures do not demand rigor, nor do they create the conditions that promote carefully considered research design; as a result, the Institute necessarily spends an inordinate amount of time mending its ways through project monitoring. Staff is often preoccupied with making tardy and frustrating fundamental design adjustments well into the implementation of the grant award or attempting to police the grantee through trivial nonsubstantive monitoring. The evidence from our review of grants and contracts files is that the monitoring process is largely ineffective and needs major adjustment. Complaints from Institute grantees suggest (and the files do not contradict them) that monitoring is often heavy-handed and preoccupied with trivia. In normal, short-term, medium-cost projects, monitoring is almost inevitably too late in detecting faults. When only three or four months are left before the end of a project, doctoring of a basic type seems out of range of the capabilities of any but the extraordinarily gifted.

Conclusions

The Committee believes that the broadest array of expertise has not been applied to setting priorities and making funding decisions because appropriate mechanisms, both internal and external, and long and short range, have not been used to fully tap that expertise.

The Institute's reliance on in-house control is in many ways understandable. When the Institute came into being, there was only a small academic community interested specifically in problems of criminal justice, few self-generated ideas, and few to provide guidance through peer review. But the Committee believes that in making both broad program and individual funding decisions, the Institute should now avail itself of the expertise of knowledgeable individuals outside the Institute.

The Committee concludes that the methods currently used by the Institute to generate and judge research rely too heavily on the judgments of its staff members, taxing both their time and skill. It also notes that the Institute has had great difficulty finding an effective means of structuring advice from users and from the public. The lack of precision and sharpness in defining programs and awarding grants and the absence of programmatic continuity are largely a result of the absence of advisory groups—with researchers and practitioners—familiar with utilization problems of research and of the absence of peer review for individual projects. Particularly since NILECJ seeks to be an applied research operation, it must ask the advice of those who will attempt to apply its research. While in-house judgments should ultimately determine the Institute's program, the agency needs to seek and take seriously advice from representatives of various groups outside the Institute. Knowledgeable individuals should be drawn from the academic community, from state and local funding agencies, from practitioners in the field, and from other interested groups.

There are many ways of structuring relationships with outside groups and a number of techniques that may be used to develop them. The objective should be to mobilize the broadest methodological and substantive expertise to each problem area and to each proposed project. Emphasis ought to be on generating quality research within defined problem areas, with all available expertise—both within and without the Institute—being brought to bear on program development and project management. Ad hoc solicitations throughout the year and piecemeal reviews do not serve this purpose well. Outside experts cannot be used effectively unless they can make comparisons among numbers of related project proposals and systematically assess development of a program area over time.

The Committee believes that the emphasis on sound review and improved design of individual projects, using peer panels and other mechanisms noted above, would help relieve the strains of monitoring. In addition, distinguishing portions of the research program that are characterized by projects of modest size and short duration from longer-term or more complex projects would separate projects whose monitoring should be relatively routine from those that require tighter control. Use of outside panels for advising selected projects can enhance the quality of the resulting products. Team monitoring can also be useful, but it should include both an advocate and a critic, with each having specific, independent reporting responsibilities.

Organizational lines should not interfere with the process of bringing all available methodological and substantive skills to bear on program planning for each problem area. Current organizational divisions do not serve the process well since they insulate methodologists from substantive experts. We recognize why LEAA and the Institute chose to set up a specific Office of Evaluation: it provided a visible and accountable way to comply with the Congressional mandate; but this historical rationale is no longer persuasive. To set up a separate evaluation office dilutes the capabilities of a good, methodologically skilled staff and isolates them from the work in other offices in which they ought to be involved. The dynamic process by which planning for research in the Office of Research Programs might use evaluation is lost because of the insularity. The territorial defensiveness that is created by the existence of separate offices exaggerates the differences in perspective and training.

The Committee is aware, however, of the specific demands of both the evaluation and dissemination efforts. Evaluation projects, especially—while designed in the context of a larger research program—must be carried out with care that they are independent of the specific research project evaluated.

The experience of the dissemination staff would also be useful in designing research, but it is seldom used in this way. The fact that staff of the Office of Technology Transfer (OTT) has been operating within its own separate office structure exacerbates the difficulties of relating dissemination to the research process. Here, too, we understand why the Institute created the office: it is a source of visibility and a buffer against outside pressures that demand obvious signs of success. But the Institute's dissemination techniques are too formal and rely too much on routine dissemination of printed materials to have much impact, and some are unrelated to research and are therefore inappropriate for a research institute. Others, like panels and conferences, are ideal for Institute attention. In this regard, a prime concern for the Institute's dissemination efforts should be to make known to researchers and practitioners what research is being done under Institute sponsorship. This effort would be greatly facilitated by closer association between research grant administration and dissemination.

The Advanced Technology Division (ATD) presents this same problem of insularity, but it is in some ways more difficult to resolve. The problems of communication have been enormous between ATD and its contractors and non-technologists in other parts of the Office of Research Programs. Yet for the process of program development, the technologists' perspective and training ought to be one among many for structuring specific research tasks: it makes no more sense for technologists alone to consider all aspects of a complex research topic than it does for psychologists alone or operations researchers alone to do so. The apparent inadequacies of the ATD program are subsumed by the more important and overriding question of the appropriateness of technological solutions to crime problems: asking a practitioner what technological innovation he or she needs has prejudged that question. Corrective measures, as have been suggested—like better management, more access to expertise, better linkage between development and producer or user—are at least secondary to the issue of whether a technological solution is appropriate in any particular case. We are sensitive to the difficulties of dispersing a staff of technologists throughout an organization where the training and outlook is different; a flexible team approach would permit consideration of both technological and nontechnological questions and issues for all research tasks.

Recommendations

9. The Committee recommends that the Institute establish formal peer review procedures and an overall advisory panel for general program planning within the structure of a three-tiered advisory system:

a. a statutory Advisory Board on Criminal Justice Research, to set overall priorities (see Recommendation 16 for details);

b. program planning panels for each of a selected set of program areas; and

c. individual project review panels.

In this advisory system both researchers and practitioners should be represented on all panels; review panels should provide for methodological and programmatic scrutiny of all projects; and panels should be set up for extended terms to establish continuity of program and should meet regularly.

The use of advisory panels within projects already under way is also helpful, though caution should be exercised so that these panels have no special investment in continuation of the particular project.

10. The Institute should employ a less obtrusive monitoring system that would allow more flexibility to grantees. With the use of dual review and improvement of project design, the need for remedial monitoring should be greatly reduced.

11. Substantive program areas (like those suggested below) should be the basis for creating the framework for program administration and budget allocation. Functional divisions, whether they relate to criminal justice operations (police, courts, and corrections) or Institute mandates (dissemination, evaluation, and technology), should serve only to provide particular expertise to program and project development, not to suggest substantive divisions.

The Institute may select from a variety of organizational modes to operate its program, including the possiblity of ad hoc task forces for different substantive areas. It should organize for planning and funding decisions around substantive research priorities and within the framework set by an overall planning advisory group and program planning panels.

12. Funding levels should not be rigidly fixed within substantive areas. With adequate advertisement and the resulting cultivation of research interest within different substantive areas, the excellence of proposals should govern the apportionment of funds, rather than the need to "move the money" within a limited selection of grantees and subjects.

13. Strict funding cycles—two or three a year—should be established and adhered to. Advertised program areas would generate wide response and require the use of effective review panels. Attention should be paid to timing so that a wide research community including academically based researchers could comfortably participate in the process.

14. The structure of NILECJ*'s research program should have appropriate evaluation, dissemination, and technology development functions integrated into the major research effort. These components should be represented on whatever decision-making mechanisms are developed to set the research agenda.*

One major function of dissemination should be to make known to researchers and practitioners ongoing Institute research. Another major function of dissemination should be to foster understanding on the part of practitioners of the contributions and limitations of research and understanding on the part of researchers of the needs and experiences of practitioners. Techniques like panels and conferences are excellent means for facilitating contact and understanding between researchers and practitioners. While such activities need expertise in dissemination techniques, they need equally the skills and knowledge of those involved in research.

Technology and the technological expertise that exists in the Institute ought to serve as one of many perspectives applied to developing research priorities. Technology staff need not be physically dispersed among program areas but should be allocated to appropriate problem areas as the analysis of the problem dictates. Above all, while people with specialized methodological skills—technological, evaluation, or any other—should interact with each other, they should not interact only with each other.

Operating Conditions

Findings

NILECJ has never had the benefit of a rich intellectual environment to provide guidance in structuring its program. LEAA has not offered a supportive environment in which to cultivate research because of its own historical struggles and pressures. Too few people with too narrow a set of interests have shown any concern for the Institute or criminal justice research—whether they were from Congress, a narrow intellectual and research community, or a narrowly drawn practitioner community. At best, the interests have been lopsided; at worst, the Institute has been unable to generate sufficient attention from a variety of sources to assist it in generating a broad and varied program. As a result, the single most dominant set of interests that has affected the Institute has been from LEAA. In large part, LEAA's mission has been the Institute's mission, and the consequences for research have been significant and largely negative.

LEAA's interests and mission have been tied directly to producing immediate solutions to problems associated with operating the criminal justice system or with directly lowering the crime rate. Its role is to service state and local practitioner constituencies, primarily through the State Planning Agencies. Its profile has been highly visible to those constituencies and to political interests. Consequently, many Institute responsibilities are tied more closely to that relationship than they are to the demands of research. Impact evaluation, mandated by Congress but a misplaced burden on Institute resources, is one example. The packaging, marketing, training, and technical assistance program for SPAS and local agencies performed by NILECJ's Office of Technology Transfer are another. Set up in separate offices, these particular evaluation and dissemination functions are only tangentially tied to research and would be better performed by the action agency rather than by a national research institute.

Many problems are traceable to the improper use of the Institute within the LEAA framework. Worse, they are traceable to the inability of the Institute to do anything more than react to the whims and changing strategies of LEAA's leadership. Crime-specific planning, Impact Cities, some examples of police hardware of questionable utility, the insistence that applied research should generate immediate solutions, and measuring the worth of Institute research in terms of changing crime rates are all illustrative of the effect of LEAA's influence.

Since the Institute is unable to pursue an independent set of strategies to cultivate research, its administrative relationship with LEAA is of first importance. LEAA conducts final review and has final (sign-off) authority to approve all Institute grants and contracts. It exercises frequent prerogatives over substantive program decisions, manipulating priorities, mandating new program undertakings, and precluding others. The research budget, the contracting process, and even the Institute's own personnel budget are outside of Institute control. Consequently, the Institute has no capacity for independent action.

Conclusions

Serious debate over the meaning and expectations for research might have provided better guidance for Institute programming. It is not clear that Congress alone could have provided this. It is clear that few others partook of the opportunity and that the minimal Congressional activity was more destructive to the Institute's ability to carefully structure research priorities than it was helpful. The Institute also might have benefited from a balanced competition of interests—both intellectual and service interests. That the Institute has not been able to attract them has exaggerated the influence and control of LEAA over the Institute's program.

The Committee finds that the dominance of LEAA has negatively affected the Institute's capacity to maintain a coherent research agenda or a coherent set of priorities and its ability to attract quality researchers. The schism between program management on substantive matters administered by the Institute staff and administrative matters managed by LEAA undermines NILECJ's capacity to conduct a coherent program. Demands to service the LEAA delivery system and respond to pressures on LEAA have led to repeated improper use of Institute resources.

There are numerous examples. Most impact evaluations are not evaluation research efforts in the strict sense: they cannot feed into the research program and they cannot provide the kinds of information that would contribute to the testing of fundamental hypotheses. They can only feed into an action program and provide bases for directing use of action funds, a function of the SPAS, which are remote from the Institute. Much of the evaluation program is the most promising and important of any in the Institute, especially the emphasis on methodological development and on comparative multi-project studies such as the National Evaluation Program. The program's defects are largely attributable to an inappropriate mandate to engage in discrete impact evaluations and technical assistance. Similarly, many of the packaging, marketing, training, and technical assistance programs of OTT, though their real impact is yet to be measured, are impressive. But the business of preparing package prescriptions for operational procedures requires the kind of close connection with operating agencies that LEAA's Office of Regional Operations should have, not an office in a national research institute.

The application of research to current social problems is, we emphasize, a reasonable and ultimately productive mission. Integrating the research mission with a separate delivery system—that is, that of LEAA—is also, we emphasize, a reasonable approach. The Committee has grappled long and hard with the task of preserving that connection. But it is equally persuaded of the necessity for a degree of insularity from the destructive pressure of LEAA. The Committee does not wish to diminish NILECJ's utility to the practitioner community, but it feels that the Institute's service role is only theoretically, and in no important way practically, enhanced by LEAA's dominance. The Institute must be able to readjust its relationship with LEAA so that LEAA becomes a service agent to disseminate ideas to the criminal justice community, not a source of tyranny over Institute planning and activities. In short, LEAA should be a primary constituent of the Institute rather than its administrator.

The Committee believes that the mandate of a national institute should be for innovative kinds of research on the nature of crime and the potential for controlling it. This mandate includes research; certain kinds of evaluation that increase knowledge of the effects of various interventions on social processes; and certain kinds of dissemination that enhance the understanding of practitioners of the value of research and what is or is not known and enhance the understanding of researchers of the real problems and needs of practitioners.

Other kinds of research are more appropriate for, and in fact are being undertaken by, some SPAS and local operating agencies. Real and immediate problems are the natural progenitors of quick and immediately applicable policy research. When this sort of research is not being done at the local level or by SPAS, it is extremely difficult for a national institute to either encourage it or directly assist in its development. This is evidenced by the experiences of the Model Evaluation Program and many NILECJ-funded projects of mediocre quality and only local applicability. While it is difficult for a mission agency like LEAA to resist the temptation of using its Institute for this purpose, this is all the more reason why we recommend special caution in shaping appropriate roles and links between LEAA and the Institute.

If the first role for the Institute is leadership in criminal justice research and facilitating exchange of information and understanding between researchers and practitioners, the second ought to be creating the capacity for leadership by creating the intellectual bases from which useful research might emerge. The first we have said requires an independence from LEAA and a shifting of appropriate tasks for each. The second involves developing a broad base of contacts with researchers and professional organizations, and mechanisms to seek advice from a wide range of constituent groups; it also includes the administrative and intellectual task of shaping a valid and usable data system for analyzing crime.

The Committee applauds the recent Justice Department proposal to integrate and coordinate the many existing criminal justice data systems within a single bureau. If the Institute were sufficiently independent of the special interests of LEAA, as we recommend, it would be appropriate and productive to develop a close connection between the Institute and a bureau of criminal justice statistics. A major data base commands the interest of researchers and staff in the use and analysis of the data. Further, the best means of developing a productive data base is the incentive of exploring important research questions. A close organizational connection between the Institute and a bureau of criminal justice statistics would be of significant value to both.

We recognize that the work encompassed by the comprehensive responsibilities of a bureau of all criminal justice statistics could easily overwhelm the Institute in its present form. But if the Institute is going to create a rich intellectual framework, as we have suggested, if it is going to play a leadership role in criminal justice research, if it is going to broaden its focus beyond LEAA's and beyond parochial research typologies and engage a wide-ranging research community, it should also have within its mandate the many fields of criminal justice research that, by quirks of administrative and legislative history, have drifted into separate empires. In this context, and if the Institute were independent from LEAA, the Committee feels a bureau of criminal justice statistics within the Institute would be most productive.

Recommendations

15. In order to enhance the integrity of the Institute and its program, and to increase its ability to contribute objectively to LEAA *from an appropriate distance,* LEAA*'s domination over the Institute must be eliminated. At the vert least, the director must have full processing and sign-off authority over all Institute awards, control over the Institute's administrative budget and personnel, and detailed program review. The Committee also recommends that the Director should be at the level of Assistant Attorney General and should be appointed by the Attorney General of the United States.*

16. In order to assure the Institute's functional independence from LEAA, *protection from the politicization of the Attorney General's role, and guidance in its work by the principles of scientific excellence, overall program priorities should be set by a statutorily authorized criminal justice research advisory board.* Most of the members of such a board should be leading scientists from the many relevant disciplines and should also include practitioners and members of the community having substantial interest in the problems to which the research ought to apply. Authorizing legislation should specify the recommended mix of membership, as well as Presidential appointment with Senate confirmation and staggered terms to remove appointments from predominant partisan influence.

17. The director of the Institute should be chosen from candidates with significant experience and recognition in both research and research administration. These qualifications are essential if the director is to be able to attract the required research staff, to establish the necessary links to the research community, and to exercise the technical judgments that are central to the job.

18. In order to ensure coordination among the various activities closely related to the research mission of the Institute and to ensure the creation of an integrated intellectual and administrative base, the National Criminal Justice Statistical Service, the National Institute of Juvenile Justice and Delinquency Prevention, and Project SEARCH *should all be in the* NILECJ *structure. We endorse the idea of a bureau of criminal justice statistics; the ideal arrangement would be to locate this bureau within an independent* NILECJ. (See the discussion of "Common Data Needs" in the "Research Priorities" section, below.)

If the proposed bureau of criminal justice statistics remains separate, it should have within it the analytic capability characteristic of organizations like the Bureau of Labor Statistics. And while such a bureau should serve many different users, the critical need is to preserve with disinterest the integrity of the data. Structural separations within the bureau between those branches concerned with research use and those concerned with immediate policy use of the data might be helpful toward this end.

19. The Committee recommends that major functions and activities that are extraneous to NILECJ'*s substantive research program, such as formalized technical assistance to criminal justice planners and practitioners in designing and performing project evaluations, or the packaging and marketing aspects of dissemination, be located within* LEAA'*s Office of Regional Operations rather than in the Institute.*

RESEARCH PRIORITIES

The Institute should pursue a course that maximizes its capacity to contribute to the goal of crime control. This requires successfully wedding the process of a multidisciplinary approach to scientific knowledge with the substance of criminal justice practice and research. As we have already noted, one of the major obstacles that the Institute has faced is the lack of a well-developed research community. Such a community must be mobilized from the many disciplines that are relevant to the study of crime and criminal behaviors. But this kind of effort will not be effective unless the Institute develops substantive program areas that will focus the concerns of different disciplines on common problems.

Therefore, the Committee recommends that the Institute organize its research programs around program areas. These should be designed to provide a common focus on a theoretically interesting problem while at the same time exploiting the variety of perspectives that different disciplines can bring to bear. They should also be designed on the assumption that producing reliable and useful knowledge is a cumulative process. It is important that the planning for such a process be long-range, not precluding early payoff in some aspects of a problem but assuming that its complexity will require extended analysis. The planning must also take account of the developing nature of scientific research and provide for possible changes in the structure and even the focus of the program.

The staff for these program areas must have both substantive competence and the flexibility to follow up on promising developments. Furthermore, the staff in each area should have the benefit of extensive and ongoing advice from a panel of outside experts whose function is to oversee the planning and implementation of the program. In order to be

effective, these panels should include experts from the various research disciplines involved as well as representatives of practitioner and user groups. This mix of advice on a continuing basis is important in order to maximize the potential for creative exchange among the variety of perspectives needed for a better understanding of the problem being explored. Indeed, progress toward reliable and useful knowledge about crime depends upon effectively structuring the advisory process.

The Committee was not asked to develop a full research agenda for the Institute. But it does recommend that the Institute consider six program areas, briefly discussed below, as one model for a productive approach to crime research. While the six program areas are not intended to be exhaustive or exclusive, they do represent the Committee's consensus view of priorities for research on crime problems. The program areas are: data center, deterrence, rehabilitation, analyzing the consequences of change in the criminal justice system, socialization to crime, and focusing the criminal law. The Committee believes that research in these six areas can increase knowledge about criminal behaviors, system change, and the effectiveness of criminal sanctions. The six program areas were chosen not only because they are central to efforts to control crime but also because the Committee considers them a realistic focus for useful research. When defined in this way, the Institute's research program cannot produce short-term reductions in crime rates—and it should not be expected to do so. But it can provide reliable knowledge to better inform criminal justice policies and make more effective the use of the criminal law.

Data Center

Common Data Needs

Data provide a fundamental resource for all empirical research and for many administrative purposes. Even though most research projects can meet their data needs primarily by ad hoc collection of data specifically for that project, there is a common need for a wide range of standard data items that can best be collected centrally. These data provide fundamental baseline observations on which further research can build, and they stimulate a wide variety of research projects. In addition such data also have significant potential for improving the planning and operations of criminal justice programs.

Such common data should include two important classes of information: cross-sectional information on crimes and the processing by the criminal justice system of suspects, defendants, and offenders; and longitudinal information on criminal-career histories of individuals. These data are essential for the progress of research on a number of crime problems and especially for research on deterrence and recidivism questions.

The cross-sectional information should include various measures of criminal justice system performance that vary across jurisdictions like states, counties, cities, and Standard Metropolitan Statistical Areas (SMSAs). These measures should be consistently and comparably reported across jurisdictions and should include at least the following variables, detailed by crime-type categories:

1. Number of reported crimes;
2. Number of arrests (by demographic subgroups of arrestees, including age, race, and sex);
3. Number of cases held for the court of general jurisdiction and number of persons charged;
4. Number of cases disposed of by type of disposition;
5. Number of persons sent to each type of correctional institution; and
6. Average time served by those released from each correctional mode.

These data can all be derived from combinations of agency statistics and offender-based tracking records like those used in the Prosecutors Management Information System (PROMIS) or the Offender Based Transaction Statistics (OBTS) system. The critical need is for compatibility across jurisdictions in reporting structure to permit cross-sectional analysis. Once the data are available they should be organized in some form of flow model that would provide a basis for examining their values at various stages in the system.

In addition to aggregate-flow data and system statistics, it is important to have a rich collection of data characterizing the development of individual criminal careers. These are needed for the study of recidivism, which accounts for the large majority of crimes. To undertake such studies, it is necessary to have a well-documented sample of records of offenders, which includes their experience with the juvenile justice system, their encounters with the adult criminal justice system, their employment history, and their experiences with various treatment and social service programs. These data need to be more detailed than is appropriate for operational use or than could be maintained on all offenders, but it is important that such detailed records be maintained

on a carefully drawn sample and that those records be updated regularly.

Because of the utmost sensitivity of such individual records, extraordinary care should be taken in developing guidelines and regulations governing the use of these data to ensure that the individuals whose records are maintained are anonymous to all users of those records. Consideration should be given to the development of legislation authorizing the use of these data for research and management purposes along with the provision of appropriate civil and criminal sanctions for their misuse.

Central Data Center

In view of the importance of the data needs identified here, it is crucial that a major effort be organized to coordinate the various common data needs and to maintain a centralized data repository to serve those needs. The Department of Justice has already indicated publicly a strong interest in such a data center. The Committee urges not only that a data center be established but also that it be made an integral part of NILECJ (see Recommendation 18). Such a data center should undertake a variety of specific functions:

1. Determine common data needs.
2. Establish data series to be collected across jurisdictions.
3. Develop reporting categories and classifications to be used consistently in those data series.
4. Develop and stimulate the use of advanced sampling, collection, and reporting methods.
5. Provide technical assistance and financial support to collection and reporting agencies, which will typically report through state statistical analysis centers.
6. Audit data reports and identify improved procedures for data collection.
7. Report on the validity and reliability of recorded and published data, and develop improved means for enhancing both.
8. Collect and maintain a data archive that retains various general criminal justice data (other than the standard series data) collected by individual investigators after the original investigator has completed use of the data. A data center should particularly maintain detailed data sets involved in any published work relating to crime or the criminal justice system so that those data sets would be available to other investigators attempting to verify or build on published work. All

federal grants involving significant data collection should require their data to be deposited in such an archive.

9. Maintain the data repository, and provide access to it for qualified users through distribution of public-use tapes and on-line retrieval at a user's terminal.

10. Undertake internal research on the data in the data base, partly for substantive results, partly as a stimulus to improved data collection, and partly to improve analytical methodology.

11. Maintain the security of the data, particularly the individual data, to protect the privacy of the individuals whose records are maintained.

The task of designing and testing such a center is itself a major research undertaking and one that properly falls within the scope of the mandate of NILECJ. As noted above, the Committee endorses the development of a criminal justice statistics center.

Deterrent and Incapacitative Effects

The questions surrounding the deterrent and incapacitative effect of the sanctions in the criminal justice system represent an important combination of basic needs in research and practical application. The subject is rich in theoretical concern that has occupied the attention of social scientists over time and in different societies. The practical importance of learning the effects of various punishments on specific behaviors is obvious. Furthermore, in terms of the recommendations of this Committee, deterrence and incapacitation research represents a particularly important example of the potential direction of research aimed at reducing crime. Recent policy-related research in deterrence has in turn stimulated disciplinary interest in the subject, particularly in the fields of sociology and economics.

Behavioral scientists, especially sociologists, have identified several different types of deterrents and deterrent effects. Separating them presents problems of research design, but also offers opportunities for creativity and for innovative reconceptualization. The relative costs and benefits of increasing punishment or increasing certainty of punishment remain to be explored. In addition to the possibilities of testing for specific deterrent and associated relationships, there is the possibility of refining and developing the geographic and other units of analysis in which results are assembled or tested. This subject of research generally suffers from obvious difficulties with the currently collected data, particularly the geographic units under which criminal statistics are subsumed, but also involving other data characteristics

that mask individual behavior and make it difficult to use the data to determine rates of crime or risks of punishment. There is considerable dispute on theoretical issues involved in the manipulation of data and on the likelihood of unraveling relationships specific enough to be useful for policy makers.

The Committee recommends the development of this subject as a major focus for Institute research:

1. The Institute should continue to work toward the development of better, more valid, accurate, and reliable statistics, with improved geographical aggregations. (Similar recommendations are to be found in the final report of the Panel on Research on Deterrent and Incapacitative Effects [National Research Council 1978], set up under the aegis of this Committee.) This work should be supervised by an ongoing committee of statistical and substantive experts.
2. The Institute should commission a variety of studies that focus more sharply on the deterrence question, by specific types of offenders and by specific groups of offenders, rather than dealing in grossly aggregated statistics.
3. The Institute should develop the capacity for immediate research, including the possibility of developing its own team of experts to take advantage of field situations and experimental and quasi-experimental events that permit the direct testing of hypotheses about deterrence, in addition to the more standard statistical manipulations and analyses.

Our recommendation that this focus be made a central subject for Institute funding comes from quite diverse philosophies and concerns among members of the Committee. As the work of the Panel on Research on Deterrent and Incapacitative Effects as well as the research contributions of several members of the Committee itself indicate, there are many complex theoretical and statistical issues involved in the study of deterrence and one's position on many of these issues determines the degree of optimism one holds as to the outcome of research on issues of deterrence. For example, there is the possibility that crime rates mutually influence each other, and the nature of these possible interrelationships should be studied.

The Committee recognizes that many perceptual questions arise in deterrence research and notes especially the paucity to date of findings on public perceptions of legal punishments. Ideally, a wide range of research efforts should be undertaken in order to develop a balanced understanding of the broad effects of social and legal sanctions, even though such research is both controversial and expensive and the payoff for policy is often uncertain. The Committee concludes that a program focused on the questions outlined above is most likely to produce valid knowledge useful to policy makers.

When and if the Institute finds diminishing returns in research on this subject, it should, of course, redefine its purposes as we have suggested it should be continuously doing. In the interim, the inherent advantages of this focus for attracting top-flight researchers, for providing exciting, intellectual problems, and for helping to refine the statistical data and tools that are necessary in the field of criminal analysis seem to make it a prime candidate for major emphasis.

Rehabilitation

The notion that an individual's propensity to repeat criminal behavior can be controlled by "treatment" has dominated correctional policy in American criminal justice for many years. This is a question of what is called specific deterrence, although it is usually discussed under the more narrow rubric of rehabilitation. The continuing high rates of recidivism make the effectiveness of our correctional policies a matter of central concerns. Unfortunately, the methodological difficulties in this area have prevented both practitioners and researchers from gaining adequate knowledge to judge either how effective these policies are or, to the extent that they are ineffective, why they have not "worked."

A research program on rehabilitation should proceed on several levels. Initially, the validity of existing evaluations of correctional programs must be addressed. Recent reviews of these evaluations have led to strongly negative conclusions about the effectiveness of a wide range of rehabilitative techniques in current use. Yet these same reviews also point to serious methodological weaknesses in the evaluations themselves, causing doubts about any inferences—negative or positive—that might be drawn from them. And, since the existing evaluations are suspect, it is critically important to carry out evaluations that do not suffer from methodological error. The lack of common measures of recidivism and contamination by experimenter bias and other variations in the treatment process are well-known problems; their continuing existence underscores the need for the Institute to develop a carefully designed, nationally controlled evaluation program for the purpose of reaching generalizable conclusions.

A second level of approach is to develop new designs and methodologies for evaluating treatment programs. We need much better data on recidivism, not only to ensure commonality in measures but also to provide a profile of the correlates of various kinds of criminal careers. The correctional setting—whether a large or small institution, some community-based facility, or the relative freedom of probation or parole supervision—is always coercive to some degree. But the degrees of coerciveness must be specified and measured in some common way if we are ever to understand the real motivational factors at work in "rehabilitation." Further, the range of settings in which correctional programs occur indicates that many different and easily biased variables must be taken into account when designing evaluations. Especially important, and often lacking in existing evaluations, are variations in the type of offender being dealt with, in the type and number of crimes committed, and in the individual offender's attitudes and capacities to learn. A concerted effort should be made to refine existing measures of behavioral variation. However, since the social scientist's most powerful tool—controlled experimentation—is necessarily limited in real settings of this nature, the Institute should also make a major effort to encourage the development of experimental research in laboratory settings.

A third level of approach should be to devise and test alternative techniques for preventing recidivism. Diversion programs of various kinds have been proliferating in recent years, and some are included among existing evaluations. But the nature of diversion strategies ranges so widely that a systematic classification of types of interventions, and a subsequent evaluation of representative types, is needed. Other techniques that should be investigated include the use of fines rather than imprisonment and requiring restitution in property crimes. The current movement to change from indeterminate sentencing to flat time or mandatory minimum sentences provides a good opportunity to test the differential effects of various sentencing strategies on the subsequent attitudes and behaviors of convicted offenders. The move to use guidelines to produce greater uniformity in sentences should also be investigated, since one of its purposes is to reduce resentment over sentencing disparities.

Policies concerned with specific deterrence—whether intended to "rehabilitate" or to punish—have been the subject of much rhetoric and ideological debate. The Institute could make a much needed contribution to clarity by challenging all assumptions and by structuring a program whose mission is research rather than action and for which reliable knowledge is the only goal. The program should be conducted not by correctional specialists—who inevitably have a stake in the results—but by multidisciplinary teams of scientists, including criminologists and experimental psychologists.

Analyzing the Consequences of Change in the Criminal Justice System

Since the advent of LEAA, much rhetoric and at least some programs have been aimed at "reforming" the criminal justice system. Theories of reform generally have in common the claim that a proposed change will have a particular, "good" impact on the system and a lack of empirical evidence for the validity of that claim. It is important, therefore, that a program be developed to provide an empirical base for predicting the consequences of any particular kind of change in the system. The consequences may have to do with the behaviors of practitioners, with the efficiency of the criminal justice system, or with the system's impact on crime and criminal behaviors.

Such a research program should develop at two levels. The first level should involve testing of proposed changes in the system. Practitioners at every stage in criminal justice processing are faced with an increasing array of alternative practices or techniques, from theories of management, from psychotherapy, from institutional behavior modification programming, from information processors, and so on. In most cases, the proposed alternatives have not been adequately tested in the various kinds of environments for which they are now intended: for example, a police administrator cannot know the possible consequences for department morale of changes in his command structure unless these changes have been tested carefully in a quasi-military setting. Furthermore, many proposed changes are argued in terms of the logic of reform: change is assumed to be good and increased efficiency is assumed to be compatible with the basic values of the system; these assumptions also need to be tested. It is critically important to provide the police, and other parts of the criminal justice system, with effective means of improving their part of the system.

A second level of research should focus on the systemic consequences of change. Much of the rhetoric of reform in criminal justice has invoked the concept of "system," either claiming systemic relationships or deploring the lack of them. For example, it is argued that changes should not be introduced in any part of the criminal justice system without careful consideration of their impact on other parts, or it is argued that changes are irrelevant to reform goals unless the changes are explicitly designed to have systemic impact. In both cases the arguments are essentially academic in the absence of reliable knowledge about relationships among the parts of the criminal justice system. As changes are introduced in one part of the criminal justice system, it is important to be able to consider their impact on other parts. The development of knowledge on the impact of such changes is essential in order to carry out the mandates of the Safe Streets Act to LEAA and to the SPAS for planning for the criminal justice system. The current capability for planning on that system-wide basis is extremely limited and involves the use of models that do not deal with the adaptation in the behavior of one part of the system to changes in another. Such a representation is less than adequate, since there is good evidence that the various parts of the system do adapt to changes in their input. Little is known, however, about the nature of that adaptation.

The first level of research requires the capacity to mount rigorously designed demonstrations in which proposed changes are made in real settings but under carefully controlled circumstances. This is not the place to argue the pros and cons of quasi-experimental design in evaluation research, but suffice it that such demonstrations would necessarily be hypothesis-testing procedures. Demonstrations of this sort should be distinguished from so-called impact evaluations; their guiding purpose must be reliable knowledge and not "intelligence" for decision makers. (It is an ironic truth about the practice of evaluation that information that is perfectly useful "intelligence" for the immediate decision-making process may not be reliable knowledge. We reiterate that the role of a national research institute should be to produce reliable knowledge.) The second level of research requires a very different kind of methodology: namely, system input-output modeling at a highly sophisticated level. Models of this sort, perhaps including econometric analyses, are needed to characterize the interactions among the different parts of the criminal justice system.

The combination of these two kinds of research on a subject provides an opportunity for integrating a variety of methodological and substantive approaches. Most important, it requires researchers from different disciplines and practitioners to deal with the kinds of information important to each group. Without this sort of exchange, neither level of research can proceed successfully. A further benefit of such a research program would be to provide the data necessary to test common assumptions about the relationship (if any) between system reform and changes in the system's capacity to deal effectively with crime problems. In any case, the focus of this research program should be on the consequences of "reform"—change—rather than on "improving" the system as an end in itself.

Socialization to Crime

Variations in the compliance behavior of different groups in our society should be of major concern to policy makers. This is a question that touches on the efficacy of particular laws, on law enforcement practices, on the level and diversity of criminal activity in the population, and ultimately on the political and social stability of the nation. Practical measures to cope with shifting crime patterns are not on the immediate horizon, in part because these patterns themselves are little understood. In order to develop a proper balance between deterring criminal activity and tolerating deviant behavior, we need to know more about the different socializing factors at work throughout our society.

This requires detailed research of two distinct kinds: first, research on types of crimes, including methods, the importance of opportunities to commit such crimes, the application of law enforcement techniques, and patterns of crime commission across crime types; and second, research on socialization processes as they vary across the different experiences of members of this society and of other societies as well. Special attention should be accorded to relatively unresearched but widespread criminal behaviors, such as white-collar crimes and official corruption. Variations across racial and ethnic subcultures, between age groups, and between individual and group behaviors should be explored.

The mix of levels of research is particularly important on this subject. Basic research on the processes of internalizing norms, exploring relationships between child-rearing practices and responses to authority, studying how rules/laws and constraints/punishments function in different cultures, surveying public attitudes toward crime and criminal behaviors, understanding variations in gang behavior over time—all can and should be focused on the question of socialization to crime. An even wider conceptual net can be achieved by including cross-cultural research on similar questions. While there is no obvious, immediate payoff for this research, a well-developed research program can, over time, provide legislators, judges, and law enforcement practitioners with a broad working understanding of propensities for crime and the potential for controlling crime in our society.

Focusing the Criminal Law

A major way in which the nation might control crime and strengthen criminal justice is through the use of criminal law as an instrument. It is a striking fact that little, if any, of the Institute's work has been devoted to changes in the criminal law. This may be due to frustration over the word-magical thinking of many law professors, legislators, and judges that the passage of a law outlawing particular acts was tantamount to the elimination of those acts. Substantial experience to the contrary has led to the abandonment of exclusive reliance on researchers in criminal law and to the involvement of researchers in other disciplines in the search for instrumental knowledge about crime control. In the course of the search, criminal law has come to be viewed as a constant. We believe, on the contrary, that it is useful to view it as a modifiable instrument, capable, if handled by properly informed lawmakers, of accomplishing much toward crime control.

The Committee recommends that systematic, interdisciplinary research concerning the impact of the criminal law—undertaken with an eye to reshaping that body of law—be carried out as part of the effort at crime control. There is a developing consensus in America that our criminal law suffers from being too diffuse in the range of acts it seeks to regulate. It provides little guidance to police and prosecutors as to which areas of behavior ought to be the focus of criminal law enforcement. Without such guidance, enforcement becomes subject to a wide range of discretion by police and prosecutors. In consequence, the administration of the criminal law is erratic, in the sense that the same acts carry diverse probabilities of apprehension and punishment, depending on the whims of particular police, the current interest of particular prosecutors, and the fluctuating state of public opinion.

It is possible that criminal law could be far more effective if it were confined more narrowly to those acts that are widely believed to represent serious violations of the minimum requirements for public order. Current research suggests that there exists a widespread consensus in all segments of the population concerning the most serious crimes—particularly crimes involving violence. Further research should be undertaken to test the extent and depth of such a consensus. Focusing the criminal sanction on such consensus serious offenses could reduce the erratic nature of criminal law enforcement and should increase the likelihood that the police and prosecutors will be supported by the public, through informed controls and information, in their efforts at crime control. The Institute could be particularly helpful in developing rigorous evaluations of various enforcement strategies. Since changes in enforcement are often politically sensitive, especially for the police department involved, the Institute should make a major effort to create cooperative relationships with police departments willing to participate in experimental ventures. Thus, research can contribute to the shaping of a uniform, enforceable, popular criminal law.

Such a program should also provide guidance on two further important issues: one, the utilization of proper and effective sanctions that will be popularly perceived as legitimate and that will prove to be functionally effective; and two, the handling through alternative means of social control (such as administrative processes and civil law) of other acts that do not fall within the sphere of the minimum, focused criminal law. Each of these issues overlaps with the central concern of two other recommended research priorities—deterrence and the consequences of introducing change in the criminal justice system—and some coordination among these concerns should result in productive exchange.

SUMMARY

This report has identified a number of problems that beset the operations and environment of the Institute. The recommendations set forth above are a product of the Committee's analysis of these problems; as such, they represent not only our judgment of what remedies are necessary but also our conception of what an effective National Institute of Law Enforcement and Criminal Justice should look like. In summary, therefore, we want to state what we believe the cumulative effects of our recommendations would be.

The mission of the Institute would be to develop reliable, generalizable knowledge about crime, criminal behaviors, and the effectiveness of crime control methods and policies. The sole reason for the Institute's existence is this service mission, which the Committee fully endorses. But since research itself can never be an instrument for solving social problems, the Institute would avoid all pretense of providing immediate solutions and instead mount a program of medium- to long-range research projects directed at producing knowledge about crime problems. As a national research institute, it would not attempt to serve a planning or "intelligence" function for SPAS, but instead would develop the resources necessary to undertake research that is not feasible or appropriate at the state or local level.

The kinds of resources required to accomplish this mission—ideas from a wide range of sources, research skills from a variety of disciplines, and data—have either been lacking altogether or in very short supply throughout the history of the Institute. Just as crime is not solely a sociological or a psychological or a political or an economic problem, neither is it solely a police, courts, or corrections problem. Flexible programs of research, directed at problems such as deterrence and rehabilitation, would mobilize the research community in the most productive way. Another crucial ingredient would be standardized data on a variety of crime-related variables; good data are a powerful incentive to productive research. The capacity to generate its own data on the basis of research needs would put the Institute in an efficacious position to attract the best scientific minds to crime research.

After mission and program, there are three other key features that follow from the Committee's recommendations: broadened access to program development, mechanisms for quality control, and measures to insulate the Institute from destructive pressures. Broadened access would open program development to a variety of perspectives on crime problems, including those of the wider social science research community, those of individuals and groups whose experiences with crime differ not only among themselves but also from the standard law enforcement view, and those of ordinary "consumers" of criminal justice activities. The Institute would actively seek the views of such diverse groups through sponsoring or participating in a variety of conferences, consultations with professional organizations, and other means that facilitate the exchange of ideas among researchers, practitioners, and users. Further, the several levels of the Institute's formal advisory system would include an appropriate mix of perspectives in order to prevent the kind of narrow approach to criminal justice research that is now characteristic of the Institute.

The Institute's advisory system would also be used (as it has not in the past) to provide quality control over the research process. The Committee's evaluation of a sample of grants and contracts awards concluded that the major source of weakness in the Institute's research program was poor project design. While the remedy for such a weakness is necessarily complex, a critical factor is the process of project review. Following the Committee's recommendations, the Institute would have all proposals (including any concept papers that are being considered seriously) reviewed by outside experts, not only for their practical value but also for their methodological soundness; this could not be done by a mail review of individual projects. The Institute would use program area panels, meeting regularly, to ensure continuity in the use of criteria and in the cumulation of knowledge, panels with a mix of researchers and practitioner/users to provide proper guidance for the long-range development of each program area. It would use sub-panels for methodological review. Broadened access and rigorous quality control can only enhance the stature and visibility of the Institute, both of which it so clearly needs.

Finally, the Institute would be insulated from destructive pressures. This report has detailed the kinds of pressures that have beset NILECJ throughout its history, ranging from unrealistic Congressional expectations in the early years to the continuing demands that the Institute perform a direct service function within the LEAA programming and delivery structure. However well intentioned these pressures might have been, they created impossible conditions for the development of a productive research program. Especially harmful was the use of crime rates to measure the effectiveness of research—a test that no research program could or should meet. The Committee has concluded that the capacity to protect the integrity of research from the pressures of action programs was never developed, largely because the director never had the authority to control the Institute program. To remedy the situation, the Institute would be reconstituted as an independent research agency within the Department of Justice and accorded final approval authority over all awards as well as control over its administrative budget, personnel, and detailed program review. Furthermore, a Criminal Justice Research Advisory Board would be established, by statute, as a final protection against any politicization of the research program.

In sum, the Committee's recommendations address five critical factors in the development of a successful research program: its mission, resources, access, quality control, and protection from the short-term pressures of a politicized environment. Because we believe that implementing these recommendations will substantially aid the Institute in its future work, we strongly urge their adoption.

We are aware, however, that these measures are necessary but not sufficient conditions for success. Rigorous review procedures, broadened access, protection from politicization are clearly important—but it would be naive to assume that they alone can guarantee effective performance in such a difficult field. The Committee of fifteen members embodies varying degrees of optimism. It is unanimous, however, in urging that a serious effort be made to implement its recommendations in order to provide the best possible conditions for socially useful criminal justice research.

References

Caplan, G. M. (1975) Statement before the Subcommittee on Domestic and International Scientific Planning and Analysis, House Committee on Science and Technology, July 18.

Caplan, G. M. (1975a) "Losing" the War on Crime. Address given at Town Hall of California, Los Angeles, December 9.

Federal Bureau of Investigation (1976) *Crime in the United States: Uniform Crime Reports, 1975*. Washington, D.C.: Federal Bureau of Investigation.

MITRE Corporation (1976) *High Impact Anti-Crime Programs: National Level Evaluation Final Report*. Eleanor Chelimsky, author. Vol. 1: Executive Summary. Vol. 2: Report. No. MTR-7148. Washington, D.C.: Law Enforcement Assistance Administration.

National Research Council (1978) *Deterrence and Incapacitation: Estimating the Effects of Criminal Sanctions on Crime Rates*. Panel on Research on Deterrent and Incapacitative Effects. Assembly of Behavioral and Social Sciences. Washington, D.C.: National Academy of Sciences.

Rogovin, C. (1973) The genesis of the Law Enforcement Assistance Administration: a personal account. *Columbia Human Rights Law Review* 5(1):9–25.

U.S. Department of Justice (1975) *Criminal Victimization Surveys in the Nation's Five Largest Cities*. National Criminal Justice Information and Statistics Service, Law Enforcement Assistance Administration. Washington, D.C.: U.S. Government Printing Office.

U.S. General Accounting Office (1976) *The Program to Develop Improved Law Enforcement Equipment Needs to Be Better Managed*. Washington, D.C.: U.S. Government Printing Office.

U.S. President (1967) *The Challenge of Crime in a Free Society*. President's Commission on Law Enforcement and the Administration of Justice. Washington, D.C.: U.S. Government Printing Office.

Yin, R. K., *et al.* (1976) *A Review of Case Studies of Technological Innovations in State and Local Services*. Santa Monica, Cal.: RAND Corp.

CASE STUDIES

Case Study—Advanced Technology

FREDRICA D. KRAMER

The Institute's sponsorship of advanced technology research and development (R&D) illustrates a number of issues: the political demands under which NILECJ has operated, the complexity and necessity of defining objectives on which to base program choices, and the necessity of maintaining vigilance over their execution. The advanced technology program is documented here by a case study, not to make special judgment on its management or substantive research, but because it illustrates clearly the implementation of a characteristic Institute stratagem—that of contracting out for whole program components—and the consequences of that approach in the particular context in which both the technology program is defined and NILECJ operates.

The case study is based on extensive interviews with NILECJ staff, examination of internal NILECJ program documents,* and an extensive 3-day meeting of Committee members and staff with representatives of NILECJ's major advanced technology contractors (the MITRE Corporation, Aerospace's Law Enforcement and Telecommunications Division, the Law Enforcement Standards Laboratory of the National Bureau of Standards, the body armor research project at Department of the Army) and NILECJ's Advanced Technology Division (ATD) staff.

*In addition to internal memoranda, actual contract documents (annual reports and annual operating plans, program and project plans, monthly progress reports, task plans, and specific project reports) were consulted.

PROGRAM STRUCTURE

Genesis of NILECJ's Advanced Technology Effort

There is no evidence that NILECJ at any time in its history chose to integrate so-called technological R&D for crime problem-solving with research activities that are based on the social and behavioral sciences. Therefore, technology R&D is planned and conducted separately from research programming for police, courts, corrections, prevention, etc.

Current ATD staff points to the President's Commission on Law Enforcement and the Administration of Justice (the Crime Commission) recommendations as a rationale for technology research as it is conceived at NILECJ. The Crime Commission* recommended that the federal government sponsor a science and technology R&D program, a federal coordinated equipment standards program (perhaps using the National Bureau of Standards), encourage operations research staff in large criminal justice agencies, and create a major scientific and technological research staff within a research institute (pp. 269–71). It also set the stage for extramural research: "The program would inevitably require technical guidance of a breadth and quality exceeding that which could be expected of any internal technical staff" (p. 270). Though the Crime Commission's report does talk about such things as police command and control systems and better statistics on recidivism in this context, it does not address the important issue of integration of technological and nontechnological research. Indeed, it deals with the need for science and technology in criminal justice only by suggesting that a discrete program for such research be established.

The legislation that mandated the National Institute was no more specific in prescribing a strategy or suggesting a need to integrate technological research with social and behavioral research. Indeed, since the Institute was an afterthought in the overall LEAA legislation, there was nothing persuasive in its legislative history—floor debate, committee work, hearings—to assist in considering such integration.

The technology program in NILECJ began and has remained structurally separate from the other research programs. Under the directorship of Henry Ruth, it was located in the Center for Criminal Justice Operations and Management (a nomenclature reminiscent of the Crime Commission recommendations). Under Martin Danziger, it was ad-

*President's Commission on Law Enforcement and the Administration of Justice (1967) *The Challenge of Crime in a Free Society*. Washington, D.C.: U.S. Government Printing Office.

ministered primarily through the Equipment Systems Improvement Program (ESIP), and currently, it is administered by the Advanced Technology Division (ATD) within the Office of Research Programs. An overriding issue relates to the isolation of technology R&D: Is it useful, or even feasible, to consider technology research and development as a separate and discrete activity? How can one assure that adequate attention is paid to nontechnological solutions to problems either through organizational structure or through mechanisms of program planning and development?

Strategy

Whatever the structure, technology research and development was originally administered, as with other NILECJ research, under many separate grants. Director Danziger offered probably the first attempt at a systematic process for analyzing technology needs and then prescribing a development and standards operation based on that analysis; each of the parts of this process were to be performed outside the Institute under contract.

The technology program under Director Danziger was called the Equipment Systems Improvement Program (ESIP). ESIP was a three-part, umbrella-contract* structure consisting of an Analysis Group, a Development Group, and a Standards Group. Under this structure, most of the planning, analysis, needs assessment, development, and some dissemination was contracted out. Of the nearly $31 million that the Institute has spent on technology research and development, almost $22 million was spent under the ESIP structure.†

The umbrella-contract structure was not singled out for advanced technology, though the umbrella-contract program in advanced technology has remained the largest, with perhaps the greatest consequence. In its original conception, the umbrella-contract structure was

*The umbrella contract is a contract in which, under broadly defined mandates, the prime contractor is largely responsible for defining the program and subcontracting pieces of that program to others under its supervision. While the prime contracts specify only, say, hardware or technology development, the pieces include development of blood analysis techniques, burglar alarms, body armor, and several other major projects with numerous subcontractors performing the work.

†The 3-day conference that the Committee's subcommittee on technology held with the major contractors therefore scrutinized the major portion of advanced technology research and development that the Institute has funded. Neither the conference nor this case study examined most of the small technology projects supported outside the umbrella contracts.

typical of other organizing modes during Martin Danziger's tenure. It was a way of correcting an earlier trend toward funding a plethora of small unrelated projects representing particular staff interests, often allegedly of poor quality and offering little payoff.* It was hoped that the three segments would provide quality products as well as a system of checks and balances for each other.

Implementation

MITRE Corporation was selected as the Analysis Group and funded for $1 million in its first year. It was to set up an elaborate field organization with selected user agencies at the local level to provide problem analysis and hardware requirements to the Institute. The Aerospace Corporation was selected as the Development Group, at $1.8 million in the same year, to begin development of specific products.

Unfortunately, analysis and development started at the same time. The rationale for simultaneous MITRE and Aerospace start-ups is unclear. Some suggest that inflated estimates of forthcoming budgets led to expectations that the Development Group would expand sufficiently to absorb the larger output of the Analysis Group, while enough critical and obvious problems existed to begin certain development projects immediately. Three consequences of the simultaneous start-up are worth noting. First, the budget did not increase as anticipated and there was soon clearly no use for the voluminous product of the Analysis Group; the effort was scrapped 14 months and about $2.6 million after start-up. Second, because the two efforts started simultaneously, the Development Group had to plan its first agenda without the benefit of the work of the Analysis Group. Third, because of the nature of many development projects—their large size and cost and long time to completion—those projects initiated through this separate planning mechanism continued despite any recommendations from the Analysis Group, and, in many cases, despite desires on the part of the Institute to make major changes in the development program. In short, commitments to early decisions and early dollars were locked in.

The first year, the Development Group undertook eight projects, five of which continued through fiscal 1975; in fiscal 1974, four new projects were begun, three of which continued through fiscal 1975.

*The use of contracts rather than grants was also intended as a measure to increase accountability for the Institute. While there are separate administrative problems associated with contract management (discussed below), the contract mechanism per se is not here in question.

Major projects have included development of a burglar alarm system, a citizen alarm system, blood and blood stain analysis, explosive detection, gunshot residue, latent fingerprint analysis,* lightweight body armor, and an improved patrol vehicle. The Development Group also provided technical and program planning support. By the end of fiscal 1975, the Group had spent between $14 and $16 million.

The third ESIP component was the Standards Group. Although conceptually part of ESIP, it was in fact created in 1971 prior to the ESIP scheme; the notion of a standards laboratory for law enforcement related back to the Crime Commission. It was contracted to the National Bureau of Standards (NBS) which set up a Law Enforcement Systems Laboratory (LESL). LESL is a technical management unit within the National Bureau of Standards that funnels law enforcement work to operating laboratories within the NBS. It has undertaken over 160 separate projects on communications equipment, security systems, protective equipment, investigative aids and other systems (like lights and sirens, buildings, vehicles), etc. Through the first 10 months of fiscal 1976, LESL completed 34 standards, 6 guidelines, 50 reports, and 7 materials. Through fiscal 1975 it had been allocated $8.03 million.

Though the three components seemed inclusive, what was not wholly contracted out and was not adequately planned for was dissemination. No clear explanation for this is apparent. Staff involved in the initial planning claim to have been concerned with dissemination but do not appear to have adequately responded to their own concern. Specifically, the responsibility was not assumed by NILECJ's Office of Technology Transfer, which does assume primary responsibility for dissemination of other NILECJ divisions. The ATD and the contractors have experienced considerable difficulty in linking up products with the user community.

While there does appear to have been some linkup at decision-making points to top management in NILECJ, there was no mandated linkup between technology and nontechnology divisions during program planning or implementation. If there were to be any real checks and balances on a substantive level they would have to be either among the very loosely related contractors or between the contractors and an Institute program staff that was at once primarily technologically oriented and quite peripheral to the operations of the program planning process.

*The Aerospace Corporation did not choose to report to the Committee on blood analysis, explosive detection, gunshot residue, or latent fingerprint analysis.

Inherent Premises

NILECJ has operated for the dominant part of its life on the premise that an agency can buy a coordinated piece of technological research and development by contracting for analysis, development, and standard-setting functions under separate, large umbrella contracts. It was assumed that it was appropriate and feasible for the Institute (the ATD staff in particular) to relinquish the opportunity to carefully consider certain broad issues of technology research and development. It was assumed further that this was a productive strategy even in light of the relatively isolated position of technological research within the Institute's organizational and administrative structure.

One question is whether nontechnological rather than technological solutions to crime will be given adequate consideration in each instance of project selection and design. Conversely, could nontechnological alternatives, if appropriate, be implemented given the isolated position of ATD? Since the program was administered solely under the Advanced Technology Division aegis, when the Analysis Group's work did prescribe nontechnological product recommendations they could not be assimilated in Institute work.

Another question is whether contractors could adequately consider or should appropriately consider issues that would normally be decided by the funding agency, such as: Who would use the research or developed product (direct clientele and indirect clientele)? What justified technological research and development in the public sector (when was research a public good, why had the private market chosen not to undertake development of certain products, who should be in the business of risk taking)? How could the research findings or products be disseminated (motivating local law enforcement agencies to use new techniques and devices, achieving cumulativeness, and creating an infrastructure to exchange ideas, generate new ones, and build on ongoing research)? The extension of this is that contractors responsible for discrete components of the total research and development package would be called upon, implicitly, to judge the usefulness—in terms of social utility, the justification for public expenditure, and appropriate consumers of products—of products they had contracted to develop. The Committee has argued in other contexts that NILECJ does not have a clear sense of mission independent of the pressures it experiences from both LEAA and a larger political arena. Therefore, in the absence of guidance from NILECJ, contractors would assess such questions in terms of their own understanding of the overall mission of NILECJ. Finally, dissemination ultimately would have to largely take care of itself since it was not formally part of the ESIP package and consequently no one took real responsibility for it.

Most important, the success of each component depended on the coordination of the whole. That coordination was solely an in-house staff function that, ironically, was dependent on the competency of a staff no longer intimately involved with planning or executing the work. And administration of the umbrella contract would likely demand more than the usual administrative and technical competence.

PROGRAM OPERATION

How well or badly the strategy actually worked can be assessed by examples in each phase of the program. It is telling that obstacles to successful program implementation were common to more than one contractor.

Generating Ideas: Where did the Technology Agenda Come From?

The Analysis Group

When it began in fiscal 1973, the Analysis Group was intended to generate ideas for the whole program. MITRE, the contractor for analysis, set up field organizations in local criminal justice agencies in seven locations to conduct operations research that would generate problems for technology research and development. MITRE developed a complicated flow process with several different levels of analysis and review ending in a so-called operational requirement or prescription for technology research. The field analysis and ATD review were together intended to translate the field work into recommendations for development.

The system met with problems in the field; as a result, lines of authority sometimes became blurred between local agency officials and MITRE headquarters and readjusting these relationships added time to start-up. The system also met with uncertain reaction by NILECJ since MITRE attempted to apply an open-ended operations research approach that often produced reports that NILECJ found difficult to apply to the task at hand. By the time MITRE's Analysis effort was terminated it had identified 138 problems and produced 4 "problem statements" and 1 "operational requirement," all of seemingly little use for prescribing hardware development ideas. And because the relationship between the analysis and development tasks was not well synchronized, an elaborate planning effort was undertaken by the development group to determine its program.

MITRE did, however, contribute to the planning process that Aerospace undertook to select candidates for development projects for fiscal 1974. MITRE was asked to create a weighting system for five major crime types using mechanisms like the Sellin and Wofgang index of seriousness and the Uniform Crime Reports data on offenses and clearance rates. MITRE also produced detailed problem analyses, and the resulting possible projects were scored according to measures of the usefulness of the approach and the significance of the crime it addressed—improving the quality of criminal justice and decreasing the incidence of the crime. Though it was a quick, single-shot effort by MITRE, it provided some data for the Aerospace planning effort.

The Development Group

Aerospace, in turn, attempted to rank order 78 different development projects using MITRE-identified problem areas, NILECJ staff input, and ideas of its own staff to generate a set of final choices for its development work. Aerospace used five evaluation criteria: the MITRE problem area priority, technical factors, application and economic factors, anticipated research and development costs, and civil factors. Civil factors were an assessment of the social, political, and legislative factors that could influence the acceptability of a proposed solution, like invasion of privacy or abridgement of civil liberties.

Interestingly, the civil factors were only scored on an up or down basis; that is, the project got a "1" if there were no civil problems and a "0" if there was. The index did not prove to be particularly discriminating. There is also some ambiguity about whose consideration of civil factors was at issue. For instance, cattle prods easily received zeros. But a citizen alarm—would citizens like it, use it, see it as an intrusive gadget in their midst even though it was intended to help them—was rated acceptable. Aerospace staff admit to their lack of expertise in making such judgments, yet because of their charge, they had to make them and without much guidance from the Institute. Some of the candidate projects that were ranked quite low on these measures were actually undertaken for other reasons: some represented prior Institute or LEAA commitment; some were already underway. But the exercise is interesting in that it represents an unusual attempt to systematically discriminate useful projects for development.

The Standards Group

To provide an initial framework for program planning, in 1972 the NBS Standards Group (the Law Enforcement Systems Laboratory, or LESL) administered an extensive Equipment Needs Survey to about 1200 police departments in the country. This provided a loose guideline for its initial choice of projects. LESL staff have expressed a deep concern for adequately reflecting user needs and used a variety of other techniques, including talking to users and surveying the literature, to set priorities. LESL also has had a particularly close relationship with ATD staff. The LESL program choices in that sense represent a joint ATD/LESL effort. But, as with other contractors, the interface with the Institute is with one individual—the program manager—on the ATD staff. In any case, the nominating procedure is essentially LESL initiated; the ATD has been primarily reactive.

In all cases, then, ideas have been generated more often than not by the contractors themselves and not by NILECJ planning.

Other Sources

In fiscal 1975, a needs assessment and formal process of generating ideas was initiated again in limited fashion through a grant to the International Association of Chiefs of Police (IACP) that is still ongoing. The IACP received a $384,000 grant to set up an Equipment and Technology Center both to assess police equipment-related needs and to disseminate equipment-related information to the police community. Included in the dissemination plans are readable standards, warnings, manufacturers' listings, and the results of new research. The IACP does not, however, see as its job the entire function of equipment-needs analysis. The IACP work is not directly related to the current development contract effort, nor will it formally relate to future development efforts. It addresses itself only to the police community. It was not directed by the Institute to look at past analysis efforts and it does not appear to be looking for a different way to set long-term priorities for new work. It is not clear whether this limited function is a result of the Institute's having re-thought its own role in analysis or simply inadequate structure of the new IACP grant.

Future Agendas

In fact, Institute staff is not currently concerned with development of new ideas for technology research. Indeed, they seem singularly uninterested in the process of generating ideas for development. ATD staff have some "back-pocket" ideas that with adequate funds they might still like to pursue, but when the current development projects run their course there is no strategy now under consideration for systematic program planning. And there is no apparent interest in achieving or resurveying former technology planning efforts.

The Institute is also not apparently concerned with spreading its technology research agenda much beyond police needs. Surely there are examples of projects that relate to other user groups and surely there are problem analyses for other contexts. But there is no systematic advisory mechanism that could bring system-wide concerns to the process of generating ideas or to setting priorities.

Setting Priorities

For whom are these projects designed? What justification is there for undertaking them? Will the products be used?

Identifying Users and Tailoring Products for Utilization

The first question in setting priorities is who should use the product? That question not only assists in clarifying appropriate products, but it assists also in assuring that appropriate links are made between production and use. The ATD defines its audience as primarily the law enforcement community. It appears that any finer distinctions have been left to the decisions of the contractors. But since the contractors' primary audience has been assumed to be the Institute, questions of ultimate usefulness and mechanisms for technology transfer have been second order.

For example, although LESL, the Standards Group at NBS, used the police to suggest useful projects, it defined its primary client as the Institute, and therefore was willing to let the Institute maintain responsibility for disseminating products back to the police. The consequence has been that standards have most often been published in a highly technical format and have been difficult for local agencies to use. The quality of the standards is not in question. Indeed, NBS's work shows a high degree of professionalism as does its concern for utilization. For instance, LESL includes in its guidelines assessments of under what conditions a standard or guideline is appropriate to be applied so as to reflect different user needs. They also express interest in compliance testing of products now on the market. But NBS produces standards for the Institute and the Institute is responsible for dissemination; it is at the juncture with the Institute that the system runs into trouble. A good example of the lack of appropriate dissemination is that state forensics laboratory standards are not traceable to NBS, although such standards are available from NBS. The rest of the system is not exploiting readily available information and the Institute, not NBS, would have to provide this link. There are other instances that underscore LESL's interest in getting their product to the ultimate user. LESL is in contact, for instance, with the National Association of State Purchasing Officials to alert them to new standards in which the Association would be interested.

But redrafting and publishing the standards have been left to an ATD staff largely ill-equipped to perform the task. The IACP grant and recent additions of a technical writer/editor to the ATD are attempts to remedy the situation. Other remedies to ensure that the products are used do not appear to be emphasized. For example, standards that LESL produces for another client agency* are made mandatory; LESL states that NILECJ has no interest in making its standards mandatory.†

Another example of the Institute's problems in reaching appropriate audiences concerns its contract with the Edgewood Arsenal. The Army has already spent about $500,000 on researching the capabilities of Kevlar 29 as body armor (and they are in the process of spending another $500,000 on further research). One objective of the research was to develop a predictive model of blunt trauma effect that would be the basis of a standard for purchasing vests. Again, however, the Army's client is the Institute. Since the Institute is responsible for dissemination, the Army has no idea whether or how their reports reach police departments or purchasing officials.

The Army's research on blunt trauma effect has gone into a second phase, testing the effect of more high-powered weaponry than is ordinarily found in urban street crime. Their rationale is that some police departments are already using and others are indicating an interest in using heavier caliber, high-velocity weapons. In addition, in 22 percent of police shootings, the officers are shot with their own weapons. Since police weapons are often high powered, the Army feels that these new data are necessary.

The justification for this further research is questionable on a number of grounds. First, development of a lightweight, bullet-proof vest was originally undertaken to offer generalized protection from unexpected

*LESL is under contract to the National Highway Traffic and Safety Administration.

†One suggestion for doing so would be to attach standards compliance to the use of LEAA Part C action funds at the state and local level.

ambush or from injury incurred during active pursuit of a criminal. Developing new armor to protect against relatively unusual threats—like the police weapon snatched by a criminal and used against the arresting officer—is not exactly compatible with the vest's original purpose. Furthermore, if protection against heavier caliber weaponry will necessitate heavier-ply fabric, then the original objective of light weight and wearability is again compromised. And, if it is simply a matter of increased ply or denser weave, the relevant question is: When has enough information been amassed for industry to extrapolate from the existing research to test a new product? Do the manufacturers of body armor have sufficient data to proceed with their work? Again, it is not the quality of the research per se that is the question: competent research on blunt trauma effect is a purchasable commodity, and the Army may have supplied it well enough. But proper guidance on the limits of the research, performance specifications, and the like is not purchasable; the Institute must provide these limits to reflect the user community's needs. A clear understanding of the limits of the research based on expectations of use of the final product does not appear to be the basis of the research.

MITRE also defined its client as the Institute, yet, as described earlier, the Institute had no adequate process by which to integrate the Analysis Group's findings and translate them into orders that could be implemented for development. Since the Institute gave no apparent guidance on the limits of the work, MITRE applied a liberal definition to its operations research task and hence produced analyses often only tangentially related to new hardware development.

In sum, the worst consequence of this blurred sense of audience is that the performers of research and development become distanced from the most critical questions of ultimate usefulness and sensibility of their work because such questions have really not been theirs to worry about.

Assessing Public Versus Private Investment

The second question in setting priorities is whether the government, and NILECJ in particular, is justified in becoming involved in development. The rationale for Institute involvement has been often as uncertain as its understanding of audience. If the Institute is to undertake particular hardware development, it should be assumed that that same research will not be undertaken by other institutions in society (private or public), that the research and development has a reasonable chance of being put to use in new product markets, and that the use to which it is put will be some social good. Several examples suggest that an exercise of discrimination on these grounds was not uniformly applied.

An analysis of the false-alarm rate in commercial burglar alarms produced a research and development effort to build a better burglar alarm. Reducing false alarms, on the face of it, is probably a social good. But the development effort did not apparently raise the overall question of why the many private companies that manufacture burglar alarms had not undertaken to develop an improved alarm. Through fiscal 1975, the Development Group's burglar alarm project had been underway for three years, it had cost over $1 million, it was not yet ready for a field test, and a private manufacturer recently produced an improved alarm system independent of the publicly sponsored effort. If the publicly supported effort is not sensitive to the speed or interest of the private sector in technological innovation, or if it cannot support risk-taking adventures that private firms will not support, its justification for research and development is not strong. The striking characteristic of much of the technological research NILECJ has funded is that it is not risk taking enough to be on the frontier of its field.

Commercial viability is a sufficiently complex problem to demand considerable attention on the part of both the Institute and the contractors. Such attention does not appear to have been given, largely, perhaps, because there is no one within the present structure who is in a position to give it. For instance, once Kevlar 29 (the nylon fiber that resists bullet impact) was developed and tested, numerous weaving and tailoring firms moved in to produce the material and the bullet-proof garments. But it remains to be seen whether bullet-proof vests will be more than a passing fad (like mace was for patrolmen a few years back) and hence whether they will remain solid market items. Ironically, since Kevlar 29 does not deteriorate rapidly, equipping police departments with bullet-proof vests made of it is likely to be primarily a one-time expense. If the Institute is concerned with assuring that the standards for vests are incorporated into production and purchasing decisions, it needs to concern itself with potential market appeal (or lack of it) of such vests. The payoff in developing marketable products is that the best vehicle for dissemination is often the producer itself.

Another example of the Institute's lack of concern with commercial viability is the improved patrol car development project. Aerospace had committed $2.6 million to the project through fiscal 1976. Automobile manufacturers are presumably both suited for and interested in producing more saleable automobiles tailored to the needs of particular clientele. Yet they have reportedly expressed distinct disinterest in the new patrol cars with fuel-saving devices and sophisticated computer equipment installations, citing the prohibitive costs of the new vehicles.

Weighing Alternative Strategies

A third question relevant to making appropriate choices for project development is whether alternative projects and strategies will be adequately considered.

The umbrella-contract structure as it now exists does not allow for an ideal mix of strategies to be assessed. An ideal process would examine nontechnological alternatives to each equipment development strategy, and it would be capable of planning cumulative approaches to broad problem areas. Contractors do not consciously do the latter; neither the structure nor the expertise available in individual contractors encouraged the former.

The isolated position of the technology program within the Institute and relative to other agencies has not afforded it real opportunity to measure its problem-solving strategies against alternatives. The hardware projects that the Institute has undertaken are not part of a repertoire of approaches to a particular criminal justice problem but rather are isolated and discrete. Problems and projects are approached as hardware questions or not hardware questions. Interest in technological research by nontechnological staff, moreover, seems to have often been affected by feelings of threat or competition.*

Numerous examples of hardware development projects speak to the limitations of a narrow technical approach. The analysis for the improved burglar alarm did not question whether nontechnical solutions alone (like stiffer sanctions for false alarms) might better correct for the squandering of police services on false alarms. It did not question whether quick response to real alarms would be sufficiently helpful in reducing burglaries to warrant development of improved hardware. Finally, Aerospace claims not to be able to know what effect new burglar alarms will have on burglaries and is content to proceed with development and hope to answer the question after development. Similarly, the question of whether citizens will be motivated to use the citizen's alarm was not considered paramount in making a decision to undertake development, nor was the question of whether police would consistently wear the improved bullet-proof vest considered prior to

*MITRE staff recalled initial, keen interest on the part of ORP corrections staff to MITRE's rape study because the study was considered potentially competitive to the other division's own work.

development. Apart from the obvious sacrifice of social or non-technological approaches, isolating technological research and development certainly adds a particular pressure to the work of the ATD staff since failure or success to problem solving will be measured by the hardware development approach alone.

Finally, the program does not appear to have been successful in ensuring a productive cumulation of knowledge both from related work in other government agencies and in the larger research community. There is no evidence of consistent coupling with other agencies doing similar work. Evidence suggests that contact between NILECJ and other government agencies or with different divisions of LEAA tends to be ad hoc and often motivated by considerations of "turf" more than indisputable appropriateness of jurisdiction. For example, although ATD has undertaken research on fingerprints, the job of advanced fingerprint retrieval has now been given to the Systems Division of LEAA's National Criminal Justice Statistical Service and ATD's work will not be pursued. For another example, although ATD staff has developed an extensive five-year plan for forensics, its future remains uncertain because forensics is a particular interest of the FBI.

Relationships with other organizations in related research can also serve as a screening mechanism to discover expenditures more appropriate to other agencies than LEAA. The police car project is a good example: it is clear that other agencies, like the Department of Transportation, or the Detroit manufacturers themselves are more adept at automobile research than LEAA. Had LEAA been talking with these organizations prior to development, it is likely that either a better project would have been prescribed or LEAA's involvement would have been considerably altered. In addition, the relationship among contractors within ATD has not been ideal. Evidence suggests that particular problems of communication have existed among the contractors, which has resulted in duplication of efforts as well as a strain on effective management of the program as a whole.*

Managing the Program

Certain issues that appear to be essentially related to management have affected program content. The umbrella-contract structure with large unit costs (estimates range from $55,000 to $90,000 per staff-year on the development contract) often creates a tendency to see projects of

*It is still unclear whether the Army's and Aerospace's body armor research is unrelated, unnecessarily duplicative, or properly additive.

questionable value through to the end to justify the large expenditure of time and effort.* The structure has often precluded simultaneously funding of varied approaches to particular problems. A review of technology-related concept papers that the Institute has rejected suggests that promising projects are rejected because they are duplicative of the large contract program. In the end, large contracts have the potential of becoming self-justifying. The Aerospace development contract includes a technical support function, which often involves review of concept papers and proposals. While the contractor surely has useful expertise on a technical level, the contract becomes the vehicle for passing judgment on the suitability of its potential competitors. It is also possible that the umbrella contracts create, in their effects, license to diffuse contractor energies into inappropriate tasks. MITRE states that during its analysis effort it reportedly received assorted ad hoc and unwritten work assignments. In short, MITRE was hired for a specific expertise, but the Institute staff saw MITRE as a general helping organization and so proceeded to approach the MITRE staff with numerous, unrelated requests for assistance that drew staff away from their assigned tasks and responsibilities.

The umbrella structure also creates a series of layers that allow decisions to be made on subcontract tasks largely out of the control of the Institute and tasks to be performed that are inappropriate to the skills of particular contractors. For example, because Aerospace is conducting the field tests of the new body armor, it is responsible for the user survey, including measurement of attitudinal and behavior changes that may accompany use of the new armor. Aerospace, by its own admission, is not expert in attitudinal research: but because Aerospace has the umbrella contract, it oversees the subcontracting to an appropriate survey research firm; and because of that structure, Aerospace rather than the Institute poses the questions to be answered. In effect, the Institute has relinquished control to an inappropriate performer.

There is also a related question about the degree to which the specific requirements of a contract are sufficient to demand and control project definition and product delivery. With many contracts, tasks are

*This study does not include a detailed analysis of the problems associated with the standard "cost plus" contract being used government wide. Documentation of these problems is becoming increasingly apparent, particularly as they relate to the reduced incentive of the contractor to hold down time and costs. Though not the subject of this study, we note that the complaints of that aspect of the contract structure have been numerous from those involved in the technology program and should be the subject of further analysis.

defined broadly enough so that the contract need not be renegotiated as work plans evolve. As a result, the contracts officer has broad control over changes and billing procedures. In fact, the success of the program depends in large measure on the relationship between the contract and program staff. For NILECJ contracts, the contract management function is within LEAA, not the Institute.

Dissemination

There have admittedly been great problems publishing the materials. For instance, MITRE reports were reviewed entirely by the Institute where, even if publication was anticipated, until very recently there was no in-house capability for technical editing. Standards, because of the necessity of complicated technical reviews, require 10 to 12 months to publication and the Standards Group has been both short-staffed and disinclined to undertake full responsibility for dissemination on nontechnical versions of its work. The unclear sense of audience has not helped motivate dissemination. Most important, any kind of active dissemination, for instance, through high-quality symposia, has been totally lacking. Hence, the kind of infrastructure that would generate fresh ideas, exchange information and ensure ongoing efforts has not developed. Equally inhibiting for high-quality research is the apparent disinterest in archiving research products—both from Institute-funded research and other related efforts—for further use. The MITRE Analysis reports remain virtually unused. There appears to be no interest in archiving information to share between contractors or with other agencies. In the end, little information and less product has reached users.

CONCLUSION

Once the Institute let the umbrella contracts, it relinquished a level of involvement and control that could have enhanced the quality of the work. It is not a question of responsibility on the part of the contractors or the Institute staff, rather the necessary process of thinking through mission, purpose, audience, validity of problem, or appropriateness of solution was mistakenly delegated to individual contractors. Without that experience, the Institute staff could not offer guidance to the performers, and the performers had difficulty divining Institute desires. The problem was heightened by the isolation of the ATD unit from other Institute work. Without a context in which the technology program could operate, not only did technology become an activity unto itself, but the contractor performing the work, rather than the Institute, determined the character and scope of the work.

As stated at the outset, the advanced technology program illustrates the political demands under which NILECJ operates. Some hardware development has apparently always been a political necessity. And certainly, visible hardware, if it works, is an attractive means to enhance political accountability. But the isolation and frustration that characterize the ATD staff suggest an ambivalence toward hardware research on the part of the Institute. At the time of this study, the Institute director had stated a flat disinterest in hardware and equipment, while the LEAA Administrator had repeatedly shown active interest in specific projects. Hardware has historically come under attack from the forces outside NILECJ and LEAA; those who believe that police forces are simply ill-equipped to deal with crime clamor for it.

The Institute has maintained between a fifth and a quarter of its budget for technology, but the nontechnology divisions neither significantly contribute to ATD's work nor help disseminate its product. It is clear that the inability to structure a technology research and development program as part of a broader strategy to solve problems in criminal justice—whether deliberate or not—created a kind of abandoned child. Although changes now under consideration result from a desire to strengthen the hand of the Institute and force more careful in-house analysis and planning, they appear to further isolate technological from other programming.*

The question that must be put to each research and development project is: Technology for what? Much of the time that question cannot be satisfactorily answered because projects have been undertaken without weighing alternative strategies. We cannot know either

*A recent study by Arthur D. Little, Inc., Washington, D.C. (prepared for the Division of Management, Office of Planning and Management, LEAA, 1976) also found significant inadequacies in the technology program, but recommended creation of a large in-house unit equal in stature to the rest of NILECJ's research program.

Two other studies, though not challenging the basic usefulness of a separate program for technology research and development, have raised critical issues—including the relationship to the private sector, the importance of marketability, and the mismatch of new hardware to current user needs. One (National Advisory Committee on Criminal Justice Standards and Goals, 1976, *Criminal Justice Research and Development: Report of the Task Force on Criminal Justice Research and Development*, U.S. Department of Justice) recommended that priority setting begin with consideration of whether a technological solution is called for and be undertaken within the context of the whole research and development program, not independently for the technology program.

whether appropriate levels have been set for technological spending, but it is clear that very little has been delivered for what has been spent so far and that there is no justification for the persistent one-quarter of the Institute's pie for technological programming. In fact, no level of spending on technology can be justified unless mechanisms are available that weigh the social implications and social benefit of every undertaking, not only through the eyes of engineers and system analysts, but also through a broad range of technical and nontechnical perspectives. In a pure sense, there is no more justification for a program division for technologists per se than there is for a division of psychologists or operations researchers, although we recognize the difficulties in homogenizing radically different disciplines for daily operations. It is crucial, however, that problems be addressed with the broadest array of perspectives and that technological solutions be a consequence of the broadest kind of analysis.

Case Study—Office of Evaluation

JUANITA L. RUBINSTEIN

Criticism of the absence of any effective evaluation of program efforts appears to be a constant in any discussion of the federal involvement in the criminal justice system. By 1973, an academic symposium on LEAA concluded that the worst flaw in its operation was the chaotic program situation resulting from a lack of useful evaluation of past projects.* Congress, in that year, included in its amendments to the Omnibus Crime Control and Safe Streets Act a mandate to NILECJ to ". . . undertake, where possible, to evaluate the various programs and projects carried out under this title. . . ." In 1974, the General Accounting Office in two reports to Congress complained of the continued inadequacy of evaluation efforts. The Institute was criticized for accomplishing little in terms of outcome evaluations for the more than 30,000 programs that had been pursued with LEAA funding. The evaluation reports that had appeared were termed inconsistent and relatively useless.

Although NILECJ records in its 1975 Annual Report that it had spent over $22 million in support of evaluation studies in its first six years of existence, evaluation was not an institutionalized function until fiscal 1974. The three major evaluations begun prior to this were ad hoc activities limited to three major programs† and were conducted, ac-

*Columbia Human Rights Law Review (1973) The Law Enforcement Assistance Administration: A Symposium on Its Operation and Impact. Conclusion. 5(1):213–19.

†The three programs evaluated were Pilot Cities, Impact Cities, and the LEAA Equipment Program.

cording to the present director of the Office of Evaluation, largely for program and management reasons.

The Caplan reorganization of the Institute in October 1973 created the Office of Evaluation (OE) with three designated divisions—Program Evaluation, Evaluation Research, and Evaluation Resources. In November of that year, LEAA Administrator Santarelli, in response to the Congressional mandate for evaluation contained in the 1973 Crime Control Act, established the LEAA Evaluation Policy Task Force. By early 1974, the LEAA Evaluation Task Force had released its report.* This report, according to Richard Linster, OE Director, was characterized by the expectation that OE would in effect be the office of evaluation for the whole of LEAA.† The Task Force had established three goals with respect to evaluation: obtain and disseminate information on the cost and effectiveness of various approaches to criminal justice problems; ensure use of performance information at each administrative level in planning and decision making; and develop a capacity for evaluation in state and local units of the criminal justice system.

The Task Force also outlined two specific programs in this report—the Model Evaluation Program (MEP) and the National Evaluation Program (NEP). This case study discusses the development of the organized evaluation effort at NILECJ from these beginnings. The NEP, an attempt to assess the effectiveness of current specific approaches in criminal justice was, for some reason, placed under the direction of the Office of Research Programs. The MEP was assigned to the Evaluation Resources Division of OE, and OE devoted many of its limited resources to MEP in the first year in which it was fully staffed and operative.‡

At its creation, OE found itself with limited resources confronting a field fraught with uncertainty and controversy. Evaluation of social action projects was a relatively new field; evaluation in criminal justice was in its infancy. OE's mandate was so broad as to be undelineated.

For its first year programming, OE appeared to follow the direction pointed out by the Task Force goals. Knowledge-building was to be addressed by the NEP program (located in the Office of Research

*U.S. Department of Justice (1974) *LEAA Evaluation Policy Task Force Report*. LEAA Evaluation Policy Task Force. Washington, D.C.: U.S. Department of Justice.

†Statement made at a meeting of the Committee's subcommittee on dissemination and evaluation, June 2, 1976.

‡According to NILECJ's Annual Reports for 1974 and 1975, evaluation as a program area received $4,414,000 (13.6% of the NILECJ budget) in fiscal 1974, and $6,572,028 (18.9%) in fiscal 1975. Of that almost $6.6 million in fiscal 1975, OE received $4,351,012 (12.5%) and NEP received $2,221,016 (6.4%).

Programs). LEAA's Office of Planning and Management was to be responsible for pursuing the goals of better management through evaluation. Therefore, OE turned its attention largely to capacity building. This move was not entirely voluntary. Capacity building at the state and local levels was in line with the Administration's "New Federalism" goals and heavy pressure evidently existed for movement in that direction.

Two million dollars and a great deal of staff time were devoted to announcing and implementing the Model Evaluation Program. The request for proposals for the MEP was designed and circulated to SPAS and Regional Planning Units (RPUS). Grants were to be awarded on the basis of the concept papers submitted. The program's goals were described as the development of model evaluation designs that could be used by the states and regions and the encouragement of evaluation in state and local agencies. Neither appears to have occurred. By the end of 1975, the Office of Evaluation had largely lost interest in the program and was moving into a new conception of its responsibilities, while MEP has continued with the 12 grants that were ultimately rewarded. In fact, due to the paucity of response (both in numbers and proposal quality), the last grant in this program was only announced in the summer of 1976.*

OE, quite obviously, was quickly disappointed in the program efforts. Its value as a reinforcement technique appears minute. Those agencies that did not have some prior knowledge of or interest in evaluation simply did not participate. Those motivated enough to submit proposals may even have found the program a negative experience. The products of MEP are also dubious. The staff monitor admits readily that "evaluation" as practiced in MEP is not classic cause-and-effect investigation but rather a form of intensive monitoring. However, he notes that a capacity to monitor is a necessary prerequisite to any attempt at impact evaluation. Further, 3 of the 12 sites selected have experienced difficulties of one sort or another and have yet to actually begin their projects. Of the remaining 9, several underwent changes of personnel or intent between the time that they submitted their proposals and were awarded grants and no longer wished to do the project outlined in their concept papers.

Perhaps OE found what it expected to find. Recognizing that it was impossible to withdraw from the program, OE appears to have considered $2 million of its funding lost. Thus, the willingness to be flexible

*OE staff reports that of a possible response from the more than 500 SPAS and RPUS, 30 concept papers were received.

in its standards for performance by SPAS and RPUS reflects a recognition of political realities and perhaps a lack of interest in local evaluation. Suggestion of future office involvement in capacity building or technological assistance is not treated in so cavalier a fashion, however. Reasons for avoiding any future involvement in that area range from the lack of staff with background in SPA operations and lack of expertise in technological aid processes to the preciousness of OE funds and the importance of other priorities. All the reasons given are valid. Nevertheless, the determination to redirect OE program activity is obvious and understandable. MEP was an ill-advised program and capacity building an inappropriate role for the Institute's Office of Evaluation. Developing the capacity of SPAS to evaluate or even monitor the projects they funded is a laudable and necessary function, but it has little to do with research and would be better situated within LEAA's Office of Regional Operations.

As MEP has receded in importance, the main thrust of OE effort has centered on program evaluation and methodology development.

In program evaluation, OE plays two basic roles. It acts as a research arm of the administrator of LEAA and the director of NILECJ in its first role, evaluating at their request any major area of LEAA programming or criminal justice initiatives of any jurisdiction considered to be of special interest.

OE follows its normal procedures in its conduct of these studies for the administrator or director. A basic design is drawn up in-house and RFPS are sent out to prospective grantees (professional associations and academic and private research institutions). At the request of the administrator, an evaluation design for the LEAA Standards and Goals Program has been drawn up this year and RFPS are now circulating. The implementation of the new Massachusetts gun law is also being studied, at the director's request. This function of OE has great potential. In fact, NILECJ should enhance its ability to take advantage of natural experiments occurring as decision makers introduce innovations in the criminal justice system.

The second role played by OE in its program evaluation function involves a partnership with the Office of Technology Transfer (OTT) in what had been the NILECJ Demonstration Programs.* The recent evolution of this role provides an interesting illustration of the conflicts endemic in the attempt to conduct applied research in an aggressive social action field and of the territorial problems arising from the

*During the June 2 meeting (see above), OTT staff indicated that the project in question would now be referred to as "field tests."

Institute's present structure. OE's original role in the joint endeavor seems largely limited to contracting for an independent evaluation of the programs at the various demonstration sites. The program itself was in large part viewed as an OTT effort to stimulate change and disseminate new techniques. The evaluations performed in the program were, of necessity, largely process measures—i.e., how difficult is the introduction and adoption of an innovation, not what effect does it have.

OE's role in the program is in the process of expanding, however, and the nature of the demonstrations themselves is thus changing. This development does not appear to be the result of normal bureaucratic expansionism, but rather a recent decision by Director Caplan that the evaluations for the program must be measures of impact or outcome.

The restructuring of the evaluation program from a process measure limited to describing the difficulty of implementing an innovation into an impact study capable of producing data on the ultimate effects an innovation had on a particular criminal justice system has had enormous ramifications. Testing a hypothesis requires structuring of conditions, selections of sites—in short, the establishment of a controlled experiment. OTT was accustomed to dealing with volunteer host agencies on a low key, non-coercive basis. Its main goals in the bureaucratic interactions that occurred were the maintenance of the good will of the local agencies and the development, within those agencies, of the feeling of "ownership" of the innovation being demonstrated. OE, on the other hand, was charged by the director with the rigorous task of structuring a controlled experiment that would result in a reasonably definitive study of a hypothesis. Furthermore, a demonstration program used as dissemination implies some value to the technique that is being disseminated. A field experiment, hypothesis testing, implies that the technique in question is just that—"in question." The potential for a great deal of tension between the two offices was present. Although the transition period,* as the two offices attempt to refashion the program, has not been completely without stress, the program has not ground to a halt. Both appear to regard the interchange as basically healthy and fruitful.

Staff at OE regard their major transitional problem as one of convincing OTT to clearly redefine the program as an experiment in their program announcement (i.e., telling local agencies "you must guarantee to adhere to the following conditions or we will not be able to test this hypothesis"). On the whole, however, OE appears to prefer to keep

*Only one program has been launched under the new conditions.

a low profile, to leave the program in OTT hands as much as possible. Currently, their involvement in the site selection is limited to the development of general guidelines; in the future, however, the staff would like to have the evaluation design completed prior to site selection and used in that process.

Basically, OE's effort in program evaluation consists of the evaluation of any criminal justice initiatives of particular interest to the administrator or director; evaluation, at the administrator's request, of LEAA activity in a specified program area; and evaluation of OTT's Demonstration/Field Testing Programs. It should be reemphasized that the studies discussed above are all performed out-of-house, with OE's responsibility in large part limited to producing the research designs and monitoring the applicable grants and contracts.

The agency's final area of commitment is in the development of methodology. Roughly one-third of the office's resources are devoted to this effort, which has been pursued primarily through the funding of unsolicited proposals. The importance of unsolicited proposals in this area (itself an unusual phenomenon at the Institute) may indicate that the agency's interest in the development of evaluation methodology has become well known in the research community. Evaluation research is currently funding work on stochastic modeling, techniques, criminal justice model building, and long-range planning techniques. There also appears to be some in-house effort at conceptualization of criminal justice modeling. This effort is decidedly small and informal, but it is one of the few examples of in-house activity not involved with the planning or grant monitoring processes. The program on methodological research is possibly the most esoteric activity in NILECJ, the most removed from the practitioner in criminal justice, and consequently the most politically vulnerable; at the same time, it is potentially of enormous importance. Along with selective program evaluation, methodological research appears to be the area that OE has carved out for its operation. Dr. Richard Linster, OE Director, concluded at a recent briefing: "The Act (Crime Control Act of 1973) could be interpreted so that millions and millions could be spent [in evaluation]. But you have to decide what you want to do with the resources you have."

The National Evaluation Program (NEP), the program designed by the LEAA Evaluation Policy Task Force to meet its knowledge goal,* is

*". . . Production and dissemination of information on the cost and effectiveness of various approaches to solving crime and criminal justice problems" (U.S. Department of Justice 1974, *op. cit.*, p. 14).

coordinated from NILECJ's Office of Research Programs. The first studies in that program were begun in fiscal 1975. Basically, NEP is NILECJ's major attempt to carry out its Congressional mandate to ". . . undertake, where possible, to evaluate the various programs and projects carried out under this title" (Crime Control Act of 1973).

In the past 8 years, 105,000 projects have been carried out with LEAA block grant funds. NEP, with a relatively small amount of money,* had to devise a way to look at a large universe and provide conclusions for decision makers, from members of Congress to local officials and police chiefs. The strategy agreed on by the Evaluation Task Force involved the purchase of phased evaluation studies of projects by topic areas. The first phase was to consist of a brief analysis of a selected program area to determine what is currently known about a criminal justice approach or topic, what further information could be provided by evaluation, and the estimated value and cost of obtaining that information. The second and less specifically defined phase would implement the evaluation design contained in the Phase I report. Dr. Richard Barnes, the NILECJ representative on the Evaluation Task Force, was named to direct the program. Topic areas covering a cluster of projects were selected by the Institute with participation of SPAS and Regional Offices (ROS). To date, 26 Phase I studies have been funded in such topic areas as pre-trial screening and specialized policy patrol. Response of the research community to the request for proposal is viewed as excellent.

NILECJ literature states that a Phase I study of any topic area must include: a state-of-the-art review; an operational description of a typical project's analysis of all available information, with conclusions about the efficiency and effectiveness of the projects in the area; an evaluation design usable by project administrators; and a design for an in-depth Phase II evaluation to fill significant knowledge gaps.

Barnes and the staff that monitor the NEP admit that the Phase I studies are not evaluations in the experimental or academic sense. However, the working goals of the program involve the identification of the universe of projects in a given topic and the establishment of a data file for each topic. The program is also seen as a chance to survey projects and their status after funding.

Despite the phrases in Institute literature about an audience for evaluation at all levels or directing the results to Congress and the people, Barnes and his staff have identified the core audience of NEP products as SPAS, RPUS, and state or local funding agencies. Though not

*As noted above, NEP in fiscal 1975 received $2,221,016 (6.4%) of the Institute budget.

a hypothesis testing experiment, Phase I studies give the prospective funder an idea of what to expect from a given project besides the glowing promises in the proposal. Consequently, dissemination of the results to decision makers is an important concern of the staff—as is the time in which the information can be processed.

To the criticism that Phase I studies are not true evaluations and that there has been no move to begin any Phase II studies (which are supposed to be more classic evaluation efforts), the staff has responded that in some criminal justice areas knowledge is at such a level that even the appropriate questions are not known and that a true evaluation in those areas could hardly be designed; Phase I activities are designed to provide that background information, and completing them should be the first priority.

A further and politically compelling response was enunciated by NILECJ staff at a meeting (June 2, 1976) with the subcommittee on dissemination and evaluation:

> Normally, when you can't find answers to a problem, your recommendation should be 'Do nothing yet.' But the public demands some action and the SPAS are sitting out there with money they must spend. We must do the best we can to give them guidance.

NILECJ's strategy in evaluation, as in most of its program, consists of putting something in people's hands right now while trying to develop a research effort. NEP is attempting to carry out the first half of the strategy while OE works on the second.

In conclusion: evaluation research is an extremely important part of the Institute's quest for reliable knowledge in the field of criminal justice; capacity building, while important, is not a function relevant to NILECJ's mission; and the National Evaluation Program is a worthwhile effort at surveying and consolidating present knowledge, an aid to an increase of cumulativeness in criminal justice research. Overall, the performance of the Office of Evaluation has been commendable but problematic—the methodological expertise of OE could be more fruitful if not structurally isolated from the Institute's planning and research functions.

Case Study—Office of Technology Transfer

JUANITA L. RUBINSTEIN

If the need to put *something* in people's hands is a motivation in the National Evaluation Program, it is the religion of the Office of Technology Transfer (OTT). Dissemination as a function has existed somewhere in its various organizational charts ever since NILECJ's inception. In fact, one of the Institute's problems has been the Congressional demand that it begin research and the dissemination of research results simultaneously.

With the Caplan reorganization of the Institute in 1973, OTT was organized as one of the Institute's three Offices (the other two being Evaluation and Research Programs). This survey of OTT will treat its activities, its view of its functions—and its blindspots—and the current attempt at reorienting its delivery. Any consideration of OTT's performance must be preceded by the realization that the office is not, and does not consider itself to be, a classic disseminator of research findings. OTT is a marketing shop. As such it produces products and services. These are the terms in which the office's staff are encouraged to think and these are the terms in which the office's director, Paul Cascarano, presents his office to the public.

OTT is composed of three divisions, which are defined by the product or service they provide. The Model Programs Development Division is characterized by Cascarano as the production component of his office. It is responsible for generating the product, the "something in people's hands." NILECJ's product line currently consists of Exemplary Projects (EPS), Prescriptive Packages (PPS), and Monographs and Validation reports. (These are discussed in greater detail below.) The Training and Testing Division (formerly Training and Demonstration) is considered OTT's sales division. As such, it is responsible for conducting training seminars on selected topics for decision and policy-makers in the field; for the Field Testing Program (formerly the Demonstration Program); for liaison with the Regional Offices and State Planning Agencies; for arranging exhibits; and for coordination of the new Host Program (described below). The Reference and Dissemination Division is regarded at OTT as the warehouse. This division coordinates the National Criminal Justice Reference Service and its clearinghouses, administers the NILECJ Reading Room and the LEAA Library, and performs special information searches at the request of the director or administrator.

Despite the marketing analogy, it is apparent to the observer that OTT relies on very traditional forms of dissemination. The dissemination of written materials, demonstration programs, and training conferences comprise the whole of OTT's strategy. It is still problematic whether the written communication of ideas, which works well enough within the research community, actually has much effect in transferring research findings to the practitioner community. There has been little systematic effort to gauge the impact that written accounts of research findings have on the behavior of practicing professionals. Some researchers theorize that criminal justice practitioners might be among the least amenable to this dissemination strategy.* Further, the ultimate success of demonstration programs as transfer mechanisms is still being debated.†

OTT does not confine itself to the dissemination of research findings. OTT and its predecessor (the Technology Transfer Division) confronted a very different problem than the Office of Evaluation. While OE was faced with the challenge of carving a performable role for itself out of the nearly limitless charge that its Congressional mandate imposed, OTT can perhaps claim to have fashioned something from nothing. Results from NILECJ research did not come immediately. Even now it is debatable how many results have been sufficiently replicated to be considered reliable knowledge. What information has been produced

*RAND Corporation (1976) *Report of the Task Force on Criminal Justice Standards and Goals*. Santa Monica, Cal.: RAND Corp.

†Federal Council for Science and Technology (1975) *Directory of Federal Technology Transfer*. Washington, D.C.: National Science Foundation. Yin, R. K. (1976) *A Review of Case Studies of Technological Innovations in State and Local Services*. Santa Monica, Cal.: RAND Corp.

consists largely of findings from individual studies and is rarely in an integrated or usable format.

OTT, however, considers itself a bridge not just between the research and practitioner communities but also between the various states and localities. It has therefore gone into the field for much of its product line. OTT's role also contains a knowledge-building component that is frequently referred to in NILECJ literature and is operational in the Model Program Development Division (MPD).

The Prescriptive Package Program is one of the major product programs of MPD. Prescriptive Packages (PPS) are attractive, slickly printed manuals on the implementation of programs or techniques, such as neighborhood team policing or management by objectives in correctional settings. They were a specific response to the need to "put something in a practitioner's hands" when there was really nothing sufficiently verified to disseminate. A total of 33 PPS have been funded; 19 are now available.

According to NILECJ literature, topics for PPS are selected by OTT to fill information gaps, describe innovative approaches, or respond to practitioner demand. Staff comment indicates that this translates to: "Approaches become fashionable. Agencies want to try them and want information on them long before their impact can be verified." OTT's response is to issue a contract (normally to a consulting firm in the field*) for the production of a Prescriptive Package. The PP provides a composite model of a particular program using the best parts of various on-going projects and including variations of the model seen in the field. There is also a brief discussion of theory and procedural and evaluative material necessary to the program's implementation. It must be stressed that a composite model is used because none of the projects viewed has been found perfect. In fact, although the methods discussed may be popularly adopted, there has often been no rigorous evaluation performed on any of the projects.

Prescriptive Packages are often confused with NEP Phase I reports.† There have been various attempts to differentiate them, the simplest being the statement that a PP about a program area illustrates in detail how to establish the program, while a Phase I report surveys the state-of-the-art in that area but gives no practical information on implementation. That some confusion still remains on the issue is evidenced by the fact that in reply to this question, Richard Barnes, director of the NEP asserted that PPS implied no value judgments on the

*In this program, the contractor is required to use an advisory board of 5 practitioners.

†See previous case study on the Office of Evaluation.

quality of the innovation discussed. Mr. Cascarano, however, had earlier spoken of the increasing use of PPS as a technical assistance tool and standard, which seems to imply some judgment of value.

Exemplary Projects (EPS) are, by OTT definition: "Outstanding state or local projects which meet rigid criteria of crime reduction and/or improvement in the operations or quality of the criminal justice system." Thus far, 17 EPS have been designated; 14 of them were projects operated with LEAA funds. The brochures and manuals designed and printed about each project are considered a "product." The process of designating EPS (finding them and verifying their accomplishments) is considered one of knowledge gathering and assessment. (This description is contained in an internal memo from Gerald Caplan to James M. Gregg, Acting Assistant Administrator of LEAA.)

As in many NILECJ procedures, as much of the selection and verification as is possible is done out-of-house, with OTT staff monitoring and coordinating. EPS are selected from projects nominated by the SPAS. At OTT request, the Regional Offices periodically canvas SPAS and RPUS for Exemplary Project nominees from among the various programs operating in their area; nominations are not limited to programs funded by LEAA. Validation reports, consisting of site visits to nominated projects to check both the objective reliability of the data used in the project's original evaluation and the substantive conclusions reached by the original evaluation, are done by an independent contractor and submitted to a review board. Validation reports have themselves become a product and are distributed through the Reference Service to aid SPAS in future evaluations.

Monographs, another OTT product, are a spin-off of this process. Monographs, which are also prepared out-of-house, discuss interesting projects uncovered in the search for EPS but not granted exemplary status—often because of insufficient evaluation. To be granted EP status, a program must be proven effective, i.e., it must have been the subject of a rigorous impact evaluation. Monographs carry no judgment about the quality or impact of the programs they discuss.

Similarly to staff discussions of NEP, one of the functions ascribed to the search for EPS is the overview of the accomplishments of local agencies using LEAA funds. As one staff member remarked: "The problem in LEAA has always been to get this year's money out, without worrying about last year's. Exemplary projects look at what past funds have done." An overview of local program evaluation efforts has also been afforded by the EP selection process and has, in part, led to OTT's assumption of the technical assistance burden in evaluation, relying heavily on validation reports as technical assistance tools. It should be reemphasized that both PPS and EPS deal primarily with working projects—not research findings.

In the past, the "products" generated through the Model Programs Development Division were largely disseminated through the Reference and Dissemination Division, which coordinates the National Criminal Justice Reference Service (NCJRS) with its contractor, General Electric. The NCJRS is a computerized data bank of all NILECJ publications and all available publications in criminal justice. With its adjunct library, it services over 33,000 registered users with selected notification of new materials and, where possible, provision of requested documents.

A thorough evaluation should probably be done of NCJRS and its ultimate impact. The only information currently available results from the service's own statistics and random surveys of users. That information, however, implies that the assumption of many critics that criminal justice practitioners are not effectively reached through printed media may not be completely warranted. NCJRS data show that 73 percent of their registered users are criminal justice professionals (not including academics in the field); 42 percent are policy personnel; and 11 percent are associated with correctional agencies. The service distributes 70,000–80,000 documents monthly to registered and non-registered users. At least 17 percent of these documents are sent to individual police personnel.*

The second avenue of disseminating OTT products has been through the "sales" division functions of training and demonstration. Topics for training workshops are chosen from among the model programs, i.e., the programs treated in one of the OTT publications (products) on Exemplary Projects, Prescriptive Packages, etc. Training materials—handbooks, case studies, films—are designed, and an expert is contracted with to conduct the seminars in various regions for audiences of local senior officials.

Demonstrations are currently being held in 22 communities throughout the country. Formerly, demonstrations were implementations of new concepts by volunteer host agencies supported by OTT. Their main functions were to serve as a technology transfer mechanism for other agencies and to test the transferability of program models. Four to six host sites spread geographically throughout the country were selected for each program demonstration. This strategy assumed that dissemination of the innovative technique would occur as interested agencies

*Figures quoted at briefing by NCJRS director Joseph Cady on June 29, 1976.

throughout each region could contact participating departments for information and make on-site observations of on-going programs. Simultaneously, the introduction of one program approach into several agencies geographically distant from one another would provide evidence of the technique's inherent adaptability to local needs. As discussed earlier, however, Director Caplan's decision to alter the program to facilitate impact studies has increased the importance of the evaluation component to the point that OTT has dropped the term demonstration recently and now refers to this project as field testing. The Host Program—scheduled to begin in May 1976 and designed to enable interested criminal justice executives to spend up to one month in an on-site examination of a model program activity—appears to encompass the current demonstration effort.

Until recently, efforts of OTT thus appear to have been largely aimed at practitioners rather than at criminal justice planners in the states.* OTT appears intent on producing and marketing its own product. Connections with the rest of NILECJ at times seemed tenuous at best. Likewise, the delivery system of LEAA (i.e., the system of Regional Offices [ROS], SPAS, and RPUS) was frequently circumvented or ignored. When it was used, the results were found (and perhaps were expected to be) as disappointing as OE found the Model Evaluation Program.† The classic example of this pattern is the Promising Projects Program. OTT staff recount that the distribution of program announcements requesting nominations to the ROS and SPAS brought little response. The project recommendations only began arriving in substantial numbers following a direct mailing to practitioners themselves. The conclusion drawn by OTT staff was that the people responsible for funding do not know what is going on in their own region.

Recently, however, there has been a noticeable change of direction, at least in part due to new Deputy Administrator of LEAA, Paul Wormeli. There is now an attempt to use the LEAA system and even to improve it. OTT now emphasizes RO and SPA cooperation in the various processes for nominating projects for exemplary status and for suggesting topics for training seminars and packages. It is moving to make training conferences available for the use of the SPAS and ROS. Liaison and technical assistance are now frequently used terms. OTT Director Cascarano speaks of using EPS and PPS as technical assistance tools, of having SPAS evaluate their technical assistance needs, and of moving to

*OTT literature repeatedly describes their "products" as practical and informative, with a minimum of theory.

†See the case study on the Office of Evaluation.

coordinate the use of LEAA discretionary funds with concepts highlighted in the training and demonstration program.

Capacity building has become the major approach spoken of by OTT staff. It appears that OTT may even have taken over the function of capacity building in evaluation—using validation reports as technical assistance tools and the Evaluation Clearinghouse formed in NCJRS.* OTT is suggesting to SPAs that they evaluate all of their projects on a given topic, using the EPS or PPS as models.

OTT's marketing strategy seems inappropriate to a research institute, as does its new aggressive strategy for capacity building. Many observers are uncomfortable with the over-confidence in findings and programs required for the aggressive approach—particularly in a field such as criminal justice research where there is much controversy and little perceived "truth." Also, not only is the "song and dance routine" of marketing thought to be unseemly for a research institute, but it is presumed to compromise the objectivity and disinterest of its research. Indeed, several observers, both within and outside of the LEAA system, have commented that OTT might be more effectively placed as an independent entity within LEAA. It is also questionable whether OTT is really adequately performing the task of disseminating the results of Institute-sponsored research. OTT's staff, however, views itself as an important contributor to NILECJ. At the very least they can claim to provide important political cover. "Every time Caplan or even Velde goes to the Hill they send someone to OTT to pick up material," OTT staff relate. And as Director Cascarano implied to a question on practitioner resistance: "I find people eager to grab hold of knowledge. LEAA never had a product line before. At least it provides a talking point."

In conclusion: the activities undertaken by the Office of Technology Transfer, which have been pursued with a great deal of energy, appear to be useful but their impact on the criminal justice system has never been objectively gauged.

The issue of effective dissemination of research results is one of great import for the Institute in planning a mission-oriented research program. However, the marketing and packaging function of OTT—however vigorously pursued—is totally inappropriate within the confines of an institution devoted to research. Should LEAA wish to continue its mode of reaching criminal justice practitioners, these

*This clearinghouse contains materials on project evaluations throughout the social sciences and is intended for the use of SPA staff, local policy makers, and project directors.

programs, along with the technical assistance function, would be better and more appropriately performed outside of the Institute. NILECJ's current structure seems to create territoriality disputes and the difference of perspectives originating in the various offices lead to unnecessary conflicts on research. OTT, as it presently functions, may be an energetic performer of valuable tasks, but it is an incongruous office in an institute devoted to research.

Case Study—Impact Cities

JUANITA L. RUBINSTEIN

The High Impact Anti-Crime Program is perhaps the most debated of LEAA's endeavors. A great deal has been written about Impact Cities since the program's much heralded inauguration in January 1972. However, this Study's concern with this massive, multi-faceted and controversial effort extends only to the role of Impact Cities as one of NILECJ's major research investments.

From fiscal 1972 through fiscal 1975, the Institute allocated $16,430,887 to support the crime analysis teams in the eight Impact Cities and the National Level Evaluation of the High Impact Anti-Crime Program, which was undertaken by the MITRE Corporation. This Case Study briefly sketches the background of Institute involvement and the problems encountered in the research component of the Impact Cities Program.*

GENERAL BACKGROUND

This decade was not very old before it became obvious that the "war on crime" was far from a decisive victory. Crime rates—the traditional

*Unless otherwise noted, the material for this case study was taken from MITRE Corporation (1976) *High Impact Anti-Crime Programs: National Level Evaluation Final Report*. Eleanor Chelimsky, author. Vol. 1: Executive Summary, Vol. 2: Report. No. MTR-7148. Washington, D.C.: Law Enforcement Assistance Administration.

measure of impact—continued to rise and the optimism expressed in the previous decade about the ability of the government to achieve effective social engineering through action programs had diminished considerably. LEAA had, since its establishment in 1968, funded many programs in crime control and criminal justice system improvement. However, critics in Congress and in the media were grumbling that the programs had effected no visible impact on crime.

Researchers and officials were, if anything, increasingly aware of what was unknown about crime and the criminal justice systems. The only easily accessible data were crime rates, collected locally and voluntarily. Data were thus dubious, unstandardized, and in an often inutile form; criminal justice research and its tools were underdeveloped. The criminal justice system was fragmented and resistant to coordination. Local planning on a systemic basis and evaluation of needs and priorities of criminal justice were virtually non-existent.

The then-current administration, from the President through the Attorney General, was on record as favoring a return to "law and order" and had seriously criticized the previous administration for tolerating an unacceptable level of street crime and civil disorder. Congressional inquiries during renewal debates and the Monagan subcommittee in its oversight hearings* continually deplored the fact that the activities of LEAA and its research institute were having no positive effect in the reduction of American crime. The steeply rising urban crime rates and the realization that LEAA had no way of determining the impact that its programs had on crime reduction was most embarassing. When Vice President Agnew, Attorney General Mitchell, and LEAA Administrator Leonard publicly inaugurated the Impact Cities Program on January 13, 1972, the goals announced were: the reduction of the incidence of 5 crimes (the stranger-to-stranger person crimes of murder, rape, assault, and robbery and the property crime of burglary) by 5 percent in 2 years and by 20 percent in 5 years; and the improvement of the capabilities of criminal justice systems through the demonstration of "comprehensive crime-oriented planning, implementation and evaluation cycle."† A third, although unofficial, goal was the demonstration to the American people of the national government's commitment to effectively controlling urban crime.

*U.S. Congress, House (1972) *Block Grant Programs of the Law Enforcement Assistance Administration*. House Report 92–1072. 92nd Congress, 2nd Session.
†MITRE Corp., Vol. 2, p. 19.

THE PROGRAM

The High Impact Anti-Crime Program was to take place in eight cities supposedly chosen because they possessed various crime problems. (The intrusion of political factors into the site selection process has been much discussed and is noted in *High Impact Anti-Crime Programs: National Level Evaluation Final Report*. The provision of $20 million per city was much too large an award for political pressure not to be exerted on the administration in behalf of various cities.) The cities of Atlanta, Baltimore, Cleveland, Dallas, Denver, Newark, Portland, and St. Louis were to be eligible, under this program, for a total of $160 million in LEAA discretionary funds during a two-year period. The funds were to be spent in a systematic effort to develop, implement, and evaluate projects specifically addressed to the target stranger-to-stranger crimes.

In line with the New Federalism philosophy of the administration, the program was to be administered through the LEAA block-grant structure. The State Planning Agencies were to provide the chosen cities with any needed assistance in planning and evaluation and to participate in the administrative and financial monitoring of the Impact Cities Program. The Regional Offices were to hold final approval authority for grant applications, funding awards, and master and evaluation plans for all impact projects. They were also to oversee the implementation and monitoring of the program. In Washington, the program's progress was to be monitored by the LEAA National Program Coordinator, NILECJ, a Policy Decision Group of three policy-level LEAA officials, and the National Criminal Justice Information Service.

The Impact Cities Program was to demonstrate the use of two innovations—the COPIE cycle and the Crime Analysis Team. COPIE was the Crime Oriented Planning, Implementation, and Evaluation model that the Impact Cities were to adopt. Each city was to use this sytem-wide cycle in determining that the specific problems attacked were indeed its major problems; that the program plans drawn up by each city reflected local priorities; that the necessary resources for each project were known and available; and that the success or failure of the various strategies and projects would be objectively ascertained. Implementing the COPIE cycle in each city was the task of the Crime Analysis Teams. These teams, supported by NILECJ funds, were identified or created in each of the Impact Cities. Groups of researchers and functional specialists were expected to serve as liaisons and coordinators for all local agencies involved in the Impact Cities Program and to perform, monitor, or supervise the COPIE cycle's operations in each of the eight criminal justice systems.

Six specific program goals were announced:

1. The reduction of crime—the five designated crimes were those thought to be serious but controllable by the criminal justice system.
2. The demonstration of the COPIE cycle—an attempt to integrate planning and evaluation research into the functions of the criminal justice system, resulting, it was hoped, in improved system performance.
3. The acquisition, through implementation of the COPIE cycle, of new knowledge about the effectiveness of various anti-crime strategies; the profile of specific crimes in terms of settings, offenders and victims; and the processes of innovation and evaluation within the criminal justice system.
4. The stimulation of increased inter-governmental and inter-agency cooperation and increased community participation in the planning and functioning of the criminal justice system.
5. The institutionalization of those innovations deemed effective.
6. The increase of the general capability of the American criminal justice system beyond the Impact Cities Program through the effective dissemination of the knowledge acquired during program implementation.

Ultimately, $140 million of LEAA discretionary funds were expended by the eight cities on a total of 233 action-oriented projects within their criminal justice system. Not surprisingly, in a program of this size and diversity, the results were mixed. Can one say as much for the return on NILECJ's investment in the program?

THE NILECJ ROLE

The Institute's concern with the Impact Cities Program was focused on an evaluation component that was to be both rigorous and complex.* NILECJ was to determine whether crime reductions were the result of particular projects and treatments and to expedite the dissemination process, ensuring replication of successful procedures.

*See MITRE Corp., *op. cit.*, Chapter 4, Vol. 2, for a description of the circumstances of the National Level Evaluation.

The program evaluation was to be conducted on three levels. City-level evaluations were to be supervised by the Crime Analysis Team (CAT). The CAT of each Impact City was to produce project and program findings for that jurisdiction. The national-level evaluation was to be performed by the Institute and its contractor, the MITRE Corporation, on the basis of the city-level findings. Finally, a global-level evaluation was to be based on a set of victimization surveys that the Bureau of the Census would undertake in 1972, 1975, and 1978, in cooperation with LEAA's Statistics Division. This last evaluation was expected to ascertain the effectiveness of the entire Impact Cities Program in terms of crime reduction.

The New Federalism dictated control of local evaluations by the CAT teams. The planned global evaluation disappeared from the agenda by the beginning of 1973.* Victimization surveys alone could not attribute any observed changes of victimization level in the Impact Cities to the Impact Program. Even if fewer people in the Impact Cities were victimized in incidents of the target crimes, there was no way to prove that this was the result of the Impact Program rather than of a host of unrelated factors. The national-level evaluation, the one with which NILECJ was most directly concerned, was scheduled to be completed before the 1975 victimization survey. Furthermore, the survey design did not provide for an assessment of the crime-reduction outcomes of the Impact Cities Program.

Evaluation planning had begun in the Institute in late October of 1971, simultaneously with the planning of the Impact Cities Program. (The entire program was evidently planned in the three months prior to its public unveiling in January 1972.) The contractor who was to perform the evaluation was not contacted until July of 1972, six months after the program began. The action programs had begun before pre-intervention conditions were ascertained, rendering any pre/post comparisons impossible. Site selection and program design were all accomplished without any input from the evaluation design (it was non-existent) or any concern for the constraints that the pursuit of rigorous evaluative research imposed.

Despite the sincere and determined efforts that were made in the Institute during November and December of 1971, the program began operations without a national-level evaluation design. In spite of the

*The MITRE final report reaches no firm conclusion on the reason for the stillbirth of the global evaluation, but speculates that the difficulties in interagency cooperation on the national level, the lack of mechanisms for working collaboration, or staff shortage might have been involved.

sustained activity, the absurd time constraints coupled with the size of the task and the press of other commitments ensured that the evaluation was sketched rather than designed. Program goals were never operationally designed. (The MITRE final report quotes internal memoranda of the Institute frantically demanding ''Five percent of what? Twenty percent of what?''*) National-level evaluation measures were not defined; a strategy was not formulated. Again and again, a reader of the MITRE report encounters the terms ''vague discussion,'' ''vaguely discussed,'' ''no mechanisms were developed.''

CONSTRAINTS ON RESEARCH

In July of 1972, when MITRE began to develop the national evaluation design, it found that the effort would be constrained by several factors.

Cost constraints rendered impossible the use of control or comparison groups of non-Impact Cities for the national-level evaluation. Thus, not only pre/post but also treatment/control studies became an impossibility. Likewise, no area-specific data collection could be undertaken within Impact Cities. This meant that resulting data would cover the entire city, prohibiting evaluation of the intra-city impact of any project or treatment. This precluded any conclusions on the displacement effect of projects or comparison of treatment effects in different areas within the cities.

Finally, MITRE could not establish a presence in the cities, because the cost was judged to be duplicative. This restriction left the national evaluation totally dependent upon the unsupervised and voluntary collection and submission of data by local agencies. (The police department in one of the Impact Cities has as yet to allow the national evaluators access to any of its data.)

The New Federalism, the administration's basic philosophy and cornerstone of the LEAA system, imposed enormous constraints on the research component of a national program. Not only was the national evaluation dependent upon the cities themselves for all of its raw data, but it was impossible to impose any designs for rigorous evaluations at the local level. Pious hopes were expressed that the guidelines for the program and the incentive funds for evaluation would encourage local efforts, but there was to be no federal coercion. Cities were to evaluate their own projects. No requirements for area-specific or base-line data collection could be imposed. No significant change in local data

*Vol. 2, p. 57.

collection could be forced. (Data collection in local criminal justice agencies in the early years of this decade was often completely inadequate. "Appalling" was the description given by a staff member of the national evaluation effort.)

The evaluation program called for rigorous city-level efforts, but the research agenda was to be entirely without teeth. Except for the victimization surveys conducted by the Census Bureau, all of the data to be generated by this massive program was to come from the cities involved. Yet there was to be no mechanism to ensure that similar strategies of data collection were followed within the 8 cities or even to monitor local data-collection efforts.

A final result of the New Federalism restraint at the national level was the number and variety of program innovations and system improvements attempted with Impact City funds. Despite the program's guidelines, the evaluation report makes clear that there was little actual limitation on the manner in which the cities spent the Impact funds for their criminal justice systems. The resulting diversity swamped any effort to evaluate system improvement in the cities involved.

CONCLUSION

MITRE studied the restrictions on research inherent in the Impact Cities Program and quickly determined that any experimental or even quasi-experimental design for the national evaluation was entirely out of the question. In an attempt to make the best of the situation, MITRE decided to concentrate on process and to address questions about what happened when those 8 cities, provided with significant sums of money and guidance, attempted system-wide planning, implementation, and evaluation.

This Case Study makes no attempt to evaluate the worth or success of the program as a whole, nor does it argue that no interesting observations were recorded on the progress of the COPIE cycle and CAT teams in the Impact Cities. One conclusion seems inevitable, however. Given NILECJ's mandate ". . . to encourage research and development. . ." [Omnibus Crime Control and Safe Streets Act of 1968, Part D, Sec. 402(A)], its participation in the Impact Program was inappropriate, indeed, a corruption of the purposes of research and development. Defenders of the program, and the evaluation report itself, repeatedly point out that basic knowledge acquisition was never intended to be a primary goal, that the program was by design, and by political necessity, an action program, a broad-based effort at system improvement.

The acceptance of these assertions renders even more evident the conclusion that NILECJ's involvement was an inappropriate use of a large portion of its research funding. Director Danziger evidently judged the Impact Program to be in line with his bold attempts to produce social change and with the crime-oriented perspective then being adopted by the Institute. Large-scale commitment of resources was also the strategy then used by the Institute in an attempt to secure the largest possible payoff from research funding. Sadly, NILECJ's involvement in the Impact Cities Program represents the opposite effect.

It is not at all certain that NILECJ could have escaped the pressures exerted in favor of the program at that point. But the lesson learned from Impact Cities must be remembered: if the goal of the Institute is to produce reliable knowledge about crime and criminal behaviors, its funds should not be used in this manner. It is counter-productive to use large amounts of Institute funds in ventures that cannot produce sound research.

APPENDIXES

Appendix A
Background Material

APPENDIX A1. Legislation: Sections of the Omnibus Crime Control and Safe Streets Act of 1968 and Amendments Relevant to the National Institute of Law Enforcement and Criminal Justice

Title I, Part D—TRAINING, EDUCATION, RESEARCH, DEMONSTRATION, AND SPECIAL GRANTS*

Sec. 401. It is the purpose of this part to provide for and encourage training, education, research, and development for the purpose of improving law enforcement and *criminal justice,* and developing new methods for the prevention and reduction of crime, and the detection and apprehension of criminals.

Sec. 402.(a) There is established within the Department of Justice a National Institute of Law Enforcement and Criminal Justice (hereafter referred to in this part as "Institute"). The Institute shall be under the general authority of the Administration. *The chief administrative officer of the Institute shall be a Director appointed by the Administrator.* It shall be the purpose of the Institute to encourage research and development to improve and strengthen law enforcement *and criminal justice, to disseminate the results of such efforts to State and local governments, and to assist in the development and support of programs for the training of law enforcement and criminal justice personnel.*

(b) The Institute is authorized—

(1) to make grants to, or enter into contracts with, public agencies, institutions of higher education, or private organizations to conduct research, demonstrations, or special projects pertaining to the purposes described in this title, including the development of new or improved approaches, techniques,

*Material introduced by the Omnibus Crime Control Act of 1970 and the Crime Control Act of 1973 is italicized.

systems, equipment, and devices to improve and strengthen law enforcement *and criminal justice;*

(2) to make continuing studies and undertake programs of research to develop new or improved approaches, techniques, systems, equipment, and devices to improve and strengthen law enforcement and *criminal justice,* including, but not limited to, the effectiveness of projects or programs carried out under this title;

(3) to carry out programs of behavioral research designed to provide more accurate information on the causes of crime and the effectiveness of various means of preventing crime, and to evaluate the success of correctional procedures;

(4) to make recommendations for action which can be taken by Federal, State, and local governments and by private persons and organizations to improve and strengthen law enforcement and *criminal justice;*

(5) to carry out programs of instructional assistance consisting of research fellowships for the programs provided under this section, and special workshops for the presentation and dissemination of information resulting from research, demonstrations, and special projects authorized by this title;

(6) *to assist in conducting, at the request of a State or a unit of general local government or a combination thereof, local or regional training programs for the training of State and local law enforcement and criminal justice personnel, including but not limited to those engaged in the investigation of crime and apprehension of criminals, community relations, the prosecution or defense of those charged with crime, corrections, rehabilitation, probation and parole of offenders. Such training activities shall be designed to supplement and improve rather than supplant the training activities of the State and units of general local government and shall not duplicate the training activities of the Federal Bureau of Investigation under section 404 of this title. While participating in the training program or traveling in connection with participation in the training program, State and local personnel shall be allowed travel expenses and a per diem allowance in the same manner as prescribed under section 5703(b) of title 5, United States Code, for persons employed intermittently in the Government service;*

(7) to carry out a program of collection and dissemination of information obtained by the Institute or other Federal agencies, public agencies, institutions of higher education, or private organizations engaged in projects under this title, including information relating to new or improved approaches, techniques, systems, equipment, and devices to improve and strengthen law enforcement; and

(8) to establish a research center to carry out the programs described in this section.

(c) *The Institute shall serve as a national and international clearinghouse for the exchange of information with respect to the improvement of law enforcement and criminal justice, including but not limited to police, courts, prosecutors, public defenders, and corrections.*

The Institute shall undertake, where possible, to evaluate the various programs and projects carried out under this title to determine their impact upon the quality of law enforcement and criminal justice and the extent to which they have met or failed to meet the purposes and policies of this title, and shall disseminate such information to State planning agencies and, upon request, to units of general local government.

The Institute shall, before the end of the fiscal year ending June 30, 1976, survey existing and future personnel needs of the Nation in the field of law enforcement and criminal justice and the adequacy of Federal, State and local programs to meet such needs. Such survey shall specifically determine the effectiveness and sufficiency of the training and academic assistance programs carried out under this title and relate such programs to actual manpower and training requirements in the law enforcement and criminal justice field. In carrying out the provisions of this section, the Director of the Institute shall consult with and make maximum use of statistical and other related information of the Department of Labor, Department of Health, Education, and Welfare, Federal, State and local criminal justice agencies and other appropriate public and private agencies. The Administration shall thereafter, within a reasonable time develop and issue guidelines, based upon the need priorities established by the survey, pursuant to which project grants for training and academic assistance programs shall be made.

The Institute shall report annually to the President, the Congress, the State planning agencies, and, upon request, to units of general local government, on the research and development activities undertaken pursuant to paragraphs (1), (2), and (3) of subsection (b), and shall describe in such report the potential benefits of such activities of law enforcement and criminal justice and the results of the evaluations made pursuant to the second paragraph of this subsection. Such report shall also describe the programs of instructional assistance, the special workshops, and the training programs undertaken pursuant to paragraphs (5) and (6) of subsection (b).

Sec. 403. A grant authorized under this part may be up to 100 per centum of the total cost of each project for which such grant is made. The Administration or the Institute shall require, whenever feasible, as a condition of approval of a grant under this part, that the recipient contribute money, facilities, or services to carry out the purposes for which the grant is sought.

APPENDIX A2. Congressional Attitudes toward the National Institute of Law Enforcement and Criminal Justice

During interviews with Institute staff, instances of Congressional inquiry were always mentioned. Such instances were especially commonplace in the early years when Representative John Rooney, during his appropriations hearings, made a point of challenging Institute work. Institute staff at that time were often called upon to produce tangible evidence of useful work. Interviews evoked many recollections of preparing material for a hearing before Congressman Rooney. Charles Rogovin, first Administrator of LEAA, commented (Rogovin 1973, p. 19):

> [Associate Administrator] Velde persuaded me that the jaundiced view of the Institute by certain members of Congress, particularly members of the Appropriations Sub-Committee with authority over the agency budget, would be reflected in continuing inadequate funding for the Institute. . .

With regard to the usefulness of doing research on the X-Y-Y chromosome aberration, which had recently surfaced in court debate over causality of criminal behavior, the following exchange took place (U.S. Congress, House 1969, p. 1038; hereinafter referred to as Rooney Hearings 1969):

ROGOVIN: . . . the aberration of the chromosome structure within the individual defendant, it is an X-Y-Y aberration, would account for their violent tendencies and thereby be a defense to the legal responsibility for the commission of a crime. Courts are being confronted with this sort of thing and there is no scientific resolution yet.

ROONEY: Surely you are not going into the scientific area to find those answers, are you?

ROGOVIN: We would hope to stimulate that kind of resolution.

ROONEY: I think we should leave that to the scientists.

ROGOVIN: Properly so, sir; the scientific research people. However, this is within the Institute which exists under the statute.

ROONEY: Rather than to lawyers who have never known how to pick a jury.

ROGOVIN: It is a tough proposition at best.

ROONEY: I don't know about that. You should get 12 men tried and true who can understand the main issues in the case and properly resolve them. This can all be covered by the judge's charge. I still don't know what this chromosome business has to do with your program.

A few minutes later, Rooney broadened his comments (pp. 1040–1):

ROONEY: . . . You ought to tell my friends what I also said in that letter of a few days ago? Do you recall?

ROGOVIN: Yes, sir, I recall it vividly. Your comment was, I think, that in your judgment the agency could function with six persons and a checkwriter.

ROONEY: That is right, and I think the same as I sit here right now. Whoever had an idea that this outfit was going to go off into the scientific development area and into some of these other things we have heard of?

ROGOVIN: I think there are other kinds of things that the Institute program could explore.

ROONEY: I thought all you needed was somebody to see to it that the checks are sent to the right addresses and that one of the people knows how to run a checkwriter.

ROGOVIN: I think it goes beyond that, sir.

ROONEY: I don't think so. I don't think it was ever intended that we would create another hierarchy. I thought this would be a function of the Department of Justice to get this money out.

Other instances illustrate greater interest in hardware development than basic research questions, the frustration of the committee at being unable to see any demonstrable successes in either research or development, and the belief that much of what the Institute did do might more appropriately be done by other federal agencies (e.g., development of an improved patrol car by the Department of Transportation).

In July and October 1971, Representative John Monagan held hearings of the Legal and Monetary Affairs Subcommittee of the House Committee on Government Operations; they detailed horror stories on LEAA funding programs, ranging from hardware excesses to outright corruption.

Much of what the Monagan hearings stressed had either direct or implied impact on the Institute. Of the Committee's findings (U.S. Congress, House 1972; hereinafter referred to as Monagan Report 1972), the first charged that the block grant programs had had "no visible impact on the incidence of crime in the United States" (p. 104). The second charged that "the impact on the reform of the criminal justice system has been minimal but cannot definitively be ascertained because LEAA has failed to develop standards for measuring and evaluating the effectiveness of its block grant programs" (p. 104). Moreover, its failure to evaluate, the Committee said, "stems directly from its failure to establish standard goals or objectives . . . it has developed no criteria against which to evaluate" (p. 70).

Another finding charged that "LEAA has failed to disseminate adequately the results of research and experimental projects conducted by participants in the programs. This gives rise to the strong probability that there has been duplication of such projects" (p. 106). The Institute was said at that time to be two years away from startup of its reference service (p. 76). The Committee's objections to hardware expenditures were related in part to its findings that LEAA had failed to provide standards, evaluation results, and technical assistance (p. 9). Such standards could have made hardware purchase decisions more intelligent, and it speaks directly to the halting startup of the Institute's Law Enforcement Standard Laboratory, then still two years away (p. 47).

These hearings thus became the point of departure for the Institute's new emphasis on evaluation of program impact. The Institute eventually was made responsible for major evaluation efforts throughout LEAA. More importantly, the emphasis on crime-specific planning that characterized Jerris Leonard's term as LEAA Administrator and strongly influenced Martin Danziger's term as Director of the Institute grew out of the Monagan hearings.

The instances of Congressional pressure are less important than their effects. One can argue that any federal funding should be subject to this kind of accountability. This is true, but a research program is in a special category. The pressures were for immediate solutions, and they often came from those who had little interest in or sympathy for research objectives. The effects, then, have to do with the attitudes of those trying to do the research. The continual mention in interviews of instances of responding to Congressional questioning underscores the fact that the pressures were keenly felt. The researchers were being conditioned to the hostility of the political world, and their own planning and funding decisions reflected that conditioning.

Appendix B Institute Funding Patterns

This appendix presents data that describe Institute funding patterns since 1969. Specific attention is given to the distinction between allocated and obligated expenditures: allocated expenditures reflect the component parts (e.g., grants, Pilot Cities awards, etc.) of the Institute budget for a fiscal year; obligated expenditures show what was actually spent or programmed of that component allocation. The difference between the total obligated expenditures and the appropriation for a fiscal year is carried over to the next fiscal year and added to the appropriation, which becomes the total funds available in that next fiscal year. However, these carry-over figures do not include any other money that may have been carried over due to de-obligations of funds from prior years, so that the total available funds in any given fiscal year may be marginally higher than these figures indicate.

There are several other characteristics of these data that should be noted. First, figures for obligated expenditures shown in a given fiscal year include the total cost of projects with award numbers for that fiscal year. This is somewhat different from the Institute's procedure, in which an award's fiscal year number does not necessarily reflect that award's year of programmed obligation. Beginning in fiscal 1974, the Institute sometimes obligated money for an award in a fiscal year but then gave that award a fiscal year number for the next fiscal year (when most of the money would be spent). Because it is virtually impossible to keep track of awards that are handled in this manner, the obligated expenditures shown for any fiscal year—as noted—include the awards with that fiscal year number, regardless of when the Institute obligated the money.

Second, the figures shown do not include expenditures for technical assistance and training awards or for salaries of Institute personnel, which are allocated out of LEAA's budget. Third, expenditures for expenses—e.g., travel, space, printing, supplies—while part of the Institute's budget, are not included in these data.

TABLE B-1 LEAA Appropriations History (dollars in thousands)

	1969 Actual	1970 Actual	1971 Actual	1972 Actual	1973 Actual	1974 Actual	1975 Estimated
Grants for development and implementation of comprehensive plans (Part B)	$19,000	$ 21,000	$ 26,000	$ 35,000	$ 50,000	$ 50,000	$ 55,000
Matching grants to improve and strengthen law enforcement (Part C):							
(a) State block grants	24,650	182,750	340,000	413,695	480,250	480,250	480,250
(b) Discretionary grants	4,350	32,000	70,000	73,005	88,750	88,750	84,750
Aid for correctional institutions and programs (Part E)	—	—	47,500	97,500	113,000	113,000	113,000
Technical assistance	—	1,200	4,000	6,000	10,000	12,000	14,968
Technology, analysis, development, and dissemination (National Institute of Law Enforcement and Criminal Justice[a])	3,000	7,500	7,500	21,000	31,598	40,098	45,198
Manpower development (Part D: education)	6,500	18,000	22,500	31,000	45,000	45,000	45,000
Data systems and statistical assistance	—	1,000	4,000	9,700	21,200	24,000	26,500
Management and operations	2,500	4,487	7,454	11,823	15,568 –14,200[b]	17,428	21,734
TOTAL OBLIGATIONAL AUTHORITY	60,000	267,937	528,954	698,723	841,166	870,526	886,400
Transferred to other agencies	3,000	182	46	196	14,431	149	—
TOTAL APPROPRIATED	63,000	268,119	529,000	698,919	855,597	870,673	886,400

SOURCE: Law Enforcement Assistance Administration.

[a]Budget of the National Institute.

[b]Transferred to other agencies in the U.S. Department of Justice pursuant to P.L. 93–50.

TABLE B-2 Summary Distribution of NILECJ Funds

Type of Expenditure	Fiscal 1969		Fiscal 1970		Fiscal 1971	
	Allocated	Obligated	Allocated	Obligated	Allocated	Obligated
Grants, contracts, agreements	—	2,892,000	—	7,472,000	—	7,768,000
Pilot Cities	—	—	—	—	—	—
Impact Cities	—	—	—	—	—	—
Drug Enforcement Administration	—	—	—	—	—	—
Standards and goals	—	—	—	—	—	—
Reference service	—	—	—	—	—	—
Office of Science and Technology	—	—	—	—	—	—
Regional office demonstrations	—	—	—	—	—	—
Graduate research fellowships	—	—	—	—	—	—
TOTAL EXPENDITURES		2,892,000		7,472,000		7,768,000
Appropriation	2,900,000[a]		7,500,000		7,500,000	
Carried-over money[b]	—		—		—	

TABLE B-2 *Continued*

Type of Expenditure	Fiscal 1972		Fiscal 1973		Fiscal 1974		Fiscal 1975	
	Allocated	Obligated	Allocated	Obligated	Allocated	Obligated	Allocated	Obligated
Grants, contracts, agreements	8,175,000	8,579,000	12,750,000	14,331,000	20,800,000	17,677,000	32,434,000	35,392,000
Pilot Cities	1,200,000	1,200,000	2,000,000	1,926,361	1,225,500	1,225,500	239,000	239,000
Impact Cities	7,700,000	7,000,000	5,600,000	1,949,667	2,430,887	2,430,887	700,000	700,000
Drug Enforcement Administration	2,300,000	1,326,000	6,400,000	6,400,000	7,075,000	7,075,000	9,100,000	9,100,000
Standards and goals	350,000	252,030	—	—	—	—	—	—
Reference service	700,000	408,450	—	—	—	—	—	—
Office of Science and Technology	—	—	4,958,000	1,331,341	—	—	—	—
Regional office demonstrations	—	—	—	—	1,200,000	1,200,000	1,924,000	1,924,000
Graduate research fellowships	250,000	10,482	250,000	237,814	—	—	—	—
TOTAL EXPENDITURES	21,000,000	18,775,962	31,598,000	26,176,183	32,731,387	29,608,387	44,397,000	47,355,000
Appropriation	21,000,000		31,598,000		40,098,000		42,500,000	
Carried-over money[b]	—		2,224,038		5,421,817		10,489,000	

SOURCES: *Directory of Grants, Contracts and Interagency Agreements; First Annual Report of the National Institute of Law Enforcement and Criminal Justice; 1975 Annual Report of the Institute* (mimeo); *National Institute Status of Funds Reports* (various fiscal years).

[a]This figure comes from the *First Annual Report* of the Institute, and is confirmed by other available data. However, it is different from the figure shown in Table B-1 for the same year.

[b]Prior to 1972, any surplus monies not spent or obligated were not carried-over, but were returned to LEAA. After 1972, money not obligated became part of available funds in the next fiscal year.

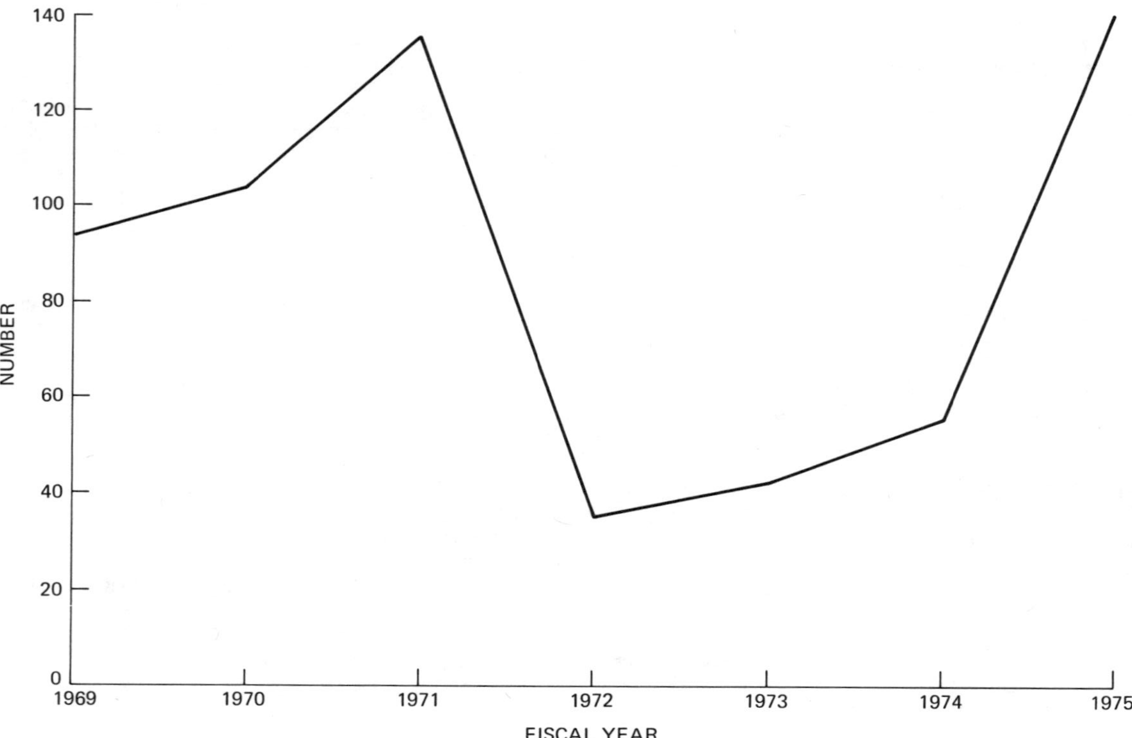

FIGURE B-1 Number of NILECJ grants, contracts, and interagency agreements per year (total: 601).

FIGURE B-2 Institute obligated expenditures for grants, contracts, and agreements (excludes pass-through money to DEA and other programs).

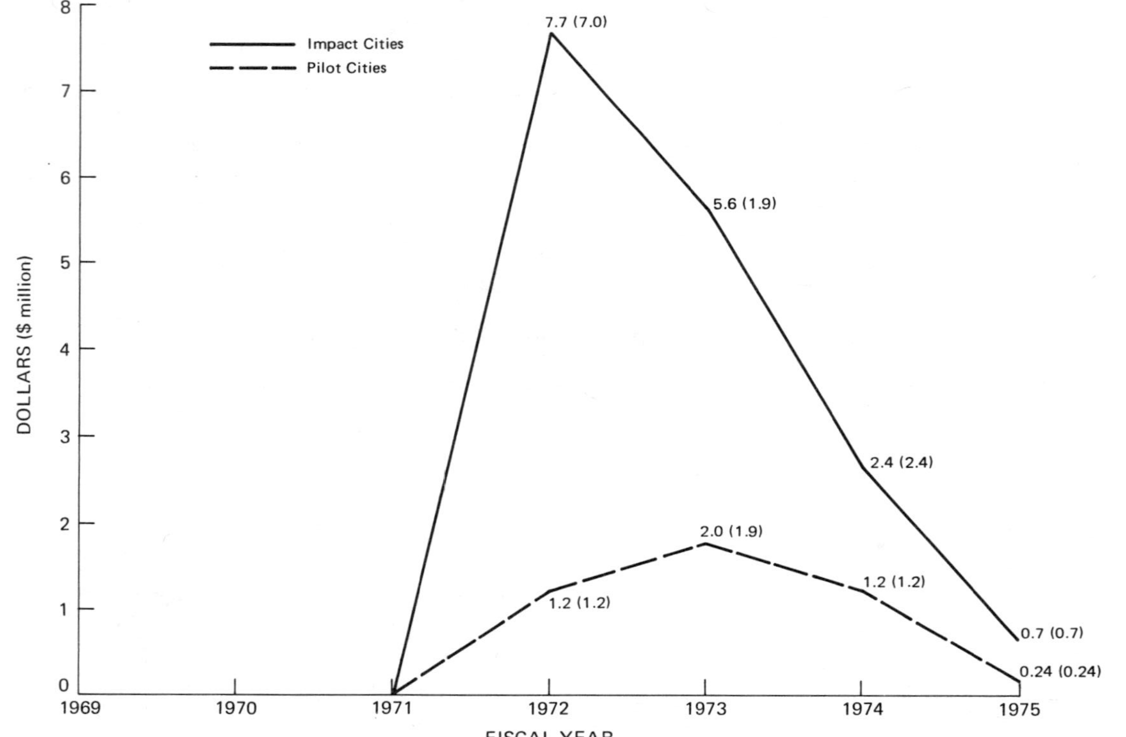

FIGURE B-3 NILECJ allocations to Impact and Pilot Cities Programs (numbers in parentheses represent amounts obligated).

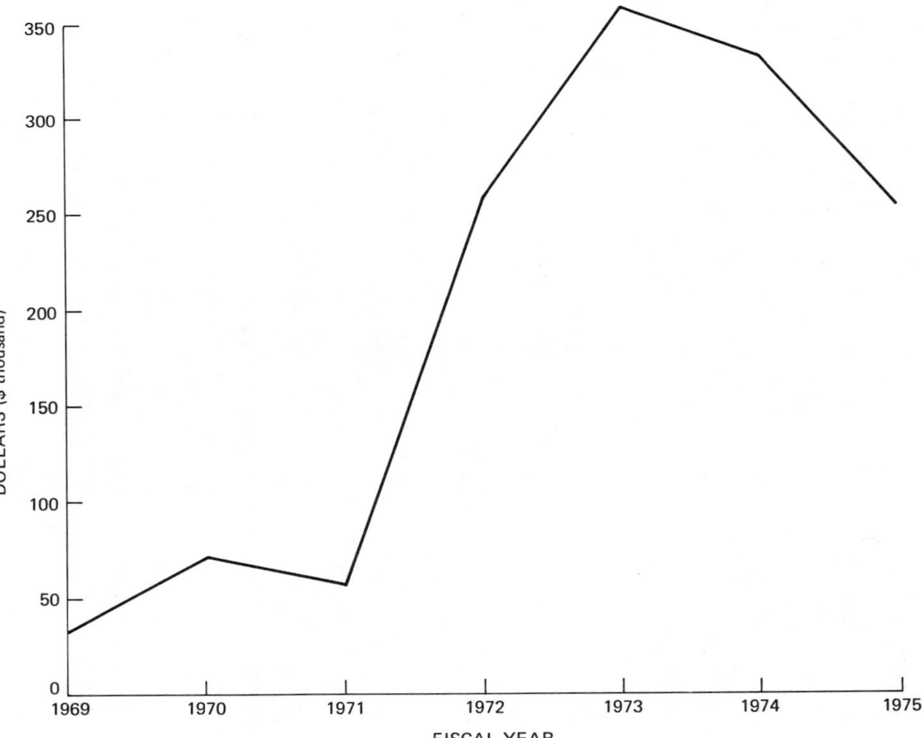

FIGURE B-4 Mean dollar amount spent on NILECJ grants, contracts, and interagency agreements.

Appendix C Designs and Questionnaires

APPENDIX C1. Grants and Contracts Sample Design

This appendix shows the sample design used by the Committee in conducting its evaluation of Institute projects funded during 1969–1975. Because we wished to particularly focus in on more recent projects and larger awards, we stratified the sample with respect to year and size of award.

In all, 627 NILECJ awards comprised the population from which the sample was drawn. Each had been previously coded by its NILECJ award identification number and other defining characteristics. We then stratified according to: (1) types of awards—grants and "other" (e.g. contracts, interagency agreements, etc.); (2) the year in which funding occurred; and (3) the dollar amount of the award. Ten different strata were needed to accommodate these award characteristics and their combinations. Although the design would have allowed us to sample each stratum 3 times (3 replications), we considered the first replication of 131 awards to be sufficient in light of our needs and resources. In addition, we sampled 7 more projects from stratum 9 of the second replication—each an award in excess of $500,000. Thus, a total of 138 NILECJ projects appeared in the sample, which was then evaluated as described in Chapter 4 of this report. A list of projects in the sample by project title appears in Appendix C3.

SAMPLE DESIGN

1. Grants

Funding in thousands of dollars	Year of Award 1969	1970	1971	1972	1973	1974	1975	TOTAL
$ 0–100	85	70	81	12	11	23	48	330
$101–500	9	28	23	14	16	21	64	175
$501+	0	0	0	0	3	0	7	10
TOTAL	94	98	104	26	30	44	119	515

2. Other (Contracts, Interagency Agreements, Technical Assistance Awards, etc.)

Funding in thousands of dollars	Year of Award 1969	1970	1971	1972	1973	1974	1975	TOTAL
$ 0–100	0	5	27	8	7	9	10	66
$101–500	0	0	4	1	5	7	11	28
$501+	0	1	0	4	2	5	6	18
TOTAL	0	6	31	13	14	21	27	112

Stratum	Type	Year	Funding in thousands of dollars	Size of Population	Size of Sample	Size of First Replication	No. of Replications	Size of Other Replications
1	Grants	1969–71	0–100	236	72	24	3	24
2	Grants	1969–71	101–500	60	36	12	3	12
3	Grants	1972–74	0–100	46	36	12	3	12
4	Grants	1972–74	101–500	51	36	12	3	12
5	Grants	1975	0–100	48	36	12	3	12
6	Grants	1975	101–500	63	36	12	3	12
7	Grants	1969–75	501+	10	10	10	1	0
8	Other	1969–75	0–100	66	36	12	3	12
9	Other	1969–75	101+	46	46	24	2	12
10*	Re-assigned			1	1	1	1	0
	TOTAL			627	345	131		

First-stage replication: N_1 = 131.
Second-stage replication: N_2 = 118.
Third-stage replication: N_3 = 96.

*This pertains to one grant that was originally incorrectly assigned to Stratum 9 when the sample was drawn.

RANDOM SAMPLING OF AWARDS WITHIN STRATA POPULATIONS

Stratum 1 (236 awards)

1st Replicate	170	46	38	116	67	184	149	192	195	16	31	133
	134	94	181	5	217	220	169	137	33	73	83	45
2nd Replicate	76	165	17	80	55	39	186	171	140	235	75	189
	86	187	219	146	106	85	175	168	32	79	29	125
3rd Replicate	148	66	159	161	110	131	229	132	103	51	21	213
	211	102	167	108	97	37	81	50	143	234	228	141

Stratum 2 (60 awards)

1st Replicate	15	52	47	60	55	17	5	45	42	59	30	4
2nd Replicate	48	1	34	38	35	16	37	8	13	19	50	9
3rd Replicate	18	20	32	11	57	53	12	29	31	43	28	49

Stratum 3 (46 awards)

1st Replicate	26	15	3	35	27	37	22	7	41	39	45	36
2nd Replicate	31	1	30	19	9	32	16	44	34	24	23	12
3rd Replicate	20	29	17	10	21	43	5	33	42	4	13	18

Stratum 4 (51 awards)

1st Replicate	33	44	22	40	50	23	21	37	4	2	9	42
2nd Replicate	51	5	14	16	8	49	12	43	19	41	24	38
3rd Replicate	26	32	35	1	6	15	29	11	27	46	34	45

Stratum 5 (48 awards)

1st Replicate	2	14	37	16	31	3	1	17	26	6	33	55
2nd Replicate	23	22	7	27	44	9	29	43	28	32	24	19
3rd Replicate	25	46	45	21	4	39	36	41	47	8	48	40

Stratum 6 (63 awards)

1st Replicate	33	16	5	31	12	46	24	53	19	38	28	60
2nd Replicate	61	8	3	42	32	41	37	50	30	35	55	43
3rd Replicate	36	29	20	63	59	4	47	27	17	40	54	21

Stratum 7 (10 awards)

Only Replicate	8	3	7	1	5	6	9	10	4	2

Stratum 8 (66 awards)

1st Replicate	54	64	44	47	13	21	15	26	11	33	41	6
2nd Replicate	25	1	23	14	40	37	46	60	32	34	28	57
3rd Replicate	50	48	62	55	39	19	63	16	42	66	36	5

Stratum 9 (46 awards)

1st Replicate	31	6	44	34	35	12	21	25	47	29	43	3
	22	20	2	8	10	42	26	14	1	32	11	19
2nd Replicate	4	24	27	33	17	38	45	46	9	13	18	15
	39	30	23	41	40	7	36	37	16	28	5	

Stratum 10 (1 award)

Only Replicate	0

AWARD CHARACTERISTICS BY STRATA— FIRST REPLICATION

Stratum 1—Grants 1969–1971 (0–$100,000): 1st Replicate

Award Identi- fication Number	Year	Amount (thousands of dollars)	Award Type*
010	69	45	1
024	69	38	1
042	69	03	1
045	69	50	1
053	69	05	1
060	69	06	1
061	69	05	1
083	69	06	1
089	69	06	1
099	69	05	1
015	70	23	1
059	70	39	1
065–14	70	10	1
065–15	70	10	1
065–18	70	09	1
084	70	56	1
024	71	06	1
025	71	04	1
049	71	46	1
055	71	09	1
074	71	05	1
082	71	36	1
115	71	09	1
123	71	01	1

*Type: 1, grant; 2, contract; 3, interagency agreement; 4, technical assistance award; 5, purchase order; 6, supplement.

Stratum 2—Grants 1969–1971 ($101,000–$500,000): 1st Replicate

Award Identi- fication Number	Year	Amount (thousands of dollars)	Award Type
009	69	102	1
031	69	102	1
023	70	313	1
027	70	121	1
078	70	200	1
028	71	121	1
050	71	298	1
078	71	153	1
087	71	195	1
122	71	110	1
151	71	109	1
160	71	123	1

Stratum 3—Grants 1972–1974 (0–$100,000): 1st Replicate

Award Identi- fication Number	Year	Amount (thousands of dollars)	Award Type
014	72	88	1
023	72	60	1
009	73	61	1
041	73	56	1
009	74	19	1
011	74	15	1
029	74	38	1
030	74	76	1
031	74	35	1
033	74	23	1
036	74	75	1
047	74	49	1

Stratum 4—Grants 1972–1974 ($101,000–$500,000): 1st Replicate

Award Identi- fication Number	Year	Amount (thousands of dollars)	Award Type
004	72	350	1
008	72	278	1
020	72	104	1
015	73	367	1
018	73	233	1
022	73	428	1
015	74	121	1
023	74	179	1
041	74	111	1
043	74	266	1
046	74	200	1
054	74	348	1

Stratum 5—Grants 1975 (0–$100,000): 1st Replicate

Award Identi- fication Number	Year	Amount (thousands of dollars)	Award Type
001	75	100	1
005	75	086	1
009	75	041	1
025	75	073	1
029	75	073	1
045	75	026	1
048	75	033	1
049	75	012	1
061	75	013	1
071	75	086	1
076	75	099	1
092	75	057	1

Stratum 6—Grants 1975 ($101,000–$500,000): 1st Replicate

Award Identi- fication Number	Year	Amount (thousands of dollars)	Award Type
007	75	395	1
019	75	187	1
023	75	254	1
031	75	147	1
042	75	164	1
060	75	336	1
069	75	241	1
073	75	252	1
080	75	368	1
096	75	249	1
105	75	109	1
118	75	197	1

Stratum 7—Grants 1969–1975 ($501,000+): 1st Replicate

Award Identi- fication Number	Year	Amount (thousands of dollars)	Award Type
019	73	0652	1
037	73	0506	1
047	73	0531	1
010	75	0791	1
011	75	0542	1
047	75	1198	1
095	75	0593	1
123	75	0600	1
127	75	0600	1
130	75	0600	1

Stratum 8—Other 1969–1975 (0–$100,000): 1st Replicate

Award Identi-fication Number	Year	Amount (thousands of dollars)	Award Type
001	71	15	3
027	71	03	3
042	71	89	3
051	71	05	3
102	71	32	3
133	71	70	3
006	72	03	5
007	73	37	3
100	73	37	4
106	73	39	4
106	74	52	4
015	75	49	2

Stratum 9—Other 1969–1975 ($101,000+): 1st Replicate

Award Identi-fication Number	Year	Amount (thousands of dollars)	Award Type
034	70	0750	3
005	71	0198	3
037	71	0400	3
001	72	1309	3
025	72	2000	3
027	72	1850	3
001	73	2147	3
011	73	0116	2
039	73	0136	3
013	74	0300	2
014	74	0800	2
016	74	0309	2
022	74	1959	2
012	74	0200	3
014	74	0325	3
111	74	0147	4
119	75	0340	4
001	75	0436	6
006	75	0195	2
024	75	0300	2
005	75	0582	3
014	75	0500	2
0361	75	0235	3
0362	75	0268	2

Stratum 10—Reassigned Cases: 1st Replicate

Award Identi-fication Number	Year	Amount (thousands of dollars)	Award Type
026	75	283	1

APPENDIX C2. List of Projects Drawn in the Sample

69–NI–99–009 (Standards) *Study of the Police Vehicle*
Grantee: Wayne State University
Award: $102,148
Investigator: H. D. Ludwig

10 (Standards) *Longitudinal Study of Psychological Test Predictors and Assessment of Patrolman Field Performance*
Grantee: Chicago Police Department
Award: $44,936
Investigator: J. Furcon

24 (Research) *Physical Environment and Urban Street Behavior*
Grantee: City University of New York
Award: $37,746
Investigator: B. P. Spring

31 (Innovation) *Model Community Corrections Program—Phase I*
Grantee: Institute for the Study of Crime & Delinquency
Award: $101,914
Investigator: R. Montilla

42 (Training) *Adoption of Scotland Yard's Mirro Electrophoresis*
Grantee: City University of New York
Award: $2,780
Investigator: A. Joseph

45 (Technical Asst.) *Conference on Computer Applications in Law Enforcement & Police Response Time*
Grantee: Franklin Institute Research Laboratory
Award: $50,000
Investigator: H. Koppel

53 (Dissemination) *Identification of Specific Factors in Dried Blood*
Grantee: Pittsburgh-Allegheny County Crime Laboratory
Award: $5,000
Investigator: C. A. McLinemoy

60 (Evaluation) *The Impact of Community Corrections Centers Upon a State Correctional System*
Grantee: Bowling Green State University
Award: $6,000
Investigator: A. C. Schnur

61 (Evaluation) *Proposal for a Retrospective Assessment of SATE*
Grantee: Scientific Analysis Corporation
Award: $5,000
Investigator: D. Miller

83 (Data Collection) *Proposed Study Concerning Juvenile Delinquency and Youth Court Reform*
Grantee: Mary Holmes Junior College
Award: $5,845
Investigators: B. Joyner and J. Maxey

89 (Research) *Research for the Endorsement of Correctional Endeavors*
Grantee: University of Virginia
Award: $6,300
Investigator: P. Low

99 (Software) *Operation Challenge—A Program for Practice Teaching by Senior Education Students*
Grantee: State of Arkansas Department of Corrections
Award: $5,370
Investigator: C. Honchin

70–NI–99–015 (Research) *Project for Security Design in Urban Residential Areas*
Grantee: Columbia University
Award: $22,960
Investigator: Oscar Newman

23 (Demonstration) *Santa Clara Criminal Justice Pilot Program*
Grantee: Institute for the Study of Crime & Delinquency
Award: $312,481
Investigator: R. Cushman

27 (Data Collection) *Study of Delinquency & Criminal Careers*
Grantee: Temple University
Award: $122,578
Investigator: M. Lalli

34–IA (Hardware Development) *Police Transceiver Development*
Grantee: U.S. Air Force Electronics Systems Division
Award: $750,000
Investigator: P. Watts

59 (Training) *The Examination and Typing of Bloodstains in the Crime Laboratory*
Grantee: John Jay College
Award: $39,057
Investigator: A. Joseph

65–14 (Research) *The Control of Shoplifting*
Grantee: University of Utah: Psychology Department
Award: $10,000
Investigator: D. Gelfand

65–15 (Research) *Human Memory and the Identification Process*
Grantee: The Research Foundation: SUNY, Albany
Award: $9,798
Investigator: K. H. Laughery

65–18 (Research) *Responses to Police Officers in Uniform*
Grantee: Stetson University: Psychology Department
Award: $9,392
Investigator: R. E. Wiley

78 (Evaluation) *Systems Study in Court Delay*
Grantee: University of Notre Dame
Award: $191,917
Investigator: L. G. Foschio

84 (Evaluation) *A Study of the Feasibility of Developing New Effectiveness Measures for Organized Crime Control Efforts*

Grantee: International Research & Technology Corporation
Award: $55,623
Investigator: D. H. Overly

71–NI–99–001–IA (Missing) *Heroin Detection Feasibility Study*
Grantee: U.S. Army Land Warfare Laboratory
Award: $15,000
Investigator: M. Cutler

05–IA (Data Collection) *Pilot Cities Victimization Survey*
Grantee: Bureau of the Census
Award: $198,000
Investigator: Richard W. Dodge

22 (Missing) *Educational Allowance*
Grantee: Brandeis University
Award: $3,500
Investigator: Unknown

24 (Dissemination) *Workshop on Forensic Applications of the Electron Microscope*
Grantee: Illinois Institute of Technology
Award: $5,726
Investigator: O. Johari

27–IA (Missing) *Latent Indented Reading–Writing Instrument*
Grantee: National Aeronautics and Space Administration
Award: $3,000
Investigator: R. J. Phillips

37–IA (Standards) *Law Enforcement Standards Laboratory*
Grantee: National Bureau of Standards
Award: $400,000

71–NI–99–042–IA (Evaluation) *A Study of Court Reporting Systems*
Grantee: National Bureau of Standards
Award: $88,623
Investigator: R. Penn

49 (Software) *Court Executive Training Program Design*
Grantee: University of Denver
Award: $46,177
Investigator: E. C. Friesen

50 (Dissemination) *Crime and Justice in Metropolitan Albuquerque: A Report of the Pilot Cities*
Grantee: Institute for Social Research & Development
Award: $297,580
Investigator: J. M. Campbell

51–IA (Feasibility) *Explosives Detecting Dogs*
Grantee: U.S. Army
Award: $5,000
Investigator: M. Cutter

55 (Evaluation) *Evaluative Research of a Community Based Probation Program*
Grantee: University of Nebraska
Award: $8,676
Investigator: D. Levine

74 (Dissemination) *Conference on Prison Homosexuality*

Grantee: Pennsylvania Prison Society
Award: $4,642
Investigator: G. R. Bacon

78 (Evaluation) *Research of Voice Identification*
Grantee: Michigan State Police Department
Award: $152,513
Investigator: W. Van Stratt

82 (Fellowship) *Educational Allowances*
Grantee: Graduate Research Fellowships
Award: $35,710
Investigator: Unknown

87 (Evaluation) *Evaluation of Community Based Correction*
Grantee: Pacific Northwest Laboratories: Batelle
Award: $194,544
Investigator: M. Matthews

102–IA (Evaluation) *Test and Evaluation of Hydronautics Explosive Vapor Detection System*
Grantee: U.S. Army
Award: $32,000
Investigator: M. Cutler

115 (Research) *Using Correctional Officers in Planned Change*
Grantee: School of Criminal Justice, SUNY, Albany
Award: $8,937
Investigator: D. Duffee

122 (Research) *Analysis of the Los Angeles District Attorney's Office*
Grantee: RAND
Award: $109,575
Investigator: P. W. Greenwood

123 (Missing) *Graduate Research Fellowship*
Grantee: O.V. Aiken
Award: $934
Investigator: O.V. Aiken

133–IA (Dissemination) *Exploratory Study of the Feasibility of Video-Taping*
Grantee: National Bureau of Standards
Award: $70,468
Investigator: R. Penn

151 (Research) *The Epidemiology of Biological Dysfunction and Violent Behavior*
Grantee: Neuro Research Foundation
Award: $108,931
Investigator: F. R. Ervin

160 (Research) *Study of Delinquency and Criminal Careers*
Grantee: Temple University
Award: $122,578
Investigator: M. Lalli

72–NI–99–001–IA (Standards) *Law Enforcement Standards Laboratory*
Grantee: National Bureau of Standards
Award: $1,309,000
Investigator: J. Diamond

04 (Demonstration) *Omaha-Douglas County Metropolitan Criminal Justice Center Program*
Grantee: University of Nebraska
Award: $349,758
Investigator: G. L. Kuchel

06–PO (Data Collection) *Behavior Modification and Corrections: Current Status*
Grantee: Institute for Applied Behavior Research
Award: $2,500
Investigator: J. Costello

08 (Research) *Evaluation of the Effects of Methadone Treatment on Crime and Criminal Addicts*
Grantee: Vera Institute of Justice
Award: $277,559
Investigator: M. Brown

14 (Evaluation) *National Assessment of Juvenile Corrections*
Grantee: University of Michigan
Award: $87,779
Investigators: R. Vinter and R. Sarri

20 (Research) *Study to Determine the Impact of Street Lighting on Crime*
Grantee: Kansas City Public Works Department
Award: $103,555
Investigator: F. A. Bond

23 (Research) *Forensic Epidemiology (Medical Epidemiology of Criminals)*
Grantee: Neuro Research Foundation
Award: $25,000
Investigator: F. Ervin

25–IA (Technical Asst.) *National Impact Program Evaluation*
Grantee: U.S. Air Force Electronics Systems Division
Award: $2,000,000
Investigator: L. Holmes

27–IA (Hardware Development) *Law Enforcement Development Group*
Grantee: Air Force and Aerospace Corporation
Award: $1,850,000
Investigator: B. Henshall

73–NI–99–001–IA (Standards) *Law Enforcement Standards Laboratory*
Grantee: National Bureau of Standards
Award: $2,146,534
Investigator: J. Diamond

07–IA (Hardware Development) *Quantitative Model of the Heroin Addiction Problem*
Grantee: Office of Science and Technology
Award: $36,500
Investigator: C. Whitehead

09 (Research) *Study of Delinquency and Criminal Careers*
Grantee: Temple University
Award: $61,416

Investigator: Michael Lalli

11–C (Data Collection) *National Narcotics Intelligence Requirements and Recommendations*
Grantee: Institute for Defense Analyses
Award: $115,991
Investigator: A. Boysen

15 (Demonstration) *Demonstration on the Reduction of Pre-Trial Delay*
Grantee: Case Western Reserve University Law School
Award: $366,637
Investigator: L. R. Kate

18 (Software) *Psychiatric Standards for Police Selection*
Grantee: Personnel Decisions Inc.
Award: $233,013
Investigator: R. W. Heckman

19 (Evaluation) *National Assessment of Juvenile Corrections*
Grantee: University of Michigan
Award: $652,471
Investigator: R. D. Vinter

22 (Evaluation) *Evaluation of the Effects of Methadone Treatment on Crime and Criminal Addicts*
Grantee: Vera Institute of Justice
Award: $427,933
Investigator: M. Brown

37 (Data Collection) *An Analysis of the Criminal Investigation Process*
Grantee: RAND
Award: $505,737
Investigator: P. W. Greenwood

39–IA (Hardware Development) *Strain Sensitive Cable Sensor Test*
Grantee: U.S. Army Material Command
Award: $136,000
Investigator: R. D. Green

41 (Dissemination) *Uniform Rules of Criminal Procedure*
Grantee: National Conference of Commissioners on Uniform State Laws
Award: $56,090
Investigator: F. Kirwin

47 (Research) *Response Time Analysis*
Grantee: Kansas City Police Department
Award: $530,656
Investigator: C. Key

73–TA–99–1000 (Dissemination) *Police Crime Analysis Units and Procedures: Prescriptive Package*
Grantee: California Crime Technological Foundation
Award: $36,500
Investigator: G. A. Buck

06 (Dissemination) *A Manual for Robbery Control Projects*
Grantee: John Jay College
Award: $39,172

Investigator: R. Ward

74–TA–99–009 (Evaluation) *Evaluation of the LEAA Courts Improvement Program*
Grantee: RAND
Award: $19,006
Investigators: P. W. Greenwood, S. Wildhorn

11 (Research) *Analysis of Classification of Young Adult Offenders*
Grantee: National Council on Crime and Delinquency
Award: $14,878
Investigator: E. A. Wenk

15 (Evaluation) *Demonstration Project for Closed Circuit Television Case Screening*
Grantee: Philadelphia District Attorney's Office
Award: $121,072
Investigator: J. Foulkes

23 (Research) *A Man Computer System for the Solution of the Mug File Problem*
Grantee: University of Houston
Award: $179,077
Investigator: B. T. Rhoades, Jr.

29 (Research) *Police Work: A Comparative Analysis of Drug Law Enforcement*
Grantee: Peter K. Manning
Award: $38,091
Investigator: Visiting Fellow

30 (Software) *History and Analysis of Legal and Administrative Policy Towards Gambling*
Grantee: Cornell University
Award: $75,805
Investigator: H. P. Baden

31 (Dissemination) *A Study of Factors Associated with Impact in Criminal Justice Evaluations*
Grantee: Stuart N. Adams
Award: $35,422
Investigator: Visiting Fellow

33 (Fellowship) *A Study of Detective Work and Procedure*
Grantee: Richard F. Sparks
Award: $23,388
Investigator: Visiting Fellow

36 (Evaluation) *Rank Change in the Metropolitan Police Department of Washington, D.C.*
Grantee: Bureau of Social Science Research
Award: $74,995

41 (Research) *Characterization and Individualization of Semen*
Grantee: University of California—Berkeley
Award: $111,110
Investigator: G. Sensabaugh

43 (Standards) *Juvenile Justice Standards Project*
Grantee: Institute of Judicial Administration
Award: $266,000
Investigator: P. A. Nejelski

47 (Research) *Youth Gang Violence*
Grantee: Harvard University Law School
Award: $48,890
Investigator: W. B. Miller

54 (Software) *The Feasibility of Guidelines for Sentencing*
Grantee: Criminal Justice Research Center Inc.
Award: $348,302
Investigator: L. T. Wilkens

J–LEAA–013–74 (Innovation) *Des Moines Community Based Exemplary Project*
Grantee: Urban and Rural Systems Associates
Award: $300,000
Investigator: N. Day

J–LEAA–016–74 (Evaluation) *National Evaluation of LEAA's Pilot Cities*
Grantee: American Institutes for Research
Award: $309,104
Investigator: R. Krug

J–LEAA–022–74 (Software) *Crime Prevention through Environmental Design*
Grantee: Westinghouse Electric Company
Award: $1,958,867
Investigator: R. Carlston

LEAA–J–IAA–012 (Hardware Development) *Feasibility Investigation and Test of Coded Taggart Materials for the Identification of Explosives*
Grantee: Atomic Energy Commission
Award: $200,000
Investigator: D. Dorn

J–LEAA–014–74 (Dissemination) *Citizen Dispute Settlement Exemplary Project*
Grantee: Abt Associates
Award: $799,506
Investigator: J. Mullen

LEAA–J–IAA–014–2 (Hardware Development) *Test and Evaluation of Less Lethal Weapons, Materials and Techniques*
Grantee: U.S. Army
Award: $325,000
Investigator: D. O. Enger

74–TA–99–1006 (Miscellaneous) *Police Family Crisis Intervention/Demonstration*
Grantee: Criminal Justice Associates, Inc.
Award: $51,590
Investigator: M. Bard

11 (Dissemination) *A Quality Control Model for Facilitating the Transfer of Technology*
Grantee: Human Resources Research Organization
Award: $146,782
Investigator: H. Wagner

75–TA–99–001 (Research) *Validity and Reliability of Detection of Deception*
Grantee: University of Utah
Award: $99,878
Investigator: D. Raskin

05 (Research) *Analysis of Deterrence for Criminal Justice Planning*
Grantee: Carnegie-Mellon University
Award: $85,811
Investigator: A. Blumstein

07 (Standards) *A National Project to Develop a Police Performance Measurement System*
Grantee: American Justice Institute
Award: $394,523
Investigator: J. Needle

09 (Evaluation) *Evaluation of Criminal Justice Planning Institute*
Grantee: American Justice Institute
Award: $40,661
Investigator: G. Taylor

10 (Evaluation) *National Assessment of Juvenile Corrections*
Grantee: University of Michigan
Award: $791,057
Investigators: R. Vinter, R. Sarri

11 (Evaluation) *Individualization and Identification of Forensically Important Physiological Fluids*
Grantee: RAND
Award: $150,077
Investigator: L. Holiday

19 (Data Collection) *In-Depth Analysis of National Defender Survey*
Grantee: National Legal Aid and Defender Association
Award: $186,721
Investigator: N. Goldberg

23 (Software) *Recruitment and Retention of Minority Correctional Employees*
Grantee: Institute for Urban Affairs and Research
Award: $254,410
Investigator: L. Brown

25 (Research) *Analysis of LEAA Victimization Surveys*
Grantee: Urban Institute
Award: $72,684
Investigator: B. Bolden

26 (Data Collection) *Residential Neighborhood Crime Control*
Grantee: Hartford Institute of Criminal and Social Justice
Award: $283,122
Investigator: B. Hollander

29 (Evaluation) *Evaluation Project: Massachusetts Community Assistant Parole Program*
Grantee: Massachusetts Parole Board
Award: $73,481
Investigator: N. Kurtz

31 (Research) *Impact of the Legal Process and Formal Sanctions on Juvenile Delinquents*
Grantee: College of William and Mary

Award: $146,710
Investigator: A. Fitch

42 (Research) *The War on Crime in the District of Columbia: 1955–75*
Grantee: American University
Award: $163,820
Investigator: J. Wilson

45 (Research) *A Study of the Detective Role in a Metropolitan Police System*
Grantee: College of William and Mary
Award: $25,988
Investigator: A. Guenther

47 (Dissemination) *Criminal Justice Symposium Series*
Grantee: Community Television of Southern California
Award: $1,197,900
Investigator: J. Witherspoon

48 (Dissemination) *Evaluation Management Workshop*
Grantee: National Conference of State Criminal Justice Planning Administrators
Award: $33,000
Investigator: H. Weisman

49 (Fellowship) *Graduate Research Fellowships*
Grantee: Center for Criminal Justice
Award: $12,000
Investigator: G. Shuman

60 (Evaluation) *Proposal for Assistance in Developing Appropriate SPA and LEAA Evaluation Systems*
Grantee: Urban Institute
Award: $336,036
Investigator: J. Wholey

61 (Dissemination) *Use of Paralegals in Defenders' Offices and in Prison Legal Aid Programs*
Grantee: Blackstone Institute
Award: $13,000
Investigator: J. Stein

69 (Data Collection) *Comparative Assessment of Alternative Policy Options in Dispute Resolution*
Grantee: University of Southern California
Award: $269,181
Investigator: E. Johnson

71 (Evaluation) *Phase I Evaluation of Pre-Trial Release Programs*
Grantee: National Center for State Courts
Award: $86,209
Investigator: B. Mahoney

73 (Research) *Evaluation of the Effects of Methadone Treatment on Crime and Criminal Addicts*
Grantee: Vera Institute
Award: $252,303
Investigator: L. Friedman

76 (Evaluation) *Early Warning Robbery Reduction Projects—Phase I*
Grantee: MITRE Corporation
Award: $99,000
Investigator: W. Eliot

80 (Evaluation) *Patrol Experimentation and Evaluation*
Grantee: Wilmington Bureau of Police
Award: $367,773
Investigator: N. Valiante

92 (Software) *Development of an Evaluation Plan for the Status Offender Program*
Grantee: Social Science Research Institute
Award: $60,892
Investigator: S. Kobrin

95 (Research) *RAP-RAND: Studies on the Habitual Criminal Offender*
Grantee: RAND
Award: $592,830
Investigator: P. Greenwood

96 (Software) *Model Evaluation Program*
Grantee: Massachusetts Committee on Criminal Justice
Award: $248,985
Investigator: R. Cole

105 (Evaluation) *Citizen Patrol Evaluation—Phase I*
Grantee: RAND
Award: $108,980
Investigator: R. Yin

118 (Research) *Study of Subcontracting of Correctional Treatment Services*
Grantee: University of Hawaii
Award: $196,631
Investigator: G. Kassebaum

119 (Miscellaneous) *National Clearinghouse for the Coordination and Evaluation of the Career Criminal Program*
Grantee: National Legal Data Center
Award: $339,545
Investigator: P. Cohen

123 (Research) *RAP-Hoover: Econometric Studies of the Criminal Justice System*
Grantee: Hoover Institution
Award: $666,666
Investigator: R. Burress

127 (Miscellaneous) *Program in Criminal Justice: Research Agreement Program*
Grantee: Yale University Law School
Award: $600,000
Investigator: S. Wheeler

130 (Miscellaneous) *Community Based Responses to Criminal Justice Needs: Research Agreement Program*
Grantee: Northwestern University

	Award: $600,000 Investigator: L. Masotti
75–CD–99–001	(Software) *Howard University Educational Development Project* Grantee: Howard University Award: $563,598 Investigator: L. Brown
J–LEAA–06–75	(Innovation) *Research of the Entire Jury Management Area and Development of Model Procedures for Jury Operations* Grantee: Bird Engineering Associates Award: $195,000 Investigator: G. Munsterman
J–LEAA–015–75	(Research) *Creation of a Research Design to Study Illegal Aliens in the U.S.* Grantee: Linton, Mields, and Coston, Inc. Award: $48,598 Investigator: D. North
J–LEAA–024–75	(Technical Asst.) *NILECJ Technical Assistance in Criminal Justice* Grantee: F.B.I. Award: $20,000 Investigator: W. Mooney
LEAA–J–IAA–005–4	(Hardware Development) *Lightweight Body Armor* Grantee: U.S. Army Award: $582,500 Investigator: N. Montanevelli
J–LEAA–014–74	(Dissemination) *Exemplary Projects Program* Grantee: Abt Associates Award: $738,617 Investigator: J. Mullen
LEAA–J–IAA–036–2	(Technical Asst.) *Equipment Systems Improvement Program* Grantee: U.S. Air Force Award: $396,000 Investigator: W. Holden
J–LEAA–008–76	(Hardware Development) *Evaluate the Utility of Dial-up Communications in the Criminal Justice System* Grantee: MITRE Corporation Award: $267,624 Investigator:
72–NI–99–026–IA	(Technical Asst.) *Equipment Systems Improvement Program* Grantee: MITRE Corporation Award: $1,000,000 Investigator: W. Hulden
73–NI–99–024–C	(Hardware Development) *Law Enforcement Development Group* Grantee: Aerospace Corporation Award: $1,850,000 Investigator: B. Henshall
J–LEAA–035–74	(Data Collection) *A Nationwide Survey of Law Enforcement and Criminal Justice Personnel Needs and Resources*

	Grantee: National Planning Association Award: $546,000 Investigator: H. Wool
LEAA–J–IAA–005–4	(Hardware Development) *Lightweight Body Armor* Grantee: U.S. Army Award: $500,000 Investigator: N. Montanevelli
LEAA–J–IAA–021–3	(Standards) *Law Enforcement Standards Laboratory* Grantee: National Bureau of Standards Award: $1,813,000 Investigator: J. Diamond
J–LEAA–033–75	(Research) *Study of the Economic and Rehabilitative Aspects of Prison Industries* Grantee: Econ., Inc. Award: $599,993 Investigator: R. Christie
J–LEAA–010–75	(Dissemination) *Operation, Maintenance and Refinement of the National Criminal Justice Reference Service* Grantee: General Electric Award: $3,481,000 Investigator: J. Cady

APPENDIX C3. Instruments Used for Evaluation of Sample

The two evaluation instruments in this appendix, representing research and dissemination activities, are presented here as examples of the 13 instruments used by the Committee to assess the sample of Institute-funded projects. Each of the 13 instruments had questions common to all categories as well as specific questions that addressed issues relevant only to particular categories. Several questions were modeled on evaluation questions developed and refined by Minnesota Systems Research, Inc.

The two examples show the kinds of issues that the Committee felt should be part of each project's file record: conceptualization, the adequacy of the research design, the overall usefulness of the project, the project's contribution to knowledge-building, and lastly, the appropriateness of the funding level. These issues formed the basis of the analysis in Chapter 4 of the report.

EVALUATION CRITERIA: RESEARCH PROJECTS

1. Evaluator Name: ____________
2. Date Evaluated: ____________
3. Project $ ____________
4. Project ID# ____________
5. Evaluator ID# ____________

6. What kinds of knowledge building are: (A) claimed by the grantee as goals of this project, and (B) in your judgment likely to result or have resulted from completion of this project? (Check all that apply in columns (A) and (B) below.)

	A	B
Administrative knowledge (e.g., ways to set up a program, deliver services, staffing needs, costs, etc.)	☐	☐
Description of characteristics of clients, population served, program, etc.	☐	☐
Assessment of the overall effectiveness of a program	☐	☐
Research exploring the relationship between measured variables	☐	☐
Tests of specific hypotheses or specific ideas	☐	☐
New substantive knowledge	☐	☐
New methodological knowledge	☐	☐
New knowledge of local conditions which might affect similar demonstration/research projects	☐	☐
Generation of new hypotheses	☐	☐
Other (specify)	☐	☐

7. Does (will) the project involve significant collection of data? If yes, answer questions 8, 9, 10, 11, 12. If no, go on to question #13.
   ☐ Yes ☐ No
8. Have the data been collected in a form which proved useful to the analysis process?
   ☐ Yes ☐ Unable to tell
   ☐ No
9. Are the data in forms that are readily usable by other researchers and scholars?
   ☐ 1. Clearly usable
   ☐ 2. Probably usable
   ☐ 3. Probably not usable
   ☐ 4. Clearly not usable
   ☐ 5. Unable to tell, or not applicable
10. Has the proposer dealt with known obstacles to validity or reliability of the data?
   ☐ 1. Shows little or no awareness
   ☐ 2. Deals with, but not effectively
   ☐ 3. Deals with many of the problems
   ☐ 4. Deals with most of the significant problems
   ☐ 5. Unable to tell, or not applicable
11. Is the collection process feasible?
   ☐ 1. Clearly feasible
   ☐ 2. Probably feasible
   ☐ 3. Probably not feasible
   ☐ 4. Clearly not feasible
   ☐ 5. Unable to tell, or not applicable
12. Is the data source selected appropriate for the issue under scrutiny?
13. Would you say that the research component of this project is incidental or central to the overall project?
   ☐ Incidental to project ☐ Central to project
14. Briefly characterize in a sentence or with key terms, the topics addressed in the project.

15. Could you characterize the perspective from which this issue is examined? (Check all that apply)

A. "Systemic Orientation"
- ☐ judges
- ☐ court administrators
- ☐ prosecutors
- ☐ defense attorneys
- ☐ probation/parole personnel
- ☐ police
- ☐ corrections
- ☐ unable to tell

B. "Service Orientation"
- ☐ functionaries within criminal justice system
- ☐ offenders
- ☐ victims
- ☐ the public

C. Other
- ☐ equity
- ☐ efficiency
- ☐ other
- ☐ inappropriate

Was that perspective appropriate?
- ☐ Yes
- ☐ No
- ☐ Unable to tell

16. Toward what type of audience are actual or anticipated findings directed? (Check all that apply)
- ☐ The funding agency staff
- ☐ Policy makers, legislators
- ☐ Administrators (of relevant information)
- ☐ Practitioners in this area
- ☐ Basic researchers, academic discipline, specialists, etc.
- ☐ Methodologists/technical specialists in instrumentation, computerization, statistics, etc.
- ☐ Other (specify)
- ☐ Unable to tell, insufficient information

17. The area(s) of major strength of this project are: (Check all that apply)
- ☐ Research Methods
- ☐ Theory
- ☐ Applied Impact
- ☐ Other (specify)
- ☐ No major strengths
- ☐ Evaluation

18. How would you describe the research aspect of this project generally? (Check all that apply)
- ☐ Natural experiment
- ☐ Lab experiment
- ☐ Field experiment
- ☐ Sample survey
- ☐ Case study
- ☐ Basic
- ☐ Applied
- ☐ Evaluation
- ☐ Exploratory
- ☐ Confirmatory (hypothesis testing, etc.)
- ☐ Synthesis or systematization of knowledge
- ☐ Theory-oriented
- ☐ Policy-oriented
- ☐ Cross-sectional
- ☐ Longitudinal
- ☐ Panel
- ☐ Ex post facto study
- ☐ Other (specify)

19. Considering acceptable methodology, given current constraints for research of this type, please give your rating of the Research component of this project on each of the selected characteristics listed below:

Conceptualization	Good	Accept-able	Poor	Not Applic-able	Unknown
1. Explanation of problem	☐	☐	☐	☐	☐
2. Operationalization of main concepts	☐	☐	☐	☐	☐
3. Explanation of research design details	☐	☐	☐	☐	☐
4. Fit of design to the problem	☐	☐	☐	☐	☐
5. Specification of model	☐	☐	☐	☐	☐
6. Discussion of germane literature	☐	☐	☐	☐	☐
7. Use of available prior knowledge	☐	☐	☐	☐	☐
8. Specification of hypotheses	☐	☐	☐	☐	☐
9. Discussion of assumptions	☐	☐	☐	☐	☐
10. Specification of unit(s) of analysis	☐	☐	☐	☐	☐
Research Design					
11. Appropriateness of unit of analysis	☐	☐	☐	☐	☐
12. Definition of population of interest	☐	☐	☐	☐	☐
13. Quantification of variables	☐	☐	☐	☐	☐
14. Pretest of procedures/ instruments	☐	☐	☐	☐	☐
15. Handling of validity issues	☐	☐	☐	☐	☐
16. Handling of reliability issues	☐	☐	☐	☐	☐
17. Use of records or existing data	☐	☐	☐	☐	☐
18. Use of multiple methods of research key topics	☐	☐	☐	☐	☐
Presentation of Findings					
19. Presentation of relevant data pro and con	☐	☐	☐	☐	☐
20. Statement of conditions under which findings are expected to hold	☐	☐	☐	☐	☐
21. Indication of policy implications of the study	☐	☐	☐	☐	☐
22. Discussion of how findings are to be utilized	☐	☐	☐	☐	☐
23. Justification of findings	☐	☐	☐	☐	☐
24. Tailoring to specific audience	☐	☐	☐	☐	☐

20. Does the research meet (hold promise for meeting) stated research objectives?
   - ☐ Yes, completely
   - ☐ Yes, to a reasonable extent given time and resource limit or study
   - ☐ Yes, some minor shortcomings (please specify)
   - ☐ No, some important major shortcomings (please specify)
   - ☐ Can't tell (briefly explain)

21. If there are important shortcomings, were they beyond the investigator(s) control?
    - ☐ No important shortcomings
    - ☐ Yes, primarily beyond investigator's control (please specify)
    - ☐ No, primarily within the investigator's control
    - ☐ Unable to tell

22. Are any of the factors listed below, in your judgment, likely to account for or "explain away" a significant part of the research findings in this project? (Check all that apply)

    A. Methodological

    1) techniques:
    - ☐ instrument decay
    - ☐ statistical regression toward the mean; subjects selected for their extremity on a criterion
    - ☐ bias due to selection and/or assignment of subjects; failure to match groups or randomly assign subjects
    - ☐ measurement problem (reliability and validity)
    - ☐ sampling design; non-representative or inadequate
    - ☐ obvious variables not measured or analyzed

    2) difficulties in objectively studying subjects:
    - ☐ prior testing of subjects
    - ☐ interaction of testing and treatment(s)
    - ☐ interaction of case selection and treatment(s)
    - ☐ multiple and confounding treatment effects
    - ☐ reactive arrangements; artificiality of experimental setting, subjects' awareness, etc.

    B. Historical/External
    - ☐ changing historic events
    - ☐ maturation of subjects; growth
    - ☐ mortality
    - ☐ differential loss of subjects from compared groups
    - ☐ interaction of case selection and maturation
    - ☐ chance

    C. Bad Implementation
    - ☐ sloppy data collection, analysis, etc.
    - ☐ failure to control likely contaminating variable(s)
    - ☐ post hoc explanations tailored to the analyzed data

    D. Others (specify)

    E. All relevant, competing explanations are reasonably handled

23. Considering the research project as a whole, how would you judge the "level of support"?

	Original Proposal	Funded Grant	Retrospective from Final Report
Not applicable	☐	☐	☐
Clearly inadequate	☐	☐	☐
Adequate, but strained	☐	☐	☐
Adequate, good fit	☐	☐	☐
Adequate, some slack	☐	☐	☐
Clearly unnecessary slack	☐	☐	☐
Can't tell	☐	☐	☐

24. Considering the research project as a whole, how would you judge the provision for expertise?

	Original Proposal	Funded Grant	Retrospective from Final Report
Not applicable	☐	☐	☐
Clearly inadequate	☐	☐	☐
Adequate, but strained	☐	☐	☐
Adequate, good fit	☐	☐	☐
Adequate, some slack	☐	☐	☐
Clearly unnecessary slack	☐	☐	☐
Can't tell	☐	☐	☐

25. Did the Institute generate opportunities for conscious reassessment, self-correction, stock-taking, getting outside suggestions, or careful readjustment of research goals and procedures during the inquiry?
    - ☐ Yes, major explicit opportunities
    - ☐ Yes, major implicit opportunities
    - ☐ Yes, minor explicit opportunities
    - ☐ Yes, minor implicit opportunities
    - ☐ No
    - ☐ Unable to tell

Any additional comments on Monitoring Process

26. On the whole how would you assess the adequacy of the project toward knowledge building?
    - ☐ Exemplary
    - ☐ Adequate
    - ☐ Minimal
    - ☐ Not adequate at all
27. On the whole, would you judge that the problem under scrutiny is, as a matter of practicality, one which is capable of solution?
    - ☐ Yes
    - ☐ No
    - ☐ Can't tell
28. Would you say that the project as it is or was being conducted is congruent with the intent of the funding?
    - ☐ Yes
    - ☐ No (please comment)
29. If project objectives changed from the original proposal, in your judgment were the changes appropriate?
    - ☐ No change in objectives
    - ☐ Appropriate changes were made (comment on reason)
    - ☐ Inappropriate changes were made (please explain)
30. If the decision were made to continue this project at approximately the same level of funding and under similar time constraints, would you recommend: (Check all that apply)
    - ☐ Expanding the current research component, increasing its share in the overall project
    - ☐ The complete re-design of the existing research component
    - ☐ Changes to correct; important methodological flaws

- ☐ An alternative methodology to that used
- ☐ Changes to improve general workmanship or procedures
- ☐ Basically no changes or only minor modifications
- ☐ Other (specify)

31. Please give other suggestions which might strengthen this research component: (optional)
32. Considering the current state of the research craft in areas and settings such as that addressed by this project, would you consider the research component to be overall:
    - ☐ Far better than average
    - ☐ Somewhat better than average
    - ☐ About average
    - ☐ Somewhat below average
    - ☐ Far below average
33. How familiar are you with the specific substantive issues and area(s) addressed by this research project?
    - ☐ Not at all familiar
    - ☐ Superficially familiar
    - ☐ Moderately familiar
    - ☐ Quite familiar
34. How familiar are you with the methodological techniques mentioned in this documentation?
    - ☐ Not at all familiar
    - ☐ Superficially familiar
    - ☐ Moderately familiar
    - ☐ Quite familiar
35. Did you have prior knowledge of the investigators involved in this project?
    - ☐ No
    - ☐ Yes, but only through literature
    - ☐ Yes, from personal contact
36. Did you have prior knowledge of the project before rating?
    - ☐ No
    - ☐ Yes
37. Considering the state of *knowledge* in the field, would you rate the theoretical or empirical contribution to be:
    - ☐ Far above average
    - ☐ Somewhat above average
    - ☐ Average
    - ☐ Somewhat below average
    - ☐ Far below average
38. Considering the *utility for others and its importance* with respect to social problems and priorities, would you rate the project as:
    - ☐ Far above average
    - ☐ Somewhat above average
    - ☐ Average
    - ☐ Somewhat below average
    - ☐ Far below average

Additional Questions:

1. In sum, if it were your decision to fund this project, would you have funded it?
   - ☐ 1. Yes
   - ☐ 2. Only with changes as specified
   - ☐ 3. No
2. Please record summary comments about the project in the space below:

EVALUATION CRITERIA: DISSEMINATION PROJECTS

1. Evaluator Name: ________________ 4. Project ID# ________________
2. Date Evaluated: ________________ 5. Evaluator ID# ________________
3. Project $ ________________
6. What are the goals of this project claimed by the grantee?
   - ☐ New administrative knowledge (e.g., ways to set up a program, deliver services, staffing needs, cross, etc.)
   - ☐ New substantive knowledge
   - ☐ New methodological knowledge
   - ☐ Description of characteristics of clients, population served, program, etc.
   - ☐ Assessment of the overall effectiveness of a program or method
   - ☐ New knowledge of local conditions which might affect demonstration/research projects
   - ☐ Generation of new ideas (as in an exploratory conference)
   - ☐ Other (specify)
7. Briefly characterize in a sentence or with key terms the topic(s) addressed in this project:
8. What was the mode of presentation?

☐ case study	☐ MIS
☐ model standard	☐ computer systems
☐ model statutes/codes	☐ discussion/"airing of subject"
☐ program guidelines	☐ curricula
☐ policy recommendations	☐ staffing recommendations
☐ performance measures	

   Was it appropriate?
   - ☐ Yes
   - ☐ No
   - ☐ Not applicable

   Comments

9. What was the medium?

☐ General Report	☐ Briefing
☐ Conference Report	☐ Seminar
☐ Book	☐ Reference Service; Clearinghouse
☐ Manual	☐ Laboratory
☐ Guide	☐ Media Techniques
☐ Conference	☐ Other

10. Is dissemination component incidental or central to overall project?
    - ☐ Central ☐ Incidental

11. Toward what type of audience are actual or anticipated findings directed? (Check all that apply)

A. Direct Audience

Criminal justice practitioners
- ☐ judges
- ☐ court administrators
- ☐ prosecutors
- ☐ defense attorneys
- ☐ police officers
- ☐ police administrators
- ☐ correctional institution staff
- ☐ other

Educators
- ☐ police academy
- ☐ high school
- ☐ college
- ☐ law school
- ☐ specialized (other)

General public
- ☐ citizens action groups
- ☐ citizen "understanding"
- ☐ other

Research community
- ☐ academic
- ☐ consulting firms
- ☐ other
- ☐ unable to tell

B. Indirect Audience

Criminal justice practitioners
- ☐ judges
- ☐ court administrators
- ☐ prosecutors
- ☐ defense attorneys
- ☐ police officers
- ☐ police administrators
- ☐ correctional institution staff
- ☐ other

Educators
- ☐ police academy
- ☐ high school
- ☐ college
- ☐ law school
- ☐ specialized (other)

General public
- ☐ citizens action groups
- ☐ citizen "understanding"
- ☐ other

Research community
- ☐ academic
- ☐ consulting firms
- ☐ other
- ☐ unable to tell

12. Was the medium employed effective for reaching the audience intended?
- ☐ 1. Clearly most effective
- ☐ 2. Effective, though other media may have been better
- ☐ 3. Probably not effective
- ☐ 4. Clearly inappropriate
- ☐ 5. Unable to tell, or not applicable

13. If yes on #12 (3, 4, or 5), what would have contributed to more effective dissemination?

14. Could you characterize the perspective in which this project is designed?

A. "Systemic Orientation"
- ☐ judges
- ☐ court administrators
- ☐ prosecutors
- ☐ defense attorneys
- ☐ probation/parole personnel
- ☐ police
- ☐ corrections
- ☐ unable to tell

B. "Service Orientation"
- ☐ functionaries within criminal justice system
- ☐ criminal justice system
- ☐ offenders
- ☐ victims
- ☐ the public

C. Change desired requires
- ☐ equipment
- ☐ techniques
- ☐ "understanding"
- ☐ more research
- ☐ more efficient allocation of resources

Was that perspective appropriate?

☐ Yes ☐ No ☐ Unable to tell

15. Was the dissemination activity based on previous NILECJ funding activity?
    - ☐ Yes
    - ☐ No
    - ☐ Unable to tell

    If yes, what project?

16. Was the dissemination activity based on any other research known by you or cited?
    - ☐ Yes
    - ☐ No
    - ☐ Unable to tell

    If yes, please describe and assess its adequacy as data source:

17. Judging the product as an example of its own type, would you rate its content as:
    - ☐ 1. Far above average
    - ☐ 2. Above average
    - ☐ 3. Average
    - ☐ 4. Below average
    - ☐ 5. Far below average
    - ☐ 6. Unable to tell, or not applicable

18. Considering the research project as a whole, how would you judge the "level of support"?

	Original Proposal	Funded Grant	Retrospective from Final Report
Not applicable	☐	☐	☐
Clearly inadequate	☐	☐	☐
Adequate, but strained	☐	☐	☐
Adequate, good fit	☐	☐	☐
Adequate, some slack	☐	☐	☐
Clearly unnecessary slack	☐	☐	☐
Can't tell	☐	☐	☐

19. Bearing in mind the state of the art of dissemination and judging the project as a whole, was it in your judgment:
    - ☐ 1. Far above average
    - ☐ 2. Above average
    - ☐ 3. Average
    - ☐ 4. Below average
    - ☐ 5. Far below average
    - ☐ 6. Unable to tell, or not applicable

20. Is there any evidence that in fact an effective transfer of technology took place?
    - ☐ 1. Yes, a significant transfer
    - ☐ 2. Some transfer
    - ☐ 3. Little transfer
    - ☐ 4. None
    - ☐ 5. Unable to tell, or not applicable
21. Considering the *utility for others and its importance* with respect to social problems and priorities, would you rate the project as:

22. Did the Institute generate opportunities for conscious reassessment, self-correction, stock-taking, getting outside suggestions, or careful readjustment of research goals and procedures during the inquiry?
    - ☐ Yes, major explicit opportunities
    - ☐ Yes, major implicit opportunities
    - ☐ Yes, minor explicit opportunities
    - ☐ Yes, minor implicit opportunities
    - ☐ No
    - ☐ Unable to tell

    Please add any additional comments on Monitoring Process:

23. How familiar are you with the specific substantive issues and area(s) addressed by this research project?
    - ☐ Not at all familiar
    - ☐ Superficially familiar
    - ☐ Moderately familiar
    - ☐ Quite familiar
24. How familiar are you with the methodological techniques mentioned in this documentation?
    - ☐ Not at all familiar
    - ☐ Superficially familiar
    - ☐ Moderately familiar
    - ☐ Quite familiar
25. Did you have prior knowledge of the investigators involved in this project?
    - ☐ No
    - ☐ Yes, but only through literature
    - ☐ Yes, from personal contact
26. Did you have prior knowledge of the project before rating?
    - ☐ No
    - ☐ Yes
27. Considering the research project as a whole, how would you judge the provision for expertise?

	Original Proposal	Funded Grant	Retrospective from Final Report
Not applicable	☐	☐	☐
Clearly inadequate	☐	☐	☐
Adequate, but strained	☐	☐	☐
Adequate, good fit	☐	☐	☐
Adequate, some slack	☐	☐	☐
Clearly unnecessary slack	☐	☐	☐
Can't tell	☐	☐	☐

Additional Questions:

1. In sum, if it were your decision to fund this project, would you have funded it?
   - ☐ 1. Yes
   - ☐ 2. Only with changes as specified
   - ☐ 3. No
2. Please record summary comments about the project in the space below:

APPENDIX C4. Sample Design for Rejects

As a complement to its analysis of a sample of Institute-funded projects, the Committee examined a sample of 137 applications for funding that were rejected by the Institute. Because these rejects are filed for the years 1972–75 according to their state of origin and the year in which they were submitted, the Committee constructed a sample design stratified by year and state. The tables on the following pages show this procedure. The frequency distribution shows how many rejected applications were received from each state for each year, and the cumulative frequency distribution shows the sum of all applications for each year. The sampling plan shows the individual rejects that were randomly drawn in the sample for every state and year. A total of 117 rejects were sampled in this manner.

In addition to the rejects drawn in this sample, there were two more small classes of rejects examined by the Committee. For 1971, a different filing method was used by NILECJ, and therefore the Committee randomly selected 10 of the 85 rejects for that year. Similarly, the Community Crime Prevention Division began its own filing system for rejects in 1975, and so 10 of the 43 rejected applications were sampled. The entire sample of rejected funding requests totaled 137.

FUNDING APPLICATIONS DISAPPROVED BY NILECJ: 1972–1975

	Frequency Distribution				Cumulative Frequency Distribution			
STATE	1972	1973	1974	1975	1972	1973	1974	1975
Alabama	1	0	3	3	1	0	1–3	1–3
Alaska	2	1	0	1	2–3	1	—	4
Arizona	3	0	6	5	4–6	—	4–9	5–9
Arkansas	0	0	0	0	—	—	—	—
California	40	41	48	22	7–46	2–42	10–57	10–31
Colorado	4	0	2	3	47–50	—	58–59	32–34
Connecticut	4	8	2	3	51–54	43–50	60–61	35–37
Delaware	0	0	1	1	—	—	62	38
D.C.	16	25	45	18	55–70	51–75	63–107	39–56

STATE	Frequency Distribution 1972	1973	1974	1975	Cumulative Frequency Distribution 1972	1973	1974	1975
Florida	14	5	17	7	71–84	76–80	108–124	57–63
Georgia	6	6	7	1	85–90	81–86	125–131	64
Hawaii	0	2	0	0	—	87–88	—	—
Idaho	0	0	0	0	—	—	—	—
Illinois	20	13	20	6	91–110	87–101	132–151	65–70
Indiana	2	0	3	4	111–112	—	152–154	71–74
Iowa	2	1	2	0	113–114	102	155–156	—
Kansas	1	0	1	0	115	—	157	—
Kentucky	2	0	8	4	116–117	—	158–165	75–78
Louisiana	2	2	2	1	118–119	103–104	166–167	79
Maine	0	1	2	2	—	105	168–169	80–81
Maryland	6	8	15	13	120–125	106–113	170–184	82–94
Massachusetts	16	12	16	16	126–141	114–125	185–200	95–110
Michigan	8	8	12	6	142–149	126–133	201–212	111–116
Minnesota	5	2	8	1	150–154	134–135	213–220	117
Mississippi	0	0	0	1	—	—	—	118
Missouri	13	7	8	3	155–167	136–142	221–228	119–121
Montana	1	0	2	0	168	—	229–230	—
Nebraska	1	2	1	3	169	143–144	231	122–124
Nevada	1	1	0	1	170	145	—	125
New Hampshire	2	1	0	0	171–172	146	—	—
New Jersey	9	2	7	11	173–181	147–148	232–238	126–136
New Mexico	0	2	1	0	—	149–150	239	—
New York	34	25	35	28	182–215	151–175	240–274	137–164
North Carolina	4	1	5	0	216–219	176	275–279	—
North Dakota	0	1	0	0	—	177	—	—
Ohio	8	6	5	8	220–227	178–183	280–284	165–172
Oklahoma	2	0	4	1	228–229	—	285–288	173
Oregon	5	5	2	3	230–234	184–188	289–290	174–176
Pennsylvania	13	9	15	13	235–247	189–197	291–305	177–189
Rhode Island	0	0	0	0	—	—	—	—
South Carolina	0	0	1	2	—	—	306	190–191
South Dakota	0	1	1	4	—	198	307	192–195
Tennessee	5	5	8	6	248–252	199–203	308–315	196–201
Texas	6	0	2	0	253–258	—	316–317	—
Utah	5	0	1	0	259–263	—	318	—
Vermont	0	0	1	0	—	—	319	—
Virginia	8	15	16	12	264–271	204–218	320–335	202–213
Washington	2	3	6	7	272–273	214–221	336–341	214–220
West Virginia	2	0	0	0	274–275	—	—	—
Wisconsin	2	2	3	3	276–277	222–223	342–344	221–223
Wyoming	0	0	0	0	—	—	—	—
Subtotal	277	223	344	223	X	X	X	X
Other Counties	0	1	4	3	—	224	345–348	224–226
TOTAL	277	224	348	226				

FUNDING APPLICATIONS DISAPPROVED BY NILECJ: 1972–1975 SAMPLING PLAN

State	1972	1973	1974	1975
Alabama				
Alaska				
Arizona				2
Arkansas				
California	18, 19, 20, 21, 22, 25, 29	5, 7, 9, 13, 18, 28	1, 27	8, 12, 19
Colorado				2
Connecticut				3
Delaware				
D.C.	13	8, 10, 21	13	12, 13, 18
Florida	10		4, 10	3
Georgia				
Hawaii		2		
Idaho				
Illinois	3, 9, 19, 20	2, 3, 10, 13	11	
Indiana				1, 3
Iowa	1		2	
Kansas				
Kentucky			3, 6	
Louisiana		2	1, 2	
Maine				
Maryland	1, 5, 6	3, 5	4, 11, 15	4, 11
Massachusetts	11, 13, 16	8, 9		3, 5, 16
Michigan		5	1, 4, 12	6
Minnesota			4	
Mississippi				
Missouri	1, 8	5, 7		1
Montana				
Nebraska			1	
Nevada				
New Hampshire				
New Jersey	7		2	11
New Mexico				
New York	1, 15, 20	11, 12, 14, 19	1, 7, 34	8, 19
North Carolina				
North Dakota				
Ohio				
Oklahoma				
Oregon		3		3
Pennsylvania	8		4, 11, 12	2, 6, 7
Rhode Island				
South Carolina				
South Dakota				
Tennessee	1			
Utah				
Vermont				
Virginia	6	7, 10, 13	12, 14	1
Washington				4
West Virginia				
Wisconsin			3	1
Wyoming				

EVALUATION CRITERIA—REJECTED APPLICATIONS

1. Evaluator Name — Date Evaluated
2. Originating State
3. Year
4. Name of Principal Investigator
5. Name of Prospective Grantee
6. Type of Grantee

(enter appropriate letter)

   a. Federal Government agency
   b. State Government agency
   c. City government agency
   d. Other government agency
   e. University
   f. Research institute
   g. Professional or trade assoc.
   h. Private research corporation
   i. Other private corporation
   j. Individual
   k. Can't tell
7. Type of Paper

(enter appropriate letter)

   a. Concept paper
   b. Proposal
8. Description of Document
   a. Number of pages
   b. Proposed budget
   c. Issue/problem (describe briefly)

   d. Relationship to academic disciplines:

   (enter appropriate number)

      1) Psychology
      2) Law or Political Science
      3) Economics, Statistics
      4) Sociology
      5) Engineering
      6) Computer Science
      7) Biology, Chemistry
      8) Social Ecology (e.g., Geography, Anthropology)
      9) Other
   e. Type of project:
      1) data collection
      2) evaluation
      3) research
      4) hardware development
      5) software development
      6) training
      7) innovation
      8) dissemination
      9) demonstrations

10) technical assistance
11) standards
12) feasibility
13) fellowship

9. Review process

(enter appropriate letter)

a. Internal
b. External

10. What NILECJ division reviewed it?
a. RAD or ROD
b. Advanced Technology
c. Community Crime Prevention
d. Police
e. Courts
f. Corrections
g. Juvenile Delinquency
h. Evaluation
i. Technology Transfer
j. Technical Assistance
k. Can't tell

11. Who should have logically handled it?
a. RAD or ROD
b. Advanced Technology
c. Community Crime Prevention
d. Police
e. Courts
f. Corrections
g. Juvenile Delinquency
h. Evaluation
i. Technology Transfer
j. Technology Assistance
k. Can't tell

12. What was Institute response to concept paper?

(enter appropriate letter)

a. Reviewed only by staff person who first received it
b. Reviewed beyond initial staff receiver
c. Request of re-work of concept paper
d. Combined with another concept paper or suggested integration with another effort
e. Proposal refused
f. Can't tell
g. Recommended application be presented to other government agency
h. Other (explain)

13. Summarize any correspondence or routing slips (internal to NILE or LEAA)

14. Was concept paper solicited?
Yes
No
Don't know

15. If yes, by what mechanism?

(enter appropriate letter)

a. Sole source contract
b. Informal solicitation
c. Limited solicitation
d. Open solicitation
e. RFP
f. Can't tell

16. Did the final letter of rejection specify any of the following reasons for not funding?

(enter appropriate letter)

a. General budgetary constraints
b. Not a high priority item
c. Unrelated to Program Plan
d. Duplication
e. Bad design/methodology
f. Too "experimental" for Institute priorities
g. Concept paper too sketchy
h. Budget already exhausted in particular program area of proposal
i. Budget cut in particular program area

17. Were there different reasons stated in internal documents, or in reviews for the rejection?
a. No
b. Unclear impact or possibilities for implementation
c. "Fuzzy" statement
d. Other (specify)

18. Given the information contained in this concept paper, would you have agreed with NILE's decision not to fund?
a. Yes, for the reasons given above
b. Yes, but for different reasons (specify)
c. No (please comment)

19. Summarize strengths and weaknesses of this concept paper as you perceive them.

NILECJ REJECTED APPLICATIONS—EVALUATION DISTRIBUTION DATA

States Distribution—Rejects (137 total)	No.	(%)
California	22	(16.1)
New York	16	(11.7)
District of Columbia, Maryland	11	(8.0)
Illinois	10	(7.3)
Pennsylvania	09	(6.6)
Virginia	08	(5.8)
Florida, Massachusetts, Michigan	05	(3.6)
New Jersey	04	(2.9)
Wisconsin	03	(2.2)

	No.	(%)
Indiana, Iowa, Kentucky, Louisiana, Missouri, Montana, Oregon, Tennessee, Washington	02	(1.5)
Arizona, Colorado, Connecticut, Georgia, Hawaii, Maine, Minnesota, Nevada, North Carolina, Texas	01	(0.7)
Year Distribution		
1971	11	(8.0)
1972	25	(18.2)
1973	27	(19.7)
1974	35	(25.5)
1975	39	(28.5)
Type of Grantee Distribution		
University	56	(40.9)
Private Research Corp.	25	(18.2)
City Government Agency	10	(7.3)
Professional Association	10	(7.3)
Individual	10	(7.3)
Other Private Corp.	7	(5.1)
Research Institute	6	(4.4)
State Government Agency	6	(4.4)
Other Government Agency	5	(3.6)
Unknown	2	(1.5)
Type of Paper Distribution		
Concept Paper	121	(88.3)
Proposal	16	(11.7)

Number of Pages Data

Average Number of Pages in a Concept Paper/Proposal 10.46

Budget Request Data

Average Budget Requested in a Concept Paper/Proposal $171,808

Relationship to Academic Discipline Distribution

	No.	(%)
Sociology	29	(21.2)
Engineering	15	(10.9)
Criminology	15	(10.9)
Economics/Statistics	13	(9.5)
Law/Political Science	10	(7.3)
Psychology	8	(5.8)
Biology/Chemistry	6	(4.4)
Social Ecology	4	(2.9)
Computer Science	3	(2.2)
Unknown/Not Reported	34	(24.8)

	No.	(%)
Project Type Distribution		
Research	49	(35.8)
Evaluation	22	(16.1)
Hardware	14	(10.2)
Software	10	(7.3)
Training	8	(5.8)
Demonstration	8	(5.8)
Data Collection	5	(3.6)
Innovation	4	(2.9)
Standards	2	(1.5)
Feasibility	2	(1.5)
Technical Assistance	0	
Unknown/Not Reported	7	(5.1)
Type of Review Distribution		
Internal Review Only	121	(88.3)
Both Internal and External Review	8	(5.8)
External Only	1	(0.7)
Unknown/Not Reported	7	(5.1)
Division Review Distribution		
RAD/ROD	62	(45.3)
Police	16	(11.7)
Community Crime Prevention	13	(9.5)
Courts	13	(9.5)
Corrections	9	(6.6)
Advanced Technology	6	(4.4)
Juvenile Delinquency	1	(0.7)
Unknown/Not Reported	8	(5.8)
Institute Response Distribution		
Reviewed beyond Initial Staff Receiver	75	(54.7)
Reviewed Only by Initial Staff Receiver	44	(32.1)
Suggested Integration with Another Concept Paper	2	(1.5)
Recommended Submission to Another Government Agency	2	(1.5)
Requested Re-work of Concept Paper	1	(0.7)
Unknown/Not Reported	10	(7.3)
Distribution of Concept Paper Solicitation Status/Solicitation Mechanism		
Not Solicited	136	(99.3)
Solicited (by limited solicitation)	1	(0.7)
Official Rejection Letter—Reasons for Not Funding Distribution		
Not a High-Priority Item	49	(35.8)
Duplication	32	(23.4)
Unrelated to Program Plan	27	(19.7)

	No.	(%)
General Budgetary Constraints	19	(13.9)
Budget Exhausted in Particular Program Area	7	(5.1)
Too "Experimental"	6	(4.4)
Concept Paper Too Sketchy	2	(1.5)
Unknown/Not Reported	21	(15.3)
Internal Reasons for Rejection Distribution		
No Other Reasons Than Those Officially Stated	85	(62.0)
Unclear Impact or Possibilities for Implementation	15	(10.9)
"Fuzzy" Statement	8	(5.8)
Other	4	(2.9)
Not Reported	5	(3.6)
Agreement with Rejection Decision Distribution		
Yes, Agree for Same Reasons as Institute	99	(72.3)
Yes, Agree but for Different Reasons Than Institute	21	(15.3)
No, Would Have Funded	8	(5.8)
Can't Tell/Not Reported	9	(6.6)

NILECJ REJECTED APPLICATIONS—TOPIC LIST (listed in chronological sequence)

001. gun control—informants
002. narcotics enforcement
003. witness recognition
004. police organizational development
005. terrorism research
006. industrial engineering and law enforcement
007. police dogs—develop a superbreed
008. criminal justice course for campus police
009. security windows
010. conference on role of criminal justice consultants
011. police organizational development
012. police attitudes
013. prison health care programs
014. develop techniques for municipal law enforcement agencies
015. fingerprint unit
016. women police
017. women police
018. marijuana research
019. change in the Minnesota Department of Corrections
020. drug treatment program
021. evaluations of communications projects
022. rehabilitation of public offenders
023. drug education in high schools
024. law enforcement services in the Maramec region of Missouri

025. evaluation of Montana community-based corrections program
026. attend a Criminal Justice course in London
027. gunfire detection system
028. evaluation of Sage Hill Camp program
029. policeman as a communicator
030. establish a central registry of pathology information
031. polygraph research
032. polygraph research
033. synthesize law enforcement literature
034. standards for listing police telephone numbers
035. explosives detecting dogs
036. "help" transmitter for police
037. electronic credit card identification
038. rape research
039. human cocaine tolerance
040. post-prison adjustment center
041. overview of contemporary law enforcement
042. community involvement in crime control
043. police roles and responses to alcoholism
044. municipal gun control
045. computer system for the criminal justice process
046. study of the prosecutor's office
047. polygraphs
048. youth service bureaus
049. vapor trace analyzer
050. aerosol jellyfish sting
051. fingerprint classification
052. polypeptides in hair
053. split sentencing
054. juvenile justice facilities
055. acoustic fingerprint transcription
056. establish a Cornell criminal justice institute
057. establish a central New York criminal justice resource center
058. survey of campus security
059. criminal investigation process in Kansas City
060. evaluation of laboratory support in the criminal justice system
061. personal space and human aggression
062. characterization of semen
063. helicopter bullet detection system
064. diversionary program for youth
065. classification as a total of punishment in penal institution
066. violence in Cuban exile communities
067. evaluation of Maywood Police Department
068. procedural reform in Iowa Courts
069. drug treatment for ex-offenders
070. police performance standards
071. a model for homicidal behavior
072. laboratory proficiency
073. role of mental services in deviancy
074. evaluation of Maryland indeterminate sentence concept

075. police accountability
076. public attitudes towards police
077. predicting crime in geographic areas
078. polygraph research
079. "life-options" model of crime
080. fingerprint methodology
081. politics of Orleans Parish court
082. court watching survey
083. behavior modification of police
084. employing ex-offenders
085. violence in Philadelphia prisons
086. relationships between inmates of two Philadelphia prisons
087. biorhythms for policemen
088. case studies in collective bargaining
089. jury management and utilization
090. plea bargaining in Wisconsin
091. behavior adaptation in metropolitan economies
092. net gun weapon
093. anti-crime programs and street crime
094. analysis of terminal recidivism
095. career development for law enforcement
096. consumer fraud
097. consumer fraud
098. citizen involvement in the criminal justice system
099. occupational deviance surveys
100. evaluation of regulations affecting consumers
101. a model of unequal incidence of the law
102. economics of bank robberies
103. police crime prevention bureaus
104. advocate counseling and education
105. criminal justice training for law students
106. case studies of collective bargaining
107. victim survey reporting
108. research on the theory of threats
109. forensic science effectiveness
110. the generalist investigator
111. burglary alarm system
112. study of victimless crimes
113. guidelines for juvenile court judges
114. educational community college center
115. women in criminal justice
116. standards for treating the mentally retarded in corrections
117. New England criminal justice information and placement service
118. police labor relations data
119. clearinghouse for private security
120. polygraphs
121. interpersonal skills in corrections
122. analysis of the police dispatch function
123. crime and the elderly
124. New England criminal justice information/placement center

125. women employees in the criminal justice system
126. new stenotype system
127. police behavior
128. victimology research
129. evaluation of police training programs
130. prediction of crime in Newark
131. model of the criminal justice system
132. evaluation of community corrections programs
133. regional evaluation team
134. evaluation of Federal program policy
135. evaluation of youth service bureaus
136. evaluation of halfway houses
137. system analysis of the juvenile justice process

APPENDIX C5. Personnel Questionnaire

Because of their role in procuring and monitoring research, the Institute's staff must have adequate background in research methodology in order to make informed decisions on the funding of research. The Committee administered a background questionnaire to all current NILECJ professional staff personnel to assess more accurately their level of training and experience. The questionnaire was designed to be relatively short and easy to administer although several questions were sufficiently open to permit variation in responses.

Of the 56 professional staff members in the Institute, 45 responded to the questionnaire:

- The GS level of the staff averages 12.5; 40 percent of the staff of the Office of Research Programs have GS–14 or GS–15 ratings.
- 80 percent have bachelor-level degrees; 26.7 percent have PhDs, and 13.3 percent have completed all the course work for a doctoral degree.
- 38 percent have 1–3 publications; 38 percent have never published.
- 53 percent have had 3 or more courses in some aspects of research methodology; 47 percent have had little or no methodological training.
- 60 percent have had more than 5 years of work experience in criminal justice; 20 percent have had less than 3 years work experience in criminal justice.

The Committee has doubts about the Institute's ability to adequately manage a sustained research program when only half the staff have the necessary formal training and experience to deal credibly and capably with good researchers in the field.

In addition to the question of training and experience, there is evidence that lack of stability among staff in the Institute's short history has created an atmosphere unconducive to a sustained research program: at the time of the survey, 60 percent of the staff had come to the Institute in the previous 3 years, and only 27 percent had been there more than 5 years. Thus, there is no substantial group of professionals who could create continuity between the last two Institute directors. The Committee's evaluation of grants and contracts reflects this; it showed tremendous fluctuation in managers on particular projects, which exacerbated the problem of cohesive grants management.

The questionnaire used and the tabulation of responses to the questionnaire appear on the following pages.

PERSONNEL QUESTIONNAIRE — NILECJ STAFF

1. Name of Division in NILECJ
2. GS Grade Level
3. Education

   B.S. or A.B. (specify) Year Institution

   M.A. (or other master's level degree) (specify) Year Institution

   Ph.D. (or other doctorate) (specify) Year Institution

   Other (specify) Year Institution

   Undergraduate Major:

   Graduate Major (specify by degree, if more than one graduate degree):

   Courses in Research Methodology (specify undergraduate or graduate):

   Areas of Research Methodology in these courses (e.g., design, sampling, inferential statistics, etc.):

4. Special Qualifications and Skills

   Publications:

   Areas of Research:

   Other:

5. Employment History

a. Present Position: (attach separate sheet if you have had more than one distinct job title within NILECJ)

(1) Title

(2) Date of Employment

(3) Job Description*

(4) % of current work spent in:

Program planning	______ %
Administration of grants and contracts	______
Technical/advisory review of reports, proposals, etc.	______
Analysis of secondary data for program planning	______
Program administration	______
Research (specify)	______
	______
Other (specify)	______
	100%

b. For each of last three positions:

(1) Title

(2) Dates of Employment to

(3) Job Description*

(4) Kind of business or organization:

government (specify federal, state or local)	______
educational institution	______
private business	______
research organization	______
self-employed	______

(5) % of time spent in:

Program planning	______ %
Administration of grants and contracts	______
Administration of research	______
Analysis of secondary data	______
Original research	______
Program or project administration	______
Direct criminal justice related work	______
Other (specify) ______	______
	100%

(1) Title

(2) Dates of Employment to

(3) Job Description*

(4) Kind of business or organization:

government (specify federal, state or local)	______
educational institution	______

*If you prefer, attach current resume to answer (3) of all parts of question 5.

private business ________
research organization ________
self-employed ________

(5) % of time spent in: Program planning ______ %
Administration of grants and contracts ______
Administration of research ______
Analysis of secondary data ______
Original research ______
Program or project administration ______
Direct criminal justice related work ______
Other (specify) __________ ______
100%

(1) Title
(2) Dates of Employment to
(3) Job Description*

(4) Kind of business or organization: government (specify federal, state or local) ________
educational institution ________
private business ________
research organization ________
self-employed ________

(5) % of time spent in: Program planning ______ %
Administration of grants and contracts ______
Administration of research ______
Analysis of secondary data ______
Original research ______
Program or project administration ______
Direct criminal justice related work ______
Other (specify) __________ ______
100%

6. Total number of years professional work experience ________
7. Total number of years work experience in criminal justice field ________
8. Do you believe you could (or could have when you started) expand or enhance the skills needed to perform your present job by any sort of training or professional experience?
   Yes ________ No ________
   If yes, what sort of training or professional experience?
9. Why did you come to the Institute? Were you recruited?

10. Are you doing the kind of work at the Institute that you believe you were hired to perform? Yes ________ No ________
    If not, how is it different?

PERSONNEL STUDY — MARGINAL TABULATIONS

Universe: 56
Responses: 45
Response Rate: 80%

	ORP	OTT	OE	(Director)	Total No.	Total %
# 2 GS Grade Level						
9–11	3	5	2		10	22.2
12–13	7	5	3		15	33.3
14–15	8	4	4		16	35.6
16+	1	1	0	1	3	6.7
Non-response	1				1	2.2
TOTAL	20	15	9	1	45	100
# 3 Education (Highest Degree* Held)						
Bachelor Level	2	6	1		9	20.0
Master's Level (1)	9	4	1			
(2)		1			15	33.3
Ph.D.	6	1	5		12	26.7
LL.B. or J.D.	1	1	0	1	3	6.7
Ph.D. course work	2	2	2		6	13.3
Non-response	0	0	0			
TOTAL	20	15	9	1	45	100
Undergraduate Major						
Hard Sciences	3	3	4		10	22.2
Behavioral, Social Sciences	13	9	4		26	57.7
Humanities	4	3	1		8	17.8
Non-response	0	0	0	1	1	2.2
TOTAL	20	15	9	1	45	99.9
Graduate Major						
Hard Sciences	2	0	3		5	11.1
Behavioral, Social Sciences	15	8	5		28	62.2
Humanities	0	1	0		1	2.2
Law	1	1	0	1	3	6.7
Other	0	1	0		1	2.2
No Graduate Work	2	4	1		7	15.6
Non-response						
TOTAL	20	15	9	1	45	100
Courses in Research Methodology						
None	1	4	0		5	11.1
Statistics	1	0	0		1	2.2

*Does not include advanced training work other than Ph.D. course work.

	ORP	OTT	OE	(Director)	Total No.	Total %
Design	0	0	0			
Sampling	0	0	0			
Two Courses in Any of Above	3	1	0		4	8.9
Three or More Courses in Any of Above	10	7	7		24	53.3
Basic Science Major	2	2	0		4	8.9
Basic Science Ph.D.	0	0	1		1	2.2
Uncertain						
Three or More Areas, No Course Specified	0	1	0		1	2.2
Economics Major & ADP Systems	1	0	0		1	2.2
MA & PhD Math	1	0	1		2	4.4
BA & MA Psych	1				1	2.2
No Response				1	1	2.2
TOTAL	20	15	9	1	45	100
#4 Publication*						
0	6	8	3		17	37.8
1–3	9	4	4		17	37.8
4–5	2	2	1		5	11.1
6–10	1	0	0	1	2	4.4
11+	2	1	1		4	8.9
TOTAL	20	15	9	1	45	100
Areas of Research						
Basic Science/Technology	2	1	0		3	6.7
Methodology (Econometric, Survey Research, Participant Observation, Small Group Dynamics, Soc Psych)	2	0	2		4	8.9
Police Operations	3	0	0		3	6.7
Operations Research	1	0	2		3	6.7
Prisons/Corrections	2	2	1		5	11.1
Manpower	1	0	0		1	2.2
Youth, Juvenile Justice	0	1	0		1	2.2
Criminology (Behavioral Characteristics of Offenders; Correlates of Recidivism; Alcohol, Drugs, Crime; Learning, Disabilities & Delinquency)	0	1	1		2	4.4
Other	3	4			7	15.6
No Response	6	6	3	1	16	35.5
TOTAL	20	15	9	1		100
#5 Employment history (years at NILECJ)						
0–<1	8	2	2		12	26.7
1–<2	0	4	3		7	15.6

*No judgment made as to quality or scholarliness of publication.

	ORP	OTT	OE	(Director)	Total No.	Total %
2–<3	3	2	1	1	7	15.6
3–<4	4	1	0		5	11.1
4–<5	0	1	1		2	4.4
5–<7	5	5	2		12	26.7
TOTAL	20	15	9	1	45	100

% Time spent currently in:			0%	<25%	<50%	<75%	75+	No Response
Program Planning	ORP		1	13	1	0	0	5
	OTT		4	7	1	1	0	2
	OE		2	7	0	0	0	0
								(1)*
TOTAL		100%	15.6%	60.0%	4.4%	2.2%	0%	17.8%
Administration of Grants and Contracts	ORP		1	2	4	6	2	5
	OTT		3	2	2	4	2	2
	OE		0	3	2	3	1	0
								(1)*
TOTAL		100.1%	8.9%	15.6%	17.8%	28.9%	11.1%	17.8%
Technical/Advisory Review	ORP		1	10	2	2	0	5
	OTT		3	8	2	0	0	2
	OE		0	6	1	2	0	0
								(1)*
TOTAL		100%	8.9%	53.3%	11.1%	8.9%	0%	17.8%
Analysis of Secondary Data for Program Planning	ORP		7	6	1	1	0	5
	OTT		9	4	0	0	0	2
	OE		4	5	0	0	0	0
								(1)*
TOTAL		99.9%	44.4%	33.3%	2.2%	2.2%	0%	17.8%
Program Administration	ORP		4	7	4	0	0	5
	OTT		5	7	1	0	0	2
	OE		3	4	1	1	0	0
								(1)*
TOTAL		100%	26.7%	40.0%	13.3%	2.2%	0%	17.8%
Research	ORP		14	1	0	0	0	5
	OTT		12	1	0	0	0	2
	OE		5	4	0	0	0	0
								(1)*
TOTAL		100%	68.9%	13.3%	0%	0%	0%	17.8%

*Director.

% Time spent currently in:			0%	<25%	<50%	<75%	75+	No Response
Other	ORP		10	4	1	0	0	5
	OTT		10	1	0	1	1	2
	OE		7	2	0	0	0	0
								(1)*
TOTAL		100%	60.0%	15.6%	2.2%	2.2%	2.2%	17.8%
Past Jobs:†								
#1 Program Planning	ORP		3	8	3	0	0	6
	OTT		6	2	4	0	0	3
	OE		3	4	0	1	0	1
								(1)*
TOTAL		100%	26.7%	31.1%	15.6%	2.2%	0%	24.4%
Admin A&C	ORP		10	2	1	1	0	6
	OTT		11	0	1	0	0	3
	OE		7	1	0	0	0	1
								(1)*
TOTAL		99.9%	62.2%	6.7%	4.4%	2.2%	0%	24.4%
Technical Advisory Review	ORP		7	5	2	0	0	6
	OTT		10	1	1	0	0	3
	OE		5	3	0	0	0	1
								(1)*
TOTAL		100%	48.9%	20.0%	6.7%	0%	0%	24.4%
Analysis of Secondary Data	ORP		6	6	1	1	0	6
	OTT		9	2	1	0	0	3
	OE		3	3	2	0	0	1
								(1)*
TOTAL		99.9%	40.0%	24.4%	8.9%	2.2%	0%	24.4%
Original Research	ORP		4	2	3	2	3	6
	OTT		9	1	1	0	1	3
	OE		4	1	1	2	0	1
								(1)*
TOTAL		100%	37.8%	8.9%	11.1%	8.9%	8.9%	24.4%
Program Administration	ORP		9	4	1	0	0	6
	OTT		8	3	0	1	0	3
	OE		3	4	1	0	0	1
								(1)*
TOTAL		99.8%	44.4%	24.4%	4.4%	2.2%	0%	24.4%
Criminal Justice Related	ORP		10	1	1	0	2	6
	OTT		9	0	0	1	2	3
	OE		7	0	0	0	1	1
								(1)*
TOTAL		99.9%	57.8%	2.2%	2.2%	2.2%	11.1%	24.4%

*Director.

†Does not include prior NILECJ positions.

% Time spent currently in:		0%	<25%	<50%	<75%	75+	No Response
Other	ORP	12	0	1	0	1	6
	OTT	6	1	0	1	4	3
	OE	5	0	0	0	3	1
TOTAL	99.9%	51.1%	2.2%	2.2%	2.2%	17.8%	(1)* 24.4%
#2 Program Planning	ORP	4	6	3	0	1	6
	OTT	3	3	1	0	0	8
	OE	3	2	1	0	0	3
TOTAL	99.9%	22.2%	24.4%	11.1%	0%	2.2%	(1)* 40%
Admin. G&C	ORP	10	3	1	0	0	6
	OTT	5	0	1	0	1	8
	OE	5	1	0	0	0	3
TOTAL	99.9%	44.4%	8.9%	4.4%	0%	2.2%	(1)* 40%
Technical/Advisor Review	ORP	10	0	3	1	0	6
	OTT	6	1	0	0	0	8
	OE	4	1	1	0	0	3
TOTAL	99.9%	44.4%	4.4%	8.9%	2.2%	0%	(1)* 40%
Analysis of Secondary Data	ORP	8	3	1	1	1	6
	OTT	5	1	1	0	0	8
	OE	5	1	0	0	0	3
TOTAL	99.9%	40.0%	11.1%	4.4%	2.2%	2.2%	(1)* 40%
Original Research	ORP	5	2	3	1	3	6
	OTT	6	1	0	0	0	8
	OE	2	3	0	0	1	3
TOTAL	100%	28.9%	13.3%	6.7%	2.2%	8.9%	(1)* 40%
Program Administration	ORP	9	4	1	0	0	6
	OTT	4	0	2	1	0	8
	OE	4	1	1	0	0	3
TOTAL	100%	37.8%	11.1%	8.9%	2.2%	0%	(1)* 40%
Criminal Justice Related	ORP	12	1	0	0	1	6
	OTT	4	1	0	0	2	8
	OE	6	0	0	0	0	3
TOTAL	100%	48.9%	4.4%	0%	0%	6.7%	(1)* 40%

*Director.

% Time spent currently in:			0%	<25%	<50%	<75%	75+	No Response
Other	ORP		11	0	0	1	2	6
	OTT		4	0	1	0	2	8
	OE		2	0	0	1	3	3 (1)*
TOTAL		99.9%	37.8%	0%	2.2%	4.4%	15.5%	40%
#3 Program Planning	ORP		8	4	2	0	0	6
	OTT		3	2	1	0	0	9
	OE		2	2	1	0	0	4 (1)*
TOTAL		100%	28.9%	17.8%	8.9%	0%	0%	44.4%
Admin. G&C	ORP		9	2	1	1	1	6
	OTT		6	0	0	0	0	9
	OE		5	0	0	0	0	4 (1)*
TOTAL		99.8%	44.4%	4.4%	2.2%	2.2%	2.2%	44.4%
Technical/Advisory Review	ORP		10	0	4	0	0	6
	OTT		5	0	1	0	0	9
	OE		3	1	1	0	0	4 (1)*
TOTAL		99.9%	40.0%	2.2%	13.3%	0%	0%	44.4%
Analysis of Secondary Data	ORP		8	4	2	0	0	6
	OTT		3	1	2	0	0	9
	OE		3	1	0	0	1	4 (1)*
TOTAL		99.9%	31.1%	13.3%	8.9%	0%	2.2%	44.4%
Original Research	ORP		5	2	4	0	3	6
	OTT		3	1	0	1	1	9
	OE		2	0	1	2	0	4 (1)*
TOTAL		100%	22.2%	6.7%	11.1%	6.7%	8.9%	44.4%
Program Administration	ORP		8	1	4	1	0	6
	OTT		4	1	1	0	0	9
	OE		2	3	0	0	0	4 (1)*
TOTAL		99.9%	31.1%	11.1%	11.1%	2.2%	0%	44.4%
Criminal Justice Related	ORP		12	0	0	0	2	6
	OTT		5	0	0	0	1	9
	OE		5	0	0	0	0	4 (1)*
TOTAL		100%	48.9%	0%	0%	0%	6.7%	44.4%

*Director.

% Time spent currently in:		0%	<25%	<50%	<75%	75+	No Response
Other	ORP	12	2	0	0	0	6
	OTT	5	0	0	0	1	9
	OE	3	0	0	2	0	4
							(1)*
TOTAL	99.8%	44.4%	4.4%	0%	4.4%	2.2%	44.4%

*Director.

	ORP	OTT	OE	(Director)	Total No.	Total %
Past Employment*						
#1 Type: Govt. Federal	2	7	3		12	26.7
State	3	2	1		6	13.3
Local	3	1	1		5	11.1
Educ. Inst.	1	2	0	1	4	8.9
Priv. Bus.†	2	1	1		4	8.9
Res. Org.	7	1	3		11	24.4
Self Empl.	0	1	0		1	2.2
Not Applicable or Non-response	2	0	0		2	4.4
TOTAL	20	15	9		45	99.9
#2 Type: Govt. Federal	2	4	0		6	13.3
State	2	2	1		5	11.1
Local	1	2	1	1	5	11.1
Educ. Inst.	1	1	4		6	13.3
Priv. Bus.†	6	3	0		9	20.0
Res. Org.	7	0	2		9	20.0
Self Empl.	0	0	0		0	0.0
Not Applicable or Non-response	1	3	1		5	11.1
TOTAL	20	15	9		45	99.9
#3 Type: Govt. Federal	2	2	1		5	11.1
State	0	1	1		2	4.4
Local	2	2	0		4	8.9
Educ. Inst.	3	1	3		7	15.6
Priv. Bus.†	6	3	1		10	22.2
Res. Org.	2	1	1	1	5	11.1
Self Empl.	0	0	0		0	0.0
Not Applicable or Non-response	5	5	2		12	26.7
TOTAL	20	15	9		45	100.0

*Does not include prior NILECJ positions.

†Includes some private, non-profit, not clearly designated research.

	ORP	OTT	OE	(Director)	Total No.	Total %
#6 Total Years Work Experience						
1–<2	0	1	0		1	2.2
2–<3	0	0	0		0	0.0
3–<5	3	1	1		5	11.1
5–<10	7	3	1		11	24.4
10+	10	10	7	1	28	62.2
TOTAL					45	99.9
#7 Total Years Work—Criminal Justice						
0–<1	0	0	1		1	2.2
1–<2	0	2	1		3	6.7
2–<3	2	1	2		5	11.1
3–<5	6	2	1		9	20.0
5–<10	11	8	4		23	51.1
10+	1	2	0	1	4	8.9
TOTAL					45	100.0
#8 Desire Better Training/Experience						
Yes	15	12	6		33	73.3
No	4	2	3		9	20.0
No Response	1	1	0	1	3	6.7
TOTAL					45	100.0
Type of Training:						
Research Methods, Research or Practitioner Contact	1	5	2		8	17.8
Mgt/Contracting	2	4	0		6	13.3
Criminal Justice Operations	4	0	0		4	8.9
Research in Criminal Justice	1	0	0		1	2.2
Criminal Justice System/Research Methods/Contracting	3	0	1		4	8.9
Other	4	3	3		10	22.2
No Response	1	1	0	1	3	6.7
						80.0
(No)					(9)	20.0
TOTAL					45	100.0

APPENDIX C6. Advisory Panel Questionnaire

For various advisory purposes, the Institute has used an overall Institute Advisory Committee (with 20 members), Advisory Panels (which have involved about 260 individuals), and individual reviewers engaged on an ad hoc basis; they represent a mix from both the practitioner and academic communities. Advisory Panels are concerned with individual projects; they review initial concept papers, recommend changes during the course of ongoing studies, and review the findings of final reports. The Advisory Committee's role deals more with offering general advice on Institute program policies and procedures.

As a means of gaining a broad base of information about the Institute's research program, a questionnaire was developed (see below) and sent to all individuals who had served in a formal advisory capacity to NILECJ during the past two fiscal years. Names of those surveyed were obtained from the Institute's *1975 Annual Report* (pp. 66–77). All of the questions were open-ended and were designed to focus individuals' observations about their specific advisory roles, the effectiveness of those roles, other tasks that could have been done by their Panel, and general impressions about NILECJ operations.

Of 274 questionnaires mailed, 84 were returned (a 31-percent response rate). Of the 84 returned, only 54 were complete: 24 respondents could not recall having served in an advisory position to NILECJ at any time, and 6 were responded to by someone other than the original addressee—noting that the individual had moved or was now deceased.

These limited responses cannot be reported as data, and we do not attempt to do so. But it should be noted that several themes emerged strongly from the responses we did receive. A number of respondents complained that they had never received feedback from Institute staff concerning the matters about which their advice had been sought. Respondents also criticized the Institute's practice of requesting advice on a project after it had been funded rather than at a point when their advice could have been more useful in ensuring that the project was properly designed. Another general criticism concerned the lack of a peer review system at the Institute. There was a strong consensus that the Institute should establish a system of peer review along the same lines as the successful one at the National Institute of Mental Health.

QUESTIONNAIRE: NILECJ ADVISORY PANELS

1) Please specify:
   a) The capacity in which you were asked to serve

   b) The title of the group or project

   c) The names of those with whom you served (and affiliation to the extent you recall)

d) The Institute staff and/or project staff with whom you worked (titles, no names necessary)

e) Duration of service and frequency of contact

2) What were you asked to do? (Please be as specific as possible)

3) Was the task or role you were asked to perform appropriate:
   a) For an external advisory?

   b) For the type of project?

   c) For the functions of the Institute?

4) Given your understanding of Institute operations, how effective was the role your group performed? Please take account of such factors as the mix of disciplines and/or professions in the group and the quality of feedback contact with the Institute.

5) Were there any other tasks which you think should have been or might be performed by a group such as yours? Are there other kinds of roles or groups that would be effective for the Institute's purposes?

6) Please comment on your impressions of the Institute and its work, including any suggestions for change.

NOTE: Please return as soon as possible.

Appendix D
Interviews

In preparing this report, a large number of current and former staff members of the National Institute of Law Enforcement and Criminal Justice were interviewed, both formally and informally. The Committee also consulted with many other individuals during the course of its work, including principal investigators on NILECJ contracts and other experts in criminal justice. The Committee recognizes the contributions of these individuals and is grateful to them for providing valuable exchanges of information.

NATIONAL INSTITUTE OF LAW ENFORCEMENT AND CRIMINAL JUSTICE

Directors

GERALD M. CAPLAN, *Director* 1973–1977
MARTIN DANZIGER, *Director* 1971–1973
IRVING SLOTT, *Acting Director* 1970–1971
HENRY RUTH, *Director* 1969–1970

Office of the Director

BETTY M. CHEMERS, *Special Assistant to the Director*
JOHN B. PICKETT, *Director of Planning*
PEGGY E. TRIPLETT, *Special Assistant to the Director*
CARRIE L. SMITH, *Staff Assistant*

Office of Research Programs

GEOFFREY M. ALPRIN, *Director*
RICHARD BARNES
PHYLLIS JO BAUNACH
GEORGE BOHLINGER
SYDNEY EPSTEIN
DAVID FARMER
LAWRENCE GREENFIELD
FRED HEINZELMAN
JOSEPH KOCHANSKI
JOAN LEWIS
CHERYL MARTORANA
WARNER J. MERRILL
KAY MONTE
MICHAEL MULKEY
GEORGE SHOLLENBERGER
LESTER SHUBIN
JOHN SULLIVAN
JAN TRUEWORTHY

Office of Evaluation

RICHARD LINSTER, *Director*
HELEN ERSKINE
JOEL GARNER
VICTORIA JAYCOX
PAUL LINEBERRY
RICHARD RAU
JOHN SPEVACEK
MARSHALL WHITHEAD
EDWIN ZEDLEWSKI

Office of Technology Transfer

PAUL CASCARANO, *Director*
MARY ANN BECK, *Director,* Model Program Development Division
JOHN CARNEY, *Director,* Reference and Dissemination Division
LOUIS MAYO, *Director,* Testing and Training Division
VIRGINIA BLADAU
ROBERT BURKHART
WILLIAM HEENAN
MARTIN LIVELY

Former NILECJ Staff and Fellows

JERRY CLARK
KAREN CLARK
JOHN GARDINER
MICHAEL MALTZ
WESLEY SKOGAN
DANIEL SKOLER
CHARLES WELLFORD

LAW ENFORCEMENT ASSISTANCE ADMINISTRATION

CHARLES WORK, *Deputy Administrator*
PAUL WORMELI, *Deputy Administrator*
JAMES GREGG, Office of Planning and Management
HARRY BRATT, National Criminal Justice Information and Statistics Service
ELIZABETH POWELL, National Criminal Justice Information and Statistics Service
FREDERICK NADER, *Deputy Assistant Administrator,* Office of Juvenile Justice
DENNIS MURPHY, Office of Regional Operations
CHARLES STRAUB, Office of Regional Operations
JAMES SWAIN, Office of Regional Operations
GEORGE CAMPBELL, *Regional Administrator,* Boston
RAIMOND BOWLES, *Deputy Regional Administrator,* Boston
DAVID POWELL, New York Regional Office

DEPARTMENT OF JUSTICE—OFFICE OF POLICY AND PLANNING

RONALD L. GAINER, *Director*
HARRY SCARR, *Assistant Director*
ROBERT DAVIS
EDWARD D. JONES III

UNITED STATES CONGRESS

JOHN CONYERS, *Chairman,* Subcommittee on Crime, House Committee on the Judiciary

JAMES H. SCHEUER, *Chairman,* Subcommittee on Science and Technology, Committee on Domestic and International and Scientific Planning, Analysis, and Cooperation

KENNETH FEINBERG, Legislative Assistant to Senator Edward M. Kennedy

As discussed in Appendix E, a number of Committee and staff members interviewed or held informal conversations with State Planning Agency (SPA) staff in various states. All of these conversations were helpful, but the following individuals gave particularly of their time and advice:

ROBERT E. CREW, JR., *Executive Director,* Minnesota Governor's Commission on Crime Prevention and Control

FRAN DODD, *Planning Director,* Texas Criminal Justice Council

DAVID FOGEL, *Executive Director,* Illinois Law Enforcement Commission

DIONISIO MANZANO, *Director,* Puerto Rico Crime Commission

BETSY REVEAL, *Planning Director,* Minnesota Governor's Commission on Crime Prevention and Control

ARNOLD R. ROSENFELD, *Executive Director,* Massachusetts Committee on Criminal Justice

DAVID SHERWOOD, *Courts Planner,* Connecticut Planning Committee on Criminal Administration

CONSTANCE TREADWELL, *Director of Evaluation,* Connecticut Planning Committee on Criminal Administration

CYNTHIA TURNURE, *Director of Research,* Minnesota Governor's Commission on Crime Prevention and Control

HENRY G. WEISMAN, *Executive Secretary,* National Conference of State Criminal Justice Planning Administrators

Others who gave of their time for interviews and informal conversations are:

BARBARA BOLAND, Criminal Justice Research Program, The Urban Institute

BERTRAM BROWN, *Director,* National Institute of Mental Health

SARAH CAREY, Lawyers Committee for Civil Rights

ELEANOR CHELIMSKY, *Department Head,* Criminal Justice System Research, The MITRE Corporation

ROBERT ENGEL, Consultant on Rehabilitation and Training Programs

MARC FURSTENBERG, formerly, *Assistant Director,* Police Foundation

ROGER HANSON, *Criminal Justice Planner,* Denver Regional Council of Governments

JOHN HEAPHY, *Assistant Director,* Police Foundation

ORAM KETCHUM, *Judge,* Superior Court of the District of Columbia

THOMAS LALLEY, *Deputy Chief,* Center for Studies of Crime and Delinquency, National Institute of Mental Health

MICHAEL MICHAELIS, Arthur D. Little, Inc.

PATRICK MURPHY, *President,* Police Foundation; formerly, *Police Commissioner,* City of New York and *Director,* Office of the Office of Law Enforcement Assistance

VICTOR NAVASKY, *Staff Reporter, Law Enforcement: The Federal Role,* Twentieth Century Fund Task Force on the Law Enforcement Assistance Administration, 1976

RICHARD RETTIG, *Senior Staff Member,* Task Force on Criminal Justice Research and Development of the Law Enforcement Assistance Administration (RAND Corp.)

CARLOS R. RIOS, *Secretary of Justice,* Puerto Rico

CARL STENBERG, *Staff Member,* Advisory Commission on Intergovernmental Relations

MICHAEL D. TATE, Arthur D. Little, Inc.

ROBERT K. YIN, *Executive Director,* Task Force on Criminal Justice Research and Development of the Law Enforcement Assistance Administration (RAND Corp.)

Appendix E
A View of the Institute from the States

As part of its efforts to assess the usefulness of Institute work, the Committee developed information from several sources about the relationship of the Institute to the LEAA structure in the states, the State Planning Agencies (SPAS). In our many interviews and conferences with Institute staff, we always asked for their opinions of the SPAS and of the Institute's potential for being helpful to LEAA programming. The attitudes of Institute staff were invariably negative, although they described many efforts on their part to consult with and be helpful to SPAS. On the other hand, we found that the Institute does not have a well-defined image among SPA staff, who were generally indifferent to or uninformed about Institute efforts. Most knew little about the Institute, except its National Criminal Justice Reference Service, and generally had no expectation that the Institute could help the SPAS develop workable programs. Those who had a well-defined view of the Institute sometimes expressed disappointment that it had not been helpful and sometimes complained that the Institute was intruding on SPA prerogatives by supporting a project in their state.

Our conclusions are based on three sources of information about SPAS. First, we interviewed a number of individuals who were either staff of SPAS or had knowledge of SPA attitudes and procedures, including current observers who have recently published reports on LEAA: Victor Navasky, staff reporter for the Twentieth Century Fund's *Law Enforcement: The Federal Role*,* and Carl Stenberg, a staff

*Twentieth Century Fund Task Force on the Law Enforcement Assistance Administration (1976) *Law Enforcement: The Federal Role*. New York: McGraw Hill.

member of the Advisory Commission on Intergovernmental Relations, which issued a report entitled *Safe Streets Reconsidered: The Block Grant Experience 1968–1975*.*

Second, several Committee members have discussed the issue of the contribution of research to state and local planning with SPA staff over the years: Alfred Blumstein, in his capacity as a member of Allegheny Regional Planning Council of the Pennsylvania Governor's Justice Commission and consultant to various SPAS; Eugene Eidenberg, who was vice chairman of the Illinois Law Enforcement Commission from 1973 to 1974 and chairman from 1974 to 1977; Malcolm Feeley, who advised the Connecticut Planning Committee on Criminal Administration on evaluation and court planning from 1973 to 1976; Samuel Krislov, who has had informal discussions with SPA staff at the Minnesota Governor's Commission on Crime Prevention and Control since 1969; and Beryl Radin, who has informally advised staff at the Texas Criminal Justice Council. In addition, Susan White, Study Director for the Committee, has had extensive advisory and research contacts with SPAS and other LEAA staff for six years, including interviews with staff of LEAAS Office of Regional Operations, the New England and New York Regional Offices, and the Maine, New Hampshire, Vermont, Massachusetts, Connecticut, Rhode Island, Illinois, Puerto Rico, Minnesota, New York, and District of Columbia SPAS.

Third, a special report on the SPA view of the Institute, which follows, was submitted to the Committee by Malcolm Feeley and Austin Sarat.

The comments gleaned from these various sources represent the best information that presently exists on this subject. The Committee regrets that more direct measures are not available and again urges (see Chapter 4) that an extensive survey be made of both SPA and practitioner use of Institute products.

REPORT to the Committee on Research on Law Enforcement and Criminal Justice by Malcolm Feeley and Austin Sarat

During the winter and summer of 1976, we visited SPAS in 8 states and conducted lengthy interviews with the heads of their planning and evaluation units. While the interviews were wide-ranging and covered a number of

*Advisory Commission on Intergovernmental Relations (1977) *Safe Streets Reconsidered: The Block Grant Experience 1968–1975*. Washington, D.C.: U.S. Government Printing Office, and *Safe Streets Reconsidered: The Block Grant Experience 1968–1975*. Part B, Case Studies. Washington, D.C.: U.S. Government Printing Office.

different topics, we always included a series of questions about NILECJ. We were interested in finding out how the Institute was viewed from the perspective of the states, what Institute functions were most valued by the SPA planning and evaluation staffs, and what additional functions they thought the Institute might perform.

The 8 states were: Massachusetts, Connecticut, Pennsylvania, Kentucky, North Carolina, Illinois, Minnesota, and California. Six of them were selected because they had been visited by a study team from the federal Advisory Commission on Intergovernmental Relations (ACIR), which had prepared lengthy case studies on the operations of their SPAS; Connecticut and Illinois were selected because of previous personal contacts with their staffs. While not randomly selected nor perfectly representative of the nation as a whole, these states constitute a wide cross-section of types of states. Still, our observations are illustrative and should not be generalized beyond the confines of our limited sample.

One consistent finding was that the Institute has no well-defined "image" among the SPA planning and evaluation staffs. Generally, the Institute was not regarded as particularly important to them. Some people did not know what the acronym NILECJ stood for, others were initially confused when we asked about the "National Institute," and still others were only vaguely aware that it was "some part of LEAA in Washington." Even some evaluation specialists whose offices have received special awards from the Institute had no clear idea of the purpose of the awards and could not identify the major functions of the Institute. One reason for this appears to be the high rate of turnover in these offices. (There were, however, some notable exceptions of this, most particularly in those few "stable" SPAS, which have had little turnover of their top staff and have assumed an aggressive role in developing plans for the state's share of LEAA money.)

The Institute's low visibility was paralleled by the lack of intense reaction—pro and con—it evoked. After probing and occasionally a reminder, most people interviewed thought it was a "good idea" and could often cite some beneficial functions it had provided them. Its information service, the National Criminal Justice Reference Service, was most frequently cited as being a good idea. Many people also said they benefited from conferences they had attended that they thought had been sponsored, at least in part, by the Institute.

There were few intense negative responses to the Institute. However, a number of people raised two sets of objections: they felt that much of the printed materials on LEAA-sponsored projects was self-serving "PR stuff," which was not helpful to them (several cited the Exemplary Project and Prescriptive Package brochures in this vein); they noted the problems people had when requesting technical assistance. A number of people reported that the Institute technical assistance (TA) staff lacked experience and was not knowledgeable enough to be of much use to them. A frequently heard complaint was "we know more about the topic than they do." Another frequently voiced complaint about the Institute's TA capacity might be stated as such: "By the time we explained all the intricacies of our particular project, we could have solved the problem by ourselves." More generally, the two sets of complaints about the Institute hinge around the tension between the general and the specific: in order for the Institute's materials to appeal to a wide audience, they must be general, but SPA planners and evaluators often find that their most pressing problems are with specifics—particular people, projects, and programs. So, when they turn to the Institute for help, it is not surprising they are frustrated.

When queried as to how the Institute might be of more help to them, the SPA evaluation and planning staffs provided widely varying responses. Some suggested that the Institute could never be of much immediate use to them and suggested that it concentrate its efforts on scholarly studies on the causes and conditions of crime rather than on trying to promote implementation of specific ideas. Others felt just the reverse, that the Institute was too "theoretical" and "abstract" and should instead provide aid in developing packaged programs to promote crime reduction, rehabilitation, etc. One planner even suggested that the Institute subsidize several SPAS and develop model planning and evaluation programs so that the other SPAS could learn what "they [i.e., national LEAA officials] want us to do."

In conclusion, while the SPAS are a constituency of the Institute, they are not a well-defined or salient constituency. The Institute has a low visibility among the SPAS; it is generally perceived as a useful—but not very helpful—organization. Beyond this general feeling, the SPAS have few expectations about the Institute, and there is certainly no single set of SPA views. Furthermore, the SPA staffs do not have any clear and consistent vision as to what the Institute might do to be of greater use to them. The same bewildering variety of ideas on functions and purpose held by various officials within the Institute is found among the various SPA staff members.

Biographical Sketches of Committee Members and Staff

SAMUEL KRISLOV is a professor of constitutional law and judicial behavior and Chairman of the Department of Political Science at the University of Minnesota. He attended Western Reserve University and New York University and received a PhD from Princeton University. He has served on the faculty at the University of Oklahoma and Michigan State University and as a visiting professor at Columbia University, Tel Aviv University, and the University of Wisconsin. He is President of the Law and Society Association and is a former editor of *Law and Society Review*. He is the author of numerous articles and books, which include *The Supreme Court and the Political Process* and *Compliance and the Law* (co-author).

ALFRED BLUMSTEIN is a professor and the Director of the Urban Systems Institute in the School of Urban and Public Affairs of Carnegie-Mellon University. He received a Bachelor of Engineering Physics and a PhD in operations research from Cornell University. In 1968, while at the Institute for Defense Analyses, he directed a study group that formulated the first plan for the research program of the National Institute of Law Enforcement and Criminal Justice. In 1966–1967, he served as Director of the Science and Technology Task Force of the President's Commission on Law Enforcement and Administration of Justice. He was a member of the Allegheny Regional Planning Council of the Pennsylvania Governor's Justice Commission and has consulted for many criminal justice agencies. He is also serving as the

Chairman of the Committee's Panel on Research on Deterrent and Incapacitative Effects.

DONALD T. CAMPBELL is Morrison Professor of Psychology at Northwestern University. He received a BA and a PhD in psychology from the University of California at Berkeley and previously taught at Ohio State University and the University of Chicago. His research has been a major influence in developing methodologies for program evaluation in the social sciences. He was elected to the National Academy of Sciences in 1973; made a fellow of the American Academy of Arts and Sciences in 1973; and elected president of the American Psychological Association in 1975. He is the author of numerous books and articles, among them *Experimental and Quasi-Experimental Designs for Research* (co-author) and *Unobtrusive Measures: Nonreactive Research in the Social Sciences* (co-author).

DONALD R. DESKINS, JR., is a professor of geography and Chairman of the Department of Geography at the University of Michigan. He received a BA, an MA, and a PhD in geography from the University of Michigan. He specializes in urban geography and teaches courses on urban crime problems. His principal research has focused on the effects of city structure, spatial imbalance, and social inequities on urban crime.

EUGENE EIDENBERG is Deputy Undersecretary for Intergovernmental Affairs in the U.S. Department of Health, Education, and Welfare. He received a BA from the University of Wisconsin and an MA and a PhD in political science from Northwestern University. From 1972 to 1977, he was Vice Chancellor of the University of Illinois in Chicago and also served as Vice Chairman and later Chairman of the Illinois Law Enforcement Commission. Other positions he has held include deputy to the mayor of Minneapolis in 1968–1969, and Assistant Vice President for administration at the University of Minnesota.

MALCOLM M. FEELEY is a professor of political science at the University of Wisconsin at Madison. He received a BA from Austin College in political science and a PhD from the University of Minnesota in political science. He has held positions at New York University and Yale Law School, where he was associated with the program in law and the behavioral sciences of the Russel Sage Foundation and the Guggenheim Program in Criminal Justice. His most recent research interests include the administration of justice in the lower criminal courts and the problems of implementing reforms and innovations in the criminal courts.

JACK P. GIBBS is a professor of sociology at the University of Arizona at Tucson, where he has been a member of the faculty since 1973. He is also co-director of a U.S. Public Health Service project on juvenile delinquency. He received a PhD from the University of Oregon and was employed as a research associate at the University of California at Berkeley. He has taught at the University of Texas and Washington State University, where he served for a time as Chairman of the Department of Sociology. His teaching and research interests include the sociology of law, criminology and deviance, social control, and human ecology.

CHARLES M. HERZFELD is Technical Director of the Aerospace Electronics Components and Energy Group of the International Telephone and Telegraph Corporation. He received a BS in chemical engineering from Catholic University and a PhD in chemical physics from the University of Chicago. He has lectured in chemistry at Catholic University, in general science at the University of Chicago, and in physics at DePaul University in Chicago and was a professor and lecturer in physics at the University of Maryland. He has worked in the Army Ballistic Missile Lab, the Naval Research Lab, and was Director of the Advanced Research Projects Agency of the Department of Defense. He has been a consultant to the National Security Council and the U.S. Energy Research and Development Administration.

ROBERT M. IGLEBURGER is the retired Director of Police for the city of Dayton, Ohio. As head of the department from 1967 to 1973, he was responsible for the department's experiments with team policing, conflict management, neighborhood assistance officers, and community service officers. He received an MA in public administration from the University of Dayton in 1976. He was Visiting Police Administrator in Residence at the Law School of the University of Wisconsin at Madison, 1973–1974. He was Director of the LEAA Pilot City Program in Dayton from 1974 until its conclusion in 1975.

GARY G. KOCH is professor of biostatistics at the School of Public Health, University of North Carolina at Chapel Hill, where he has served on the faculty since 1968. He received a BS in mathematics, an MS in industrial engineering from Ohio State University, and a PhD in statistics from the University of North Carolina. His principal research interest has been the development of statistical methodology for the analysis of categorical data and corresponding applications to a broad range of research settings, including criminal justice statistics.

BERYL A. RADIN is a faculty fellow in the Office of the Assistant Secretary for Planning and Evaluation in the U.S. Department of Health, Education, and Welfare. She is on leave from the LBJ School of Public Affairs at the University of Texas at Austin. She received a BA in history from Antioch College, an MA in American Studies from the University of Minnesota, and a PhD in social policies planning from the University of California at Berkeley. Her principal research focuses on policy implementation in areas of social policy, particularly education, welfare, and social services. The agencies that she has worked with or consulted for include the U.S. Commission on Civil Rights, the Police Foundation, and the Social Security Administration.

SIMON ROTTENBERG is professor of economics at the University of Massachusetts at Amherst. He received a BA from George Washington University and a PhD in economics from Harvard University. He has been a member of the faculty of the University of Puerto Rico, the University of Chicago, Catholic University of Chile, the State University of New York at Buffalo, and Duke University. He has held visiting professorships at Lake Forest College, the University of Manchester, and the Law School of the University of Virginia. He has done research and published papers on the economics of criminal behavior and the social response to crime.

RICHARD D. SCHWARTZ is Ernest R. White Professor of Law at the College of Law at Syracuse University. He was formerly Dean of the Law School at the University of New York at Buffalo from 1971 to 1976. He received a BA and a PhD in sociology from Yale University and was a postdoctoral fellow at the Institute of Human Relations at Yale from 1951 to 1954. Since then, he has taught sociology and law at Yale University and Northwestern University. He is a former editor of *Law and Society Review*. His publications include *Behavior Theory and Social Science, Unobtrusive Measures: Nonreactive Research in the Social Sciences* (co-author), and *Society and Legal Order*.

MARVIN E. WOLFGANG is Director of the Center for Studies in Criminology and Criminal Law at the University of Pennsylvania. He received a BA from Dickerson College and an MA and a PhD from the University of Pennsylvania. He was formerly Chairman of the Department of Sociology at the University of Pennsylvania. He has served as consultant to the President's Commission on Law Enforcement and Administration of Justice, as Director of Research for the Commission on the Causes and Prevention of Violence, and has been President of the American Society of Criminology and the American Academy of Political and Social Science. His extensive publications include works on violence, delinquency, crime, and justice.

COLEMAN A. YOUNG is the mayor of Detroit, Michigan. He is also a member of the executive board of the Urban Economic Policy Committee of the U.S. Conference of Mayors. Formerly, he was Michigan state senator from 1964 to 1973 and delegate to the Michigan State Constitutional Convention in 1961–1962. As mayor, he is responsible for the Ad Hoc Group on Juvenile Crime, composed of members of the criminal justice system and the community who made proposals designed to streamline the system of juvenile justice.

SUSAN O. WHITE, who was Study Director to the Committee on Research on Law Enforcement and Criminal Justice, is an associate professor of political science at the University of New Hampshire (on leave, 1975–1977). She received a BA from Bryn Mawr College and an MA and a PhD in public law from the University of Minnesota. Her publications include work on police behavior, the administration of justice, and criminal justice reform. She has served on the Research and Evaluation Subcommittee of the New Hampshire Governor's Commission on Crime and Delinquency and has been a consultant on evaluation to the New England Regional Office of the Law Enforcement Assistance Administration.

FREDRICA D. KRAMER was Research Associate to the Committee on Research on Law Enforcement and Criminal Justice. She received a BA in political science from the University of California at Berkeley and an MA in urban planning from Hunter College, City University of New York. She has worked as a legislative assistant on social legislation. For the New York Addiction Services Agency, she developed legislative programs, including programs for drug abusers in the criminal justice system and research on legal services for the treatment population.

MICHAEL A. ROSSETTI was Research Assistant to the Committee on Research on Law Enforcement and Criminal Justice. He received a BA in economics and political science from Boston College and an MA in economics from Pennsylvania State University. He has been involved with criminal justice research at the federal and state levels.

JUANITA L. RUBINSTEIN was Research Assistant to the Committee on Research on Law Enforcement and Criminal Justice. She received a BA and an MA in public administration from the University of New Hampshire. As a public policy analyst, she has specialized in criminal justice issues and intergovernmental relations.